Who

Marshall McLuhan?

Exploring a Mosaic of Impressions

Barrington Nevitt
with Maurice McLuhan

Editors

Frank Zingrone   Wayne Constantineau
Eric McLuhan

Stoddart

- To
H.C.E.

Published in 1995 by
Stoddart Publishing Co. Limited
34 Lesmill Road
Toronto, Canada
M3B 2T6
Tel. (416) 445-3333
Fax (416) 445-5967

First published in 1994 by Comprehensivist Publications

Stoddart Books are available for bulk purchase for sales
promotions, premiums, fundraising, and seminars. For details,
contact the **Special Sales Department** at the above address.

ISBN: 0-7737-5768-6

Printed and bound in Canada

*Stoddart Publishing gratefully acknowledges the support of the Canada
Council, the Ontario Ministry of Culture, Tourism, and Recreation, Ontario
Arts Council, and Ontario Publishing Centre in the development of writing
and publishing in Canada.*

ACKNOWLEDGMENTS

We should like to thank the Ontario Arts Council for their initial grant that enabled us to cover the cost of communicating with our contributors and to undertake preparation of our manuscript.

We are also very grateful to Dennis Murphy, Alan Thomas, and Eric Wesselow for their active help and suggestions.

We recognize our boundless debt not only to the multicultural traditions of our planet, but also to teachers and friends who remain anonymous. Most of all, we thank the many contributors who accepted our invitation to participate in our Mosaic by offering free use, in whole or in part, of their copyrighted material; for together, we created this celebration in Marshall's living spirit.

Contents

THE MAN

Styles of perception alter the object. Great men are misperceived as their mounting celebrity distorts their image. Time also adds to the skew. Our instinct is to communicate; to know more is to be more, our genes insist. Story, like hunger, and the quest for love is an irreducible form of human need. Its subjects live on in us.

In these rich reprises we find the action of McLuhan catalyzing the process of learning in a wide array of others and in this process his living spirit endures, long after his death. This interaction is an art — the art of failing less and less to find his whole mind and spirit by assembling a pattern of the totality of his effects in the intellectual mosaic of those his ideas touched.

The post-modern bias takes us back to the Cynics and satirists who knew that everything is both true and not true at the same time. We are always being undercut in our attempts to create new meanings by the shifts in context created by media forms. McLuhan's approach to understanding this fundamental problem still excites many as the most productive set of questions yet assembled to guide us through the age of electric process.

In spite of all the 'improvements' in our means of communication, the ineffable identity of the subject remains intact, even mysterious, as the revelations of those he touched most mount in number and proliferate in detail.

Yet some are positioned best to initiate and explain the action that gels the pattern that supplants the man.

THE EXPLORERS

MAURICE MCLUHAN

As boys growing up together in Winnipeg, Maurice and his brother Marshall were inseparable until their paths divided at university. Marshall took his degree at Cambridge while Maurice graduated from the University of Toronto. Maurice then spent a year abroad at Marshall's urging, where he attended classes at the Sorbonne. "Red," began to find his own identity:

As the younger brother of "Mars," I spent much of my early life trying to match his performance rather than to make my own identity. As I can now see by rereading his *Letters*[5] this powerful influence continued until the mid-1930s. Thereafter, as our paths separated more widely, I constantly admired evidence of his further growth from student to "artist," as in *The Gutenburg Galaxy* and *Understanding Media:* he was "... the man in any field, scientific or humanistic, who grasps the implications of his actions and of new knowledge in his own time. ... the man of integral awareness."[6] In the early 1960s, when Marshall was deeply involved in probing the nature of our rapidly changing environment, I was completing twenty years of ministry in the United Church of Canada. The cultural revolution had already ushered in Hippies and Flower Children, new drug cultures and communes that forced me to question my own assumptions. In his words, I "dropped out to get back in touch" with the new situation.

Maurice therefore welcomed Marshall's invitation in 1969, after the retirement of artist Harley Parker, to become his research assistant at the Centre for Culture and Technology at the University of Toronto.

Maurice frequently served to represent the Centre for Marshall as keynote speaker at conferences in Canada and the USA. Consistently, he received outstanding recognition for his thoughtful presentations including the White House Conference on Education, in Washington D.C. where his "rich contributions" to the conference were remarked by the Nixon administration coordinator. After Marshall's death, Maurice continued to use his ideas to explore himself and the world, which led to a publisher's suggestion that he write a book about his brother.

In 1972, I left the Centre for a teaching appointment in Communication Studies at Sheridan College in Oakville, Ontario. I tried to pass on to my students what I had learned while at the Centre: any medium has the power to restructure our minds in a unique way by imposing its own mode of thought.

In 1988, a publisher asked me to consider writing a book about my brother. I approached Barrington, a good friend of both Marshall and myself, to see whether he might be interested in collaborating; and he agreed, if we could use Marshall's "mosaic approach." I also recognized that Barry's long collaboration with Marshall meant that he would bear the main burden for composing this work.

Maurice McLuhan's guidance and grounding for the project have been indispensible for its success as a truer picture of the main subject, his older, celebrated brother.

Barrington Nevitt

Barry was one of the closest and most creatively complementary of Marshall McLuhan's collaborators. He co-authored *Take Today: The Executive As Dropout* with McLuhan in 1972 and many groundbreaking articles as well. He worked through the 60's and 70's in intellectual tandem with McLuhan operating variously as high powered conversant, co-conspirator, fan and foil. In the years since McLuhan's death (1980) several colleagues have continued to explore and develop the work he pioneered. More than anyone else Barry Nevitt has stood at the centre of the effort to preserve the work and extend its intellectual influence and development.

Friend, colleague, confidant and co-author, Barry has continued to explicate and embellish profoundly the system of thought which we associate with the Innis/McLuhan thrust. Nothing is closer to the source or more adept in deep understanding than Nevitt's own remarkable work in *The ABC of Prophecy, The Communication Ecology, Keeping Ahead of Economic Panic,* and more. He was not infrequently a co-creator of the complex and influential ideas on electric process and its human effects. Those who come after Marshall McLuhan are indebted to Barrington Nevitt for his efforts in keeping the vision intact against the dissipations of exploiters who have too often used the work with specious understanding for selfish ends. The half-understood pieties of the faithful hangers-on have also made necessary the clear adjudications of Nevitt's comprehensive vision of the electronic paradigm.

Barry was born in 1908 near Niagara Falls, Canada, and throughout his childhood was fascinated by and wholly absorbed in the spectacular new technology of electric process in all its forms. In his teens he built "wireless" telegraphs and radios, familiarizing himself with the magical properties of the electro-magnetic spectrum. And in his spare time he attended school and acquired a wireless operator's licence and a bush-pilot's training. Like only a handful at that time he was transfixed by the possibility of catching the world in electric nets.

In his early twenties (1932-33) Barry went to Leningrad to experience the excitement of the Soviet revolution at work and to help in the development of VHF measurement techniques for their budding communications efforts. Escaping that volatile situation, narrowly missing serious trouble, he returned to Canada and went to work for Northern Electric where he made a significant contribution to the growth and development of that important Canadian company. Later (1939-44) Nevitt spent his war years doing sensitive and invaluable government communications work with Canadian Pacific and Defence Communications Ltd (a typical war-time Crown Corporation including all peace-time competitors). Toward the end of the war he was seconded to RCA to develop radio teletype systems for the Bureau of Ships in Washington D.C. Subsequently, he remained in New York to train their engineers in the latest technologies for world-wide use. 1947-60 he spent with L.M. Ericsson Telephone Company of Sweden in combining the efforts of government and private organizations to expand their national and international communication networks. For example, networking the new capital Brasilia to all of its provincial capitals and the outside world.

After returning to Canada in 1960, Barry was appointed consultant to Canada's Royal Commission on Government Organization that recommended the establishment of a Ministry of Communication. As a private consultant, he also played an important role in the adoption of Canada's satellite communications programme as well as establishing Northern Electric Company's international division. From 1963-76, Nevitt was also involved in establishing the Ontario Development Corporation, especially in technological assessment and management training of entrepreneurs to obtain financing for projects such as the Canadian IMAX film technology. All the while he was working persistently and intensely with McLuhan.

Latterly, Barrington Nevitt's outstanding contributions to Canada and the world has been recognized in his twice being Canada's selected candidate for the UNESCO Teleglobe Award (the "Nobel" of Communications) which is dedicated to the memory of Marshall McLuhan. Old friends meet in wonderful ways.

THE EDITORS

"Old men ought to be explorers
Here and there does not matter
We must be still and still moving
Into another intensity ..."

TSE

CHAPTER A

EXPLORATIONS

I first met Marshall by telephone at the end of 1964, to suggest founding a branch of the Society for General Systems Research, for combining my own approach to teaching the Philosophy of Science with the insights of *Understanding Media* — a pre-Christmas present from my wife (Constance). Instead, Marshall invited me to attend the first Monday-night session of 1965 at his Centre, then a temporary building, next to the campus observatory. That was it!

From then to the end of 1980, when he left history to enter eternity, I continued to grow with him as a fellow explorer, for our knowledge was complementary. Through shared tradition, we were both already aware of how to avoid the "booby trap" of technological determinism and its imperatives, as we continued to learn from each other, while discovering what neither of us had previously known.

I remember that during the 1970s, when giving oral examinations on books his students had chosen from the reading list (Appendix A), Marshall used to say

> Don't tell me what's in the books. I've read them. Tell me what you learned that you didn't already know. Then, we may both learn something new.

I also recall what Marshall wrote to Ann Landers in 1969, about a proposed biography comparing the lives of twins

> What is needed is a great collection of anecdotes minus any point of view. The anecdote can yield multitudes of diverse insights unsuspected by the narrator of the anecdote.[1]

In reading Stéphane Mallarmé with Marshall, we had confirmed that "To define is to kill. To suggest is to create." In writing with him, we also learned how the interplay of anecdotal "figures" could reveal a "ground" of process patterns that gave them meaning. We now celebrate Marshall's living spirit. It began by asking everybody willing to share our exploration with two basic questions that they were free to modify.

WHO WAS MARSHALL McLUHAN?

What did you learn from Marshall McLuhan that you didn't already know? (*What effects did he have on your Thinking?*)

What anecdotes or personal experience demonstrate Marshall's humanity? (*What influence did he have on your Feeling?*)

Thus, by using Marshall's broad mosaic approach, we hope to make manifest the message of his own life. We look at his life and work not merely through some definable "text" in a limited literate "context," but as an indefinable figure in the boundless ground of human existence. We believe he would welcome a growing multitude of "parallel actions" to shed light on and through the plots and subplots of this book, for that was his method.[2] In his words:

> For many years, until I wrote my first book, *The Mechanical Bride,*[3] I adopted an extremely moralistic approach to all environmental technology. I loathed machinery. I abominated cities. I equated the Industrial Revolution with original sin and the mass media with the Fall. In short, I rejected almost every element of modern life in favour of a Rousseauvian utopianism. But gradually I perceived how sterile and useless this attitude was, and I began to realize that the greatest artists of the 20th century — Yeats, Pound, Joyce, Eliot — had discovered a totally different approach, based on the identity of the processes of cognition and creation. I realized that artistic creation is the playback of ordinary experience — from trash to treasures. I ceased being a moralist and became a student.[4]

Better than anyone else, Marshall reveals in his *Letters*[5] how he grew up from a brash and opinionated young man to a witty and warm-hearted sage, who grew younger with age.

By 1964, in *Understanding Media*, Marshall had already prophesied his own fate as an "artist" in the new Global Village, for that was already happening: "to reward and make celebrities of artists can, ... be a way of ignoring their prophetic work, and preventing its timely use for survival."[6]

I learned from Marshall how to explore and to gain fresh insights into my own multi-cultural experience by recognizing, at the very beginning of our association, that:

> **PERCEPTS** are unique experiences of direct encounter with present existence.

CONCEPTS are convenient packages of similar percepts of past experience that automatically convert the present into rear-view images.

ACOUSTIC SPACE is an EAR-world having centres everywhere with boundaries nowhere and is the natural habitat of non-literate cultures.

VISUAL SPACE is an EYE-world having separate centres with definite boundaries and is the civilized home of literate Western cultures — an inadvertent result of Greek phonetic literacy.

Every innovation, while *obsolescing* something present, also *retrieves* something similar, previously obsolesced. (See page 262-63)

Communicating anything new is a "miracle" — very difficult, but not impossible — more art than science.

Electric information traveling at the speed of light has eroded the Ground Rules of the literate Eye-world, while retrieving Process Patterns of the non-literate Ear-world with new meaning. Also, it enhances inner experience.

Human maturity enables us to savour the simultaneous conflicting emotions arising from our disasters.

We are constantly expanding this list and sharing it with other explorers.

By 1968, when Marshall and I began writing *Take Today*,[8] we recognized that communication satellites had ushered in a new Global Electric Theatre of the Absurd, where only the unexpected happens, precisely because old logical Thinking can no longer keep pace with new eco-logical Being. Today, effects precede causes by design and new roles constantly displace old jobs.

Electric speedup had created global crises of identity, regardless of any intent to improve human communication. These crises were manifested simultaneously in varying intensity by differing cultures as conflicts of gender, colour and creed, and young and old, as well as tribe, class and nationality that split humanity. We could no longer afford merely to wait and see the effects of innovation; human survival demanded that we now learn to anticipate the effects before creating the causes. And we set out in the tradition of

Giambattista Vico and James Joyce to create a new New Science: to anticipate, rather than merely react to what was actually happening, by instant replay with "suspended judgment."

On the way, we recognized that the prevailing Mathematical Theory of Communication (derived historically from telegraph-signaling systems) is valid only for machines; it considers communication merely as replica, matching the output "message" with the input "program" as its sole "content."

In contrast, artists are concerned with how people make sense or meaning through re-presentation, not replica. Every human artifact is a "medium" of human communication. Each user becomes its "content" to *make sense* or meaning individually, but the "message" of human communicating is always the totality of its effects, regardless of any intent (see Chapter L).

By 1971, we realized that

> For the best part of a century, we have been programming human consciousness with retrievals and replays of the tribal unconscious. The complementary of this process would seem to be the "natural" program for the period ahead: *programming the unconscious with the recently achieved forms of consciousness.* This procedure would evoke a new form of consciousness. Everybody becomes a voluntary participant in creating diversity without loss of identity. Man is the content of the environment he creates, whether of "hardware" or "software," whether of consciousness or unconsciousness. There is therefore no technical alternative to "humanism," even though for many this would include the divine grace of the superhuman.[9]

Although, as an "artist," Marshall had already foreseen that any prophetic work would be ignored by most specialists and generalists, he hoped to find a few "comprehensivists" who could bypass the visual bias of Western civilization by learning to use all their wits and senses. Marshall and his collaborators used the comprehensivist approach (not theory) for exploring the "laws" of media. Marshall taught us to use satire, paradox, and hyperbole as "probes" to stimulate thinking through dialogue to discover new knowledge, rather than to inhibit thinking by argument to defend old opinions. Since 1981, we have continued to expand this approach through work in progress (outlined in Chapters K to N). The electronic versions of our books, and future multi-media productions will offer different forms of "Virtual Dialogue," but no machine interface can ever substitute for multi-sensory face-to-face dialogue.

We hope that each reader will gain new understanding of Marshall's message by re-cognizing the new laws of their own situations through reading this mosaic aloud to each other, as we often did with Marshall in re-reading *Finnegans Wake* — the subplot of our human drama.

In our beginning is our end

Margaret Stewart, Secretary to Marshall McLuhan from 1963 to 1978, beside the entrance to his Centre for Culture and Technology at the Coach House.

Rags "putting on" Mars and Red with their mother Elsie Hall McLuhan, circa 1934.

Maurice and Barrington — The Explorers — at leisure in 1994.

Buckminster Fuller, Barrington Nevitt, and Marshall McLuhan at a plenary session of the McLuhan Emergency Strategy Seminar, Bahamas, January 1970. (Photograph by Robert Fleming, who also contributes to this book.)

For Corinne and Marshall, who already had a "carriage," their daughters presented a "bicycle built-for-two," on a special wedding anniversary, to take many a "spin" around Wychwood Park in the 1970s.

Corinne and Marshall as we like to remember them.

René Cera's Pied Piper faces Marshall's last graduating class at his Centre for Culture and Technology in 1978.

22

CHAPTER B

COACH HOUSE AT THE MARGIN

MARGARET STEWART

Longtime secretary to McLuhan, along with her husband Jim, were his close friends. Marg was the Center's most valuable asset and was almost singlehandedly responsible for organizing McLuhan's prolific output. Her quiet prowess in managing Marshall's career, was crucial to his success in extending the Coach House into the world:

I started to work for Marshall in 1963, and soon learned that the workload was tremendous. In 1964, Marshall told me that all letters for the past year had been fine, but that he could no longer read each letter, because he had to get on with the real work of the Centre. He said that he would no longer read the letters, but just sign them. I then asked if he would read any letters that I was uncertain about. He said that he would, and he certainly did. The only problem here was that, if he wrote in a correction, he would immediately sign the letter and put it in a sealed envelope for immediate mailing. ... I didn't have the correction to put on the file copy. However, it seemed to work, because we never received any complaint.

In 1964, I was appointed by the University of Toronto as the Secretary of the Centre for Culture and Technology. What that actually meant was that I was official secretary to Marshall McLuhan, because he was the Centre for Culture and Technology!

Marshall had a truly amazing mind. He worked not only on one project at a time, but on many. It was like working for three or four people all rolled into one! I worked with him for fifteen years, and during that time I received much moral support from Barrington Nevitt, Matie Molinaro (Marshall's agent) and Maurice McLuhan; they would always take time to listen, if I had a problem. That is something I will never forget!

Marshall had his moments when he could be quite testy (don't we all), but the bottom line is that he was kindly. He was not a pompous man. He always wrote to his friends, despite his heavy schedule, because he cared about them.

One thing I loved about Marshall was his great sense of humour. He collected one-liners, and often used them in his talks. I remember telling him about one that I had noticed on a nearby sign, during a weekend visit to our cottage: A STREAKER IS JUST A PASSING FANNY. Marshall loved that one, and immediately put it into his file. Sometime later, he received a letter from John Evans (then President of the University of Toronto) stating: "I hope you don't mind, Marshall, but I borrowed your one-liner about the streaker, which I used in a talk I gave recently."

In 1978, I suffered a broken hip that left me a semi-invalid and unable to work. Marshall came to the hospital several times, and when he couldn't come, he phoned. When I went home, he called me regularly. Toward the end of 1978, he kept asking me to please come back to work. That, of course, was not possible. Marshall said: "The students will carry you upstairs." I explained to Marshall that I wouldn't be doing him any favour, if I did go back, because I was no longer capable of doing the work properly.

In the early months of 1979, Marshall began telling me that he was doing a lot of his work at home because he didn't feel comfortable at the Centre. His complaints became more frequent over the next months until he finally said that the Centre was on the verge of collapse. I thought he might be exaggerating a bit, but later events proved him correct: the office files were totally messed-up and many records were missing.

Marshall suffered a stroke in the Fall of 1979. He even came to visit me then, and, although it is hard to believe, we could still communicate! Personally, I think that stroke was the result of too much stress.

I had the honour to know Marshall and to work for him. He was unique and I know I will never meet anyone like him again in my lifetime. I feel proud to say that we had a good rapport.

But I have a question that haunts me to this day: What happened to Marshall and the Centre from 1978 to 1980?

I also remember that, as Marshall's fame began to spread during the mid-1960s, Claude Bissell (President of the University of Toronto) arrived at the old Centre one evening with a group of wealthy Swiss McLuhanites. They implored him to return with them to Switzerland and become their "king"!

Although constantly harried by visitors, both attractive and otherwise, Marshall received them all in his own inimitable way: he soon excused himself "to attend to students waiting for his overdue lecture," and courteously declined most of their proposals.

We should like to add, in answer to her question, that the greatest calamity that befell the Centre, before Marshall left us, was the loss of Marg.

ALAN THOMAS

Former Chairman, Adult Education, Ontario Institute for Studies in Education, fondly remembers still earlier times.

Encountering McLuhan for the first time was unforgettable, no matter how it happened. Only individuals resident in Toronto, and particularly young and intellectually hungry ones, will remember Rohrer's Bookstore on Bloor Street, just west of Yonge — on the south side.

One could hardly imagine a greater gift to young Canadians, growing up in overgrown towns and small cities, than the invitation to a greater world of thought, imagination, and concern, that Mr. Rohrer provided in Toronto in the 1950s. It was overcrowded, stuffed with books, and intimations of far away worlds of ideas.

Here, at the very back of the store, on a magazine rack, heroically untidy, amid editions of *The Partisan Review, Daedalus,* and *Field and Stream,* we stumbled over McLuhan's first, and so far as I know, only edition of *Counterblast.*[13] It didn't matter to us in the slightest that it was somehow related to Wyndham Lewis' *Blast* from a previous generation that had a powerful meaning for McLuhan. That significance only came later.

What mattered to us was that here, in this unprofessionally, perhaps one might better say, uncommercially, printed and published, "monograph" — the word hardly captures the modest reality — was our world, expressed, indeed celebrated, in words and phrases that captured our imaginations. Maurice Richard's puck in the Montreal forum was related to other events, and forms of expression that suddenly made sense to us. My sophisticated contemporary from Montreal — a real city — provided the complete accolade. "I would rather have written that," he said, "than slept with Marilyn Monroe." You really had to be a young North American male in the 1950s to appreciate the depth of feeling.

After that, and some personal encounters with Marshall, came *Explorations.*[14] It is difficult today to convey the excitement, the anticipation, with which we greeted each successive edition. The collection stands up well to today's reading, and one notices that McLuhan, increasingly unacknowledged, contributes more and more of his world as the series moves to its conclusion. It still retains its irresistibility, its irritations, and its perplexities, just as it did thirty years ago.

McLuhan was the poet of the fifties. It was to the forms of life and thought that his imagination was attracted, and the forms that he saw emerging, much to his delight and continual astonishment, are still emerging.

On July 30, 1959, while visiting Alan's home in Vancouver, Marshall had first declared rhetorically: "The medium is the message." Marshall recognized this big breakthrough as the form of many fresh discoveries briefly indicated in this book.

Meanwhile, according to our longtime friend Mel Kranzberg, Professor of the History of Technology, Georgia Institute of Technology, and former Editor of *Technology and Culture,* Marshall chose the name of his Centre to resonate this complementarity.

Subsequently, the Centre moved to an old red-brick school house at nearby 96 St. Joseph Street, where it remained until Marshall departed to occupy the Schweitzer Chair at Fordham University, New York (during the 1967-8 academic year).

ARTHUR PORTER

Arthur Porter, a Professor of Industrial Engineering at the University of Toronto and pioneer in Operations Research, then took charge of the old Centre to pioneer its new home — a Coach House (built in 1828), beside St. Michael's library. Upon Marshall's return in 1968, the new Centre resumed its old role at the margin between University and City — between old and new media — where the action is.

Arthur's friendship with Marshall continued to grow over the years; and he generously recorded for us his first impressions of meeting McLuhan at various cocktail parties in 1961, and much more.

After leaving one of these parties, I returned home to tell my wife (Patricia) that I had met a most incredible chap. I have never met anyone like him. But I didn't know what the hell he was talking about most of the time!

26

About two meetings later, I began to get a faint glimmer what was going on. Marshall's use of language was completely different to mine, so we were at cross purposes. Then, suddenly, it struck me: here is a Professor of English who understands information theory! I had been working on that quite a bit myself.

I attended a few of Marshall's seminars (in the early 1960s) and learned that there was a real threat that we might lose him to an American University. At that time, Claude Bissell (President of the University of Toronto) set up a committee with himself as Chairman, and Marshall, Jack Sword (the University's financial V.P.), "Carl" Williams (Professor of Psychology), "Tom" Easterbrook (Professor of Economics), Malcolm Ross (Professor of English), and myself that established the new Centre for Culture and Technology.

There were also preparations for Expo '67. We started in 1964. I chaired the Committee for Science and Medicine, with Tuzo Wilson (Professor of Geology) as vice-chairman, Gerald Halpenny (a Montreal physician), Frank R. Scott (Canadian poet), and Dr. Cohen (whose first name I've forgotten). We were responsible for the theme pavilion — "Man and his Technology," "Man and the Polar Region," but we bogged down. This went on and on for about a year before it was due to open. There was the building with nothing in it! So I decided that we had to get Marshall in on this, even though I already knew that he never wanted to be part of any committee.

Nevertheless, we agreed to meet at the Board of Trade Club in downtown Toronto. The night before, Marshall had given a lecture in Chicago (at the 25th Jubilee of Continental Can Company, I believe). This was a white-tie affair, except for Marshall, for it was summer. He went in his seersucker. He had also told me he was going to be late, because he was flying back from Chicago that morning.

We had left a note, "Gone to lunch two floors up," but he didn't join us. We returned about two o'clock, and there he was in his seersucker, flat out on the chesterfield, asleep. But we soon got going.

It was a fantastic three-hour meeting. By the end of it, "Man in the Community" was there. Designers were attending, and here was the framework. After several months, and spending a fortune on consultants, the whole thing suddenly came to life. He was the catalyst. At the end of the session, he said, "Why not come home for a drink?"

Just before we set off, I asked, "What about your bag? Marshall pulled out a plastic bag with his shaving kit and toothbrush. That is what he took to Chicago. Marshall had obviously not taken seriously this white-tie affair. That was for the head table!

Afterwards, there was the NBC-TV show in March 1967. The producers arrived with an enormous transport loaded with equipment

27

and went to Simcoe Hall (the University's administrative centre). They asked where to find the Centre for Culture and Technology, but nobody knew! However, the girl at the switchboard did know that McLuhan had an office at 96 St. Joseph Street. When they got there with their equipment, the door was locked, but they knew it must be the right place from a bit of metallic tape with Marshall's name on it. The equipment was ten times the size of the Centre. As Marshall often remarked: "The media are always bigger than the event!"

CLAUDE BISSELL

When Marshall was at Fordham, Claude Bissell, President of the University of Toronto, was on sabbatical leave as a visiting Professor at Harvard. Marshall and Claude shared a close and friendly association for over thirty years. Here, Claude shares a personal note, and we will hear further details from him later (see Chapters J & Q).

I first met Marshall McLuhan in the late forties when we were both recent appointments to the English Department at the University of Toronto, he at St. Michael's College, I at University College. We lived a short distance from each other in college houses, and there was a good deal of informal visiting between the two.

From the time of the establishment of the Centre for Culture and Technology in 1963, Marshall was responsible for its operation to the central administration of the University. He was the least aggressive of divisional heads, satisfied with a modest yearly grant to cover secretarial assistance and occasional expenses. From this narrow base, he became an international figure for whom the world was indeed a global village.

On one occasion, he dropped in at our house and was received by my mother-in-law, who had recently come on a visit from Scotland. When my wife and I returned home, we wondered how Mrs. Gray, who had grown up in a Presbyterian home in the Hebrides, had got along with the visitor. Even then he was well known for his wide-ranging and startling views, and for his readiness, on all occasions, to explain them.

"Oh, just fine," said Mrs. Gray, "I didn't understand most of what he was saying, but he was such a nice man and so much interested in Scotland." (He once phoned my wife to find out where he could get an authentic plaid sports coat. "I can add the Scottish accent," he said. "You see, I'm meeting somebody about an important personal matter, and I want to make a strong impression. Scottish means business!")

From a later period I recall another domestic incident. We were spending the year at Harvard (I was a visiting professor), and were living in an apartment on the campus. Marshall, who had been at Fordham University in a specially endowed chair, came to see us to discuss his return to Toronto.

Shortly after he arrived, he said that he had to make a purchase, and would be back in a few minutes. When, after half an hour or so, he hadn't returned, I set out to find him. He had, in all likelihood, gone to Harvard Square, a short distance from where we lived. I found him standing at an intersection of the square (actually a tangle of branching streets), looking bewildered, and holding a large bouquet of roses that he was bringing to my wife, who was one of his great admirers.

Arthur Porter proceeds.

With Jack Sword (who was then acting President of the University) we agreed that the St. Joseph location was inadequate for housing this world-famous Centre. So Jack and I toured the campus, and we found a much bigger building that was vacant. On the other hand, it was too pretentious for Marshall. The nearby Coach House was also vacant and due for demolition. So we put it on the budget for complete refurbishing. That's how it happened.

Marshall complained about the new Centre too, because everything was unfamiliar. For example, he didn't like the green floor covering of the seminar room. But, soon after, his friend, mural artist René Cera covered an entire wall with "The Pied Piper" that replayed the carpet's colour, Marshall not only stopped complaining, but began to relish everything there. Now, back to Arthur Porter:

After his operation and return to Toronto in 1968, I went down to Fordham with Marshall, and stayed for a night. We had gone by train. With his hearing highly sensitized by the operation the noise was horrendous, and he took the trip with his fingers stuffed in his ears.

Mac Hillock arranged a lunch for us with half a dozen of IBM's divisional directors. Marshall soon got tuned up, and was telling them about a computer for every home, no need to visit the grocery,... Two of them said to me after lunch, "We haven't heard of anything as crazy as that!" Marshall was talking about the personal computer a dozen years before they thought of it. Here was a Professor of English more than a decade ahead of the technical people in computer evolution. He was thinking in terms of the user.

During 1971 (I think it was), on my next visit to New York, I had been asked to give the John Kershman Memorial Lecture for the American Association of Neurology and Neuro-surgery at Lennox Hill Hospital. At the dinner, on the night before, I was sitting beside Tuzo Wilson's new brother-in-law, who said: "Arthur, you know Marshall McLuhan. I think you'd like to hear from the guy who did the operation. He's in this group."

It was Dr. Lester Mount of Columbia Presbyterian Hospital. He recounted that the operation started at 5 a.m. on a Saturday morning, and went on until 2 a.m. on a Sunday morning. (Tuzo's brother-in-law said in an aside: "He's meticulous, one stitch at a time, only after careful deliberation.") Dr. Mount had also raised the brain very slowly and carefully to avoid damage, before he could excise the "benign" meningioma tumor under it. (So far as we know, this was the longest operation of its kind in medical history.)

Marshall was then taken to the recovery room, where, normally, after such an operation, people hallucinate. But Dr. Mount reported: "At about 6 a.m. I went around to see him before I left the hospital. I just saw a faint flicker of the eyelid, so I said, 'How are you feeling this morning Professor McLuhan? he replied, 'It depends how you categorize feeling!'"

That shot me sky high. How can anyone go through such a procedure without hallucinating!

Marshall completely changed my way of thinking. It was an almost upside down about face. From focusing on technology and hardware, it moved completely to: "How is it going to be used?" and "What effect is it going to have on people?" — from the hardware to the psychological and social effects, and all our ways of thinking.

Marshall used to close his eyes, and say: "No information," then touch the table with his finger, and add: "No connection." So simple, yet so profound in its implications. I became a different person. My interests changed.

Marshall exposed me to an entirely new dimension. I had never in my wildest dreams associated vision, hearing, tactility through the interplay of the senses, that artists call *synesthesia*. The miniskirt, the mesh stocking — you don't have to feel them. You see them, but they stimulate the tactile.

After reading Jonathan Miller's criticisms of *McLuhan*,[15] in 1971, I concluded that Miller didn't have a clue about "communication theory" — the whole basis of McLuhan.

Since Marshall and I admired Jonathan Miller and much

of his previous work, we could scarcely believe that he would question our approach in his book *McLuhan*.[15]

> I am grateful for the way in which McLuhan alerted me to the odd properties of the medium itself. And yet I can rehabilitate no actual truth from what I read. Perhaps McLuhan has accomplished the greatest paradox of all, creating the possibility of truth by shocking us all with a gigantic system of lies.

And that challenged us to engage in, what was for Marshall, a rare debate, via *The Listener*.[18,19]

Our replies were intended for readers who would not merely read, but could also hear, what we were trying to say with more than one wit and sense. We had hoped Jonathan might understand our attempt, but we also recognized that it could never substitute for the ongoing dialogue enjoyed with fellow explorers.[20]

I had visited Marshall in Bronxville during 1967, to discuss and obtain his approval for my monograph on "Problems of Communicating with People through Media."[16] It compared the Shannon-Weaver mathematical theory of communication with McLuhan's approach to human communication, outlined in his *Understanding Media*.[6]

Marshall and I afterwards modified this approach. Instead of considering old media as the content of new media, we recognized that people are always the content of their media (which, as users, they put on like masks). The old media comprise the program content of the new media.

In short, we distinguished between a *Transportation Theory of Communication* for machines (e.g., communication equipment and computers) and a *Transformation Approach to Communication* for people (directly and via media). In these, we contrasted the procedure of matching outputs to inputs for machine communication, and the process of making different outputs from similar inputs when people communicate.

Marshall and his colleagues also emphasized the difference in sensory experience between light on, (e.g., the reflected light from a motion picture screen) and light through (e.g., the light that emerges from a TV screen) so obvious to stained-glass window artists, like Eric Wesselow, who need no proof for the validity of their own experience. Only people can make sense of sensory inputs. Nobody can "intellectualize multi-sensory human experience" or prove the validity of anything that makes life really worth living; and, since the 1960s, Computer Communication colleagues have continued inviting me to their conferences as "devil's advocate" to discuss what computers cannot do.[17]

Although averse to disciples, who merely regurgitated his work, Marshall was fond of "fans," who participated whole-heartedly in his explorations, whether they agreed with him or not. He patiently sought dialogue with fellow explorers to organize shared ignorance for making new discoveries, but impatiently avoided mere questions of specialist knowledge that led only to argument.

WYCHWOOD PARK

Wherever Corinne and Marshall settled, their presence created a centre of urbanity. Before they left Toronto in 1967, it had been a small book-filled family home with a big backyard in the pleasantly wooded Wells Hill area. After returning to Toronto in 1968 from a year at Fordham University, it was a larger family home in Wychwood Park.

This location became a new Academe for his neo-peripatetics. But Corinne also kept it as a haven for her six entirely different, but highly talented children.

GEORGE THOMPSON

In 1972, when Maurice left the Centre, Marshall appointed George as research assistant. George, an artist at the Royal Ontario Museum, was a former colleague of Harley Parker (with whom he had shared the graphical design of *Counterblast* and the *Distant Early Warning* card deck, discussed later). George became an indispensable aide, as well as a close friend of Marshall and his family; and he gives us a key to Marshall's affinity for the Park.

Marshall loved walking in parks! This was his favourite pastime, just walking and talking. He often said: "I make the most significant discoveries while simply talking to people."

It was at such a time, while strolling through the park, that

Marshall, having listened patiently to my exaggerated remarks, admonished me: "Calm yourself George, be patient, and always remember this: don't try to explain everything — just a little. But, above all, don't expect too much of anyone!"

Marshall kept a supply of logs ready outside for fireside evenings; he often split the big ones himself, and invited male visitors to help him carry them inside.

In contrast to his formal public debates, in these informal chats, Marshall drew a clear line between argument (that he tried to cut short), and dialogue (which he stimulated among fellow explorers), and socializing in deference to family guests.

Marshall and I and other colleagues also worked together in this "fireside" atmosphere, so conducive to fruitful exploration and writing that often continued at the kitchen table. And Marshall tape-recorded anything about our work-in-progress that might be of interest to his son Eric, who was then teaching in Wisconsin.

At lunch time, Marshall would say: "Let's have something warm," and then mix a couple of cans of soup to serve with cheese and crackers. At any time, they might take a break to go downstairs for a quick look at one of his favourite TV programs (such as "Mountbatten" or "Hogan's Heroes"), or to join visiting family and friends on the front patio, most often, after 1972, to play with "laws of media."

There were also birthday parties, and TV interviews in the garden with famous journalists such as Tom Wolfe, as well as a constant stream of celebrated scholars, like John Wain, too many to mention. While some came to learn enthusiastically, others came to refute passionately, what Marshall was teaching; but he received them all with urbanity.

In April 1970, Marshall summed up in *Toronto Life* what he felt about Wychwood Park.

> The point of the park is that it has no function, no goal, no objective. It's an Agatha Christie place, unexpected, inexplicable, and it's a community in every sense.
>
> We have proximity and privacy here, both at the same time. It takes a public to create privacy, and we have that. The park, circled about the pond, is a bell, and it resonates.

> We're in a kind of theatre, aware of everybody else who
> lives here, but not obliged to any of our neighbours.
>   It was started as an artists' colony — a place to play. At
> play, man uses all his faculties; at work, he specializes.[10]

LELA WILSON

Among the McLuhans' close friends in the Park were
"Connie" and "Jack" Sword (former V.P. Finance, University
of Toronto); also Janet and John Barnes (former CBC executive) and, perhaps closest of all, the mural painter York
Wilson and his wife Lela who recalls:[11]

Late evening, often the four of us would get together for several
laps around the Park. Marshall loved a hot cup of cocoa and we usually ended the evening with that; then came the walking home, which
sometimes never seemed to end. Often conversations would get so
interesting that we would walk past each other's homes several
times.

When the McLuhans visited us in Mexico (San Miguel de Allende),
Marshall and York would retire to the roof garden, where all was
quiet, and work on ideas such as "Tetrads" (Laws of Media). Marshall
wanted York to do a book with him, but York would never allow himself much time away from painting and so it never materialized.

It was a lovely friendship, and they went to the hospital on the
same day for their last illnesses. York hung on a little longer, but he
certainly missed Marshall. York was very ill when the film about
Marshall was being made and could hardly speak, but with some
coaching from the producer (Marshall's daughter Stephanie) he finally murmured: "I think the reason Marshall and I were such close
friends was, we didn't want anything from each other." Marshall was
courted so much by people who wanted something from him, if only to
couple their names with his.

After York's death, Corinne and I found a sad entry in his diary
(written on December 31, 1980)

> Marshall McLuhan died last night in his sleep. The immedi-
> ate feeling is a sense of emptiness — a loneliness, depres-
> sion and even pessimism. What is the use of anything?
> What matters? What to do, where to go? A sense of useless-
> ness — I want to paint a tribute to Marshall — where to
> start? He is too great a man. Too close a friend. Maybe as
> time goes on I'll know what to do. Not now.

In the Foreword of *York Wilson* by Paul Duval (Wallack Galleries, Ottawa, 1978), Marshall had previously written:

> In the nuclear age abstract or non-objective art is plainly prophetic. On the phone or on the air the user of electric services has no physical body. We are discarnate people, figures in an instantaneous and invisible ground of energy and vibration. This resonant and acoustic ground is discontinuous and man-made, deeply involving and subjective yet minus any point of view or personal stress. The work of York Wilson is a notable manifestation of the new awareness of nuclear man, the shift from sight to insight.

In 1970, although never a firm adherent of any political ideology, Marshall joined an ultimately victorious political battle at the Ontario Municipal Board to preserve the integrity of Wychwood Park against construction of four 28-storey buildings.

In 1971, he played an even more active role in the successful fight to prevent extension of the Spadina expressway.

Meanwhile, in November 1970, Marshall had also appeared before the Public Works Committee at City Hall to oppose the widening of St. Joseph Street, which passes through St. Michael's College, where he taught. The following interchange is typical of his playful, yet profound, attack

MARSHALL McLUHAN:
> Moreness is not conducive to sanity or dialogue. The university is a place of dialogue, encounter, awareness. The present program of moreness may make the next dialogue impossible. There is disadvantage in dialogue with a large truck. I cannot converse with a jackhammer. Even economists see that the cult of moreness is finished. The GNP is no longer the test for health. By the time economists can see something you may be past the point of no return. They are the last to see anything. They are drunk with figures. Moreness is the alcoholic's dream of a cure. The cure is at the bottom of the next bottle.

ALDERMAN ALLAN LAMPORT:
> Couldn't we get back to the subject?

MARSHALL McLUHAN:
> Yes, the subject is the campus and what you are doing to it. The subject is moreness. You want moreness.

ALDERMAN JUNE MARKS:
May I ask the commissioner what would improve pedestrian safety, if we widen the street?

MARSHALL McLUHAN (aside):
A tunnel of love! [11]

ROBERT HITTEL

A construction contractor in Fort Lauderdale, Florida, is a "fan" at a distance. "Bob" published, at his own initiative and expense, the first available record of *The Writings of Marshall McLuhan and what has been written about him*.[12]

In replying to our questions, Bob tries to separate Marshall (his dear friend in particular) from McLuhan (the man in general).

For me to think McLuhan, it is necessary to negotiate my thoughts into a special place, a place free of the surface clatter of mundane activities that demand all of my attention. I can never find McLuhan in words or diagrams or any other direct approach. I don't think I would ever have found McLuhan, if I had not been desperately searching.

In the later sixties, I found myself, with four teenagers, in the midst of a generation gap. At the time, this was of serious concern. My fixed ideas of the world collapsed and I grabbed at anything for some form of stability. I could find nothing to answer my questions. Slowly, McLuhan came into focus. The understanding was not sudden, it took many months in and out of this special place in my mind, but McLuhan explained my children's behavior.

This special place to which I must go is where process becomes visible. Marshall understood how the printing press with moveable type had led to the literate culture — the visual bias that led to our industrial revolution and democracy. In other words, man's "free will" is not all that free. There are subtle hidden processes that direct his behavior while he is busy with the surface clatter.

So, the generation gap, involving my children, was not their will, nor my will, but something beyond our control. I did not agree with their attitudes, but now I understood them. McLuhan did that for me.

But, it is not all that simple, for I found that once you descend into the maelstrom that exposes process, there is no escape (as there was for Poe's classic hero). I keep going back to think about new technologies and the subtle processes of change that they bring about in the environment. How will they influence the "collective unconscious"?

I found that words fall far too short of explaining McLuhan; it is as if another realm must be entered for a whole perception of the man.

With environmental processes changing at such a rapid pace, I feel we are playing Russian roulette with technology. I would like to share in creating the thought space required for McLuhan.

As for anecdotes, this special thought place recalls a time when Marshall and his wife Corinne visited us. Our home is not large, but Marshall could never find the guest room. We joked about his concentration. He retorted with a story about a colleague who, on a cold winter morning, arriving a bit late for his lecture and hastily hanging up his coat, discovered in front of the class that he had forgotten his trousers.

The story was about Marshall's close friend and colleague, Bernard Muller-Thym, who taught philosophy at Saint Louis University during the 1940s. Maurice met him there on a visit to Marshall, who thought Bernie a "genius" in spite of his absent-mindedness.

Bernie later became famous among his clients as "the oral Peter Drucker;" for both had graduated from Bennington College and had finally become management consultants.

Bernie, made an important contribution to NASA in their attempt to catch up with, and surpass *Sputnik*. He discouraged the writing of memos to neighbouring colleagues by removing the material and mental walls between them. And he conducted seminars everywhere, but never wrote a book anywhere until a wise Japanese publisher, recognizing Bernie's "aural-oral" bent, sent him a charming bilingual secretary; he gladly articulated for her *The Physiology of Management* — a "best-seller" in Japanese.

I first met Bernie as a fellow consultant with John Culkin, "Bucky" Fuller, and Harley Parker at the *McLuhan Emergency Strategy Seminar* in the Bahamas (January, 1970). I also participated with Bernie in the *International Council of Societies of Industrial Designers* (ICSID '73) in Kyoto, Japan; and afterwards, during his long and fatal illness, stood by for him in seminars on "New Frontiers of Management" at the University of Michigan, Ann Arbor.

Donald Forgie

Library Science professor and a good friend of McLuhan recalls that, after lunching at the Centre sometime in 1972, he finally convinced Marshall to enter the precincts of "Fort Book" (the new Robarts library at U of T), a monster whose birth Marshall had done his utmost to frustrate. Just after they entered, as if in protest against Marshall's invasion, the power failed and the lights went out.

This breakdown led Marshall immediately to comment upon human "sensorial balance" in general: how lowering the visual raised the audile-tactile that led to lowering the voice level. By the time lighting was restored, we had agreed to try out the "hi-tech" hardware of the new lecture theatre by moving the Centre's seminars there for the next semester. These seminars attracted larger audiences, as well as more "outside" speakers, by providing much better motion picture and TV projection facilities (not to mention seating) than at the coach-house.

After an unforgettable demonstration of the theatre's electronic music capability, a lady stood up and said to the composer: "I think there is something wrong with electronic music. Can you tell me how it differs from other music? The composer was unable to answer immediately, so she began to sing a haunting Gaelic melody, and, in about a minute, added: "That is the difference!" Everybody knew what she meant.

Although a fruitful experience, the theatre's environment reduced fresh discovery by substituting electronic monologue for face-to-face dialogue. Ultimately, that induced Marshall to return to the intimacy of the Coach House.

Robert K. Logan

A physics professor at the University of Toronto, was a colleague of Marshall's who co-authored two articles with him, "Alphabet, Mother of Invention" and "The Double Bind of Human Communication."

Arthur Porter introduced me to Marshall by telephone and McLuhan immediately invited me to lunch at the Coach House. He wanted to discuss an interdisciplinary course I was teaching called the Poetry of Physics and the Physics of Poetry. At lunch he asked me a hundred questions about physics theory. I was astounded by his grasp of the most profound aspects of my discipline and by the level of questions that he asked. My head was spinning during that first encounter. His mind darted in and out of so many different corners. At that lunch we began a collaboration which was to last the rest of his life.

I told him of my theory that science began in the West and not the East despite all of the inventions of the Chinese because of the influence of monotheism and codified law. "What else do you find in the West which is not present in China?", he challenged me. I was dumbfounded. I couldn't think. I was so awestruck by his insights and the speed at which ideas were coming at me. "I give up", I gulped. "The alphabet", he said chortling and within five minutes we had the essence of the first paper we published together called "Alphabet, Mother of Invention". In that article, which formed the basis of a book entitled *The Alphabet Effect,* we developed the hypothesis that the phonetic alphabet, monotheism, codified law, abstract science and deductive logic were ideas unique to the West which created an environment for their mutual development.

The next six years of my life were the richest I experienced working with Marshall and serving as his science advisor. What I enjoyed the most of all was his good humour and warm friendship which I can illustrate with the following episode. He and I were arguing over the telephone about whether or not the Hebrew alphabet which contained only consonants was the first phonetic alphabet or whether that honour belonged to the Greek alphabet which also included the vowels. He said to me, "we will never settle this over the phone, come on over to the house for lunch." I rushed over and was greeted by Marshall wearing an apron with the Hebrew alphabet emblazoned all over it and grinning from ear to ear. We sat down in his kitchen where he served me a bowl of alphabet soup (Roman letters by the way), crackers and a bottle of beer. By the time the beer and soup were consumed we had cheerily resolved our dispute and were pushing on into new territory.

Marshall often called me on the telephone, day or night, to discuss new ideas. He loved bouncing his ideas off his friends and all those he met in the course of his interesting life. He had many different research colleagues ranging from Andy Warhohl to Prime Minister Trudeau.

One day, he asked me to chair the weekly Monday night seminar because he was having dinner with the Prime Minister and he planned to bring him to the seminar after our usual 8 o'clock starting time. He swore me to secrecy so that he could have the fun of surprising the group. Sure enough 45 minutes into our seminar I heard the sounds of the PM's motorcycle escort pulling up to the coach house. In strode Marshall with the Prime Minister and his entourage in tow and brazenly announced to the startled gathering of seminar participants, "Ladies and Gentleman, the Prime Minister of Canada." The discussion that evening included bilingualism and Quebec separatism, subjects of intense interest to Marshall. And he and I continued a dialogue with the Prime Minister on these themes primarily by letters which Marshall dictated to Marg Stewart.

I certainly have wonderful memories of my days with Marshall and some sad ones, particularly, during the last year of his life when he suffered the terrible fate of a stroke that left him aphasic. His struggle to communicate despite his horrible handicap has always been an inspiration to me. I have attempted to continue the work that I started with Marshall. And, as Marshall said of his relation to the work of Harold Innis, I am pleased to think of my own work as a footnote to the observations of McLuhan. He has enriched my life and I consider it a great honour to have been his friend and colleague.

CHAPTER C

A Monday-Night Seminar

Marshall had the faculty of stimulating the thinking of not only artists and scholars, but of many others, both inside and outside the University. This is amply confirmed by the Monday-night seminars which he chaired for over a decade.

Margaret Stewart's complete diary, which included a list of visitors to the Centre, was lost in the turmoil that followed her departure. Even of the famous, there were far too many either to remember, or to mention. However, Marg does recall that pianist Glenn Gould, who was both charming and shy, often came to see Marshall alone. Russian poet Yevtushenko also arranged an enjoyable "audience" with him. "Bill" Davis, while Minister of Education (afterwards Premier of Ontario), dropped in to chat; and Malcolm Muggeridge, with his wife, visited several times to share their insights on religious questions.

One Monday evening, as "Bob" Logan has just related, Prime Minister Trudeau likewise came to the Centre and discussed, in friendly informality, problems of running the government of Canada.

Professor of History, Lynn White Jr. also shared his discoveries of some revolutionary social effects of technology. For example, his investigations and discoveries of strong feudal effects from simple medieval technologies (the stirrup, the compound crank, the rattrap spring and the horse collar) led to deeply intriguing and groundbreaking insights.

We had other unforgettable evenings, for example: Harley Parker (who was then teaching at an institute for the deaf in Rochester, NY) brought along some of his students to demonstrate their powers of communication; and Eric McLuhan, who was retraining perception of former "drop-outs" at Fanshawe College (London, Ontario), also came with his students to describe what they were really capable of doing, even without using their eyes. We learned much from all of them about coping with problems of sensory deprivation.

From 1968, after we started to write *The Executive as*

Dropout (ultimately, the subtitle for *Take Today*), Marshall asked me to sit beside him during the Monday-night seminars.

My prime role in Monday's sessions (which were not always on Monday) was to kick off discussion for the first half-hour, Marshall used to say; but it was rarely for more than ten minutes. The "kick-offs" were based on "headings" regarding matters of long-term interest, or simply on current headlines discussed on the ten-minute drive with him from my home to the Centre. Marshall also expected me to "prompt" him unobtrusively on topics that might be appropriate for further discussion.

This chapter documents one of the very few seminars recorded, "Marshall McLuhan and Barrington Nevitt with Students and Guests," first reported in the *Innis Herald* of March 10, 1977, by Carl Scharfe.

MARSHALL:

One of the subjects that I had thought might be proper for tonight is one that Mr. Nevitt and I are working on — separatism. We are using a special approach. I am looking here at an item from the *Dallas Morning News*, end of November (1976), mentioning a strange aspect of nuclear warfare that shows a kind of flip characteristic. It starts: *Newsweek* said Space Battle between satellites could determine the outcome of any war on earth by crippling the orbiting early warning and ballistic missile defence systems of the losing nation, forcing it to capitulate under threat of massive nuclear attack. Some military thinkers even suggest that the super powers may ultimately be able to fight bloodless wars in space, settling the issue there without ever firing a shot on earth. That would be almost like settling a war by private combat or by a football game.

BARRINGTON:

In Latin America most of the revolutions used to be settled by counting how many soldiers or other armed forces could be lined up on each side.

MARSHALL:

A democratic method.

BARRINGTON:

People foolish enough to fight weren't soldiers, of course, they were civilians, and they got killed.

42

MARSHALL:

As war becomes impractical, in the sense that the cost of an actual battle with atom bombs and so on, would be too big to make war possible, this is a kind of sporty outlet, an alternative. Have a battle in the air with your ballistic missile defence systems, and the first system to crumble would be the end of the war. Then there would have to be a settling process. There would have to be a rearrangement of the power and territorial patterns on earth.

BARRINGTON:

As we have said in *Take Today*, The Third World War will be a war of images, but how do you settle it?

MARSHALL:

Jimmy Carter's recent election was fought by images, not policies. His image got him the black vote. Nothing was ever said in his policies to suggest any reason why the black should vote for Jimmy Carter, but his image did, and they put him in.

Mr. Nevitt and I call the electronic world, "The Fourth World." The electronic world goes around the First, Second, and Third Worlds. The Fourth World is an electronic service environment which is total. It's planetary.

All the nations of the world have transistor radios, and the Third World takes those radio programmes very seriously. There was a man in here today from the Middle East, and he said that people there listened to the radio intensely every waking hour.

A theme I have assumed with Mr. Nevitt is that radio itself (independent of its programming or content) is a very deadly instrument where you are dealing with semi-literates and non-literates, who live by ear.

This relates, by the way, to Ireland. The effect of radio in Ireland has been ferocious — an intensifying of separatism and warfare. It has exactly the same effect in the Middle East, China, or anywhere in the Third World. Radio would be bad medicine for India, Africa, China, any part of the Third World that has intense exposure to it. TV has completely different effects, politically.

French Canada is complicated by the fact that it has both radio and TV — the impulse to separate, to break away from some structure or family.

We'll pause here just to take note that the effect of radio, or electronic environments, on private individuals is alienation and splitting up; likewise on families, communities, and nations. Just why should instantaneous information have this strange effect of splitting people apart?

43

It has nothing to do with the programmes. It has to do with this service environment of instantaneous information as an ordinary, daily environmental fact. When your environment becomes instantaneous, when it becomes activated at the speed of light, it does strange things to the user.

BARRINGTON:

You don't even have to be listening to radio or looking at TV to be influenced by its effects, if you are living in a society inundated with it.

MARSHALL:

The shape of the service environment of roads affects people as much as if they owned a car. The environmental effect shapes the awareness of perceptual life and develops therefore the sorts of expectations that go with it. Nobody would question the fact that, if you lived in a very high speed motor car environment, it would have some effect on people. Yet, for some reason, the fact of living in an instantaneous, speed-of-light, environment has never been discussed. All that gets discussed are the programmes. What's on the air tonight? What's the show? They get studied, but the actual environmental service is ignored?

So, we are going to take a few spot checks on Québec under the conditions of electric service environment. When you submit people to such an environment, much depends upon the sort of people. The effect of radio on China is, presumably, not the effect that it has on Canada; and the effect on different age groups is also different.

BARRINGTON:

Also different on the village and city people.

MARSHALL:

One of the peculiarities of radio and electric technology is that it moves you instantaneously: you are everywhere at the speed of light, without a body. People using telephone, TV, or radio, or any other electric service do not have bodies; they are discarnate beings. This is easily noticed on the telephone when you are speaking to someone, a distant party. You know you don't have a body, and yet you are there, let's say, in New York; and they are here. Nobody has studied what this implies, psychologically, or otherwise.

JOE KEOGH:

Did I tell you that story about my little seven-year old Timmy calling up one of his friends and saying: "Is Dougie here?" from my house to his house.

MARSHALL:

Well, you say he's "on the phone," means he's not here. He's gone, or "on the air." When you're on the air you are everywhere at once. Incidentally, unlike angels (which, technically, can be only in one place at a time), when you are on the air you are everywhere at once. "He's on the air," means he is everywhere and anybody can pick him up; but the effect of not having a body, for most of the services in our information environment, has significance which nobody has looked into at all. I haven't. I would venture off-hand to say that people without bodies tend to be very weak in private identity, that a private identity tends to form in an interfacing of social surround. But, minus a body, the social interfacing or encounters are very weak. Again, it is very difficult to explain why the subject has never been studied.

Theologians, who should be the first to leap into the study, have never even mentioned the subject. It has a profound meaning for the future and the present of religion, not just the future. I would say off-hand it has very unfortunate meaning. But what we do in talking about these things is to study the pattern or the effect without value judgments. When you are discovering something that affects everybody it is somewhat gratuitous to impose a single private value judgment upon it.

BARRINGTON:

Philosophers feel they have to pass judgment on things...

MARSHALL:

They don't have to, but we are just explaining why we don't. If you notice that the motor car is destroying the family, that does not constitute a value judgment about the motor car. You could begin a quite violent discussion of the motor car as the destroyer of the family, if you started at that point. But to come back to Québec, an area about which I know relatively little. I've been there several times. I have many friends from there and have encountered them here at this College. At St. Mike's there are lots of French Canadians. We lived with them down in Windsor, Ontario (where there are large numbers of them), but I don't pretend to know very much about Québec. I do know that it has a very rich history, a very heavily layered and nourished history, unlike us. Our history is very thin and very porous, I would say.

French-Canadian history is very dense and rich. So is that of most European countries. The French have no problem about identity; they have an intense, very powerful identity, unlike English Canada.

Part of this is owing to their religion, their long practice of it, and their communal life in small agricultural parishes over the past 200 years. But prior to that, remember, they were the people who opened up North America — the fur traders and the explorers who opened up the whole continent, and who undertook violent forms.

They have had a very strange history, dynastically, also in their wars with and their relations with England, and France, and with the U.S. They've had their own political history in international terms.

They encountered a very strange situation when Canada became federal in the 19th century. Confederation was a very alien thing to them (entirely the product of hardware, railways, and industry), having spent their centuries with the fur traders and the world of lumber, fish, and other staples.

Now these people have suddenly encountered the Fourth World — electricity. It has happened in other Third-World areas, and it has very special effects on Third-World people.

I think one might say that Third-World people want to head for the city when the first large urbanized forms develop; they want to have a taste of the big city.

BARRINGTON:

They want to have all the products of the 19th century industry without having to go through the misery of having one.

MARSHALL:

Well that's true. Anybody would settle for that at any time, if it were possible. In all parts of the world today, there is a huge rush to the urban areas from the rural areas — a form of separatism in which the more stabilized forms of life are suddenly violated by the intrusion of new images. The images of the movies and of radio and TV programmes, advertise this impossibility — the new satis-factions of an entirely new urban life — all happening at very high speeds. This has happened around the world. It's not limited to French Canada or to North America in any way.

BARRINGTON:

The urban dweller in the USSR is now devoted to having a 19th century and all that that means — consumer goods, heavy indus-try, factories...

MARSHALL:

There is another big factor, mainly that, with the coming of indus-trialism, you have specialism in work — the job as opposed to role-playing. The villager in the country is not a job-holder; he is a role-player. Also, the time clock. Mr. Eliot devoted one of his most famous poems, "The Waste Land," to the effect of the time-kept city on the human psyche — fragmenting the individual into a clock robot. It has been in our own past too. We have often laughed at the clock watchers, people who hated their jobs, people who kept their eye on the clock; but it was a kind of revolution that most North Americans have been through. I know more about the way the English went through this period, but in a sense they never came out of it. The English are seemingly trapped in this situation (that of the industrial world, with its fragmented work, fragment-ed time patterns, fragmented people); it is still with them as a great burden.

What about the social services as an attempt to compensate for what people went through in the Industrial Age?

The industrial thing is now pretty well behind us. Wherever you have intense industrialism you can have automation. There is no highly mechanized form of work which cannot be automated. This holds, of course, the spectre of unemployment over everybody. In England they have tried to come out of 19th century fragmenta-tion by social services, which have, I expect people know, increas-ingly impoverished everybody. The unions have been one of the main pushers in the social service thing, but the result is that England has lost all momentum, all vision, all hope. A highly industrialized and tooled-up country ready to do anything, but without any opportunity to do anything.

BARRINGTON:

That is total fragmentation on all levels of government...

MARSHALL:

The fragmentation of industry has been passed along from the fac-tory to the Civil Service and to the educational system.

This brings us back to French Canada where they are bitter about centralism, Ottawa, government, service environment, civil servants. This represents total loss of freedom and human respon-sibility from their point of view: that is, for those who have lived in French rural areas, where the individual is a completely whole being, to have to encounter a bureaucrat or a civil servant (a sort of residual legatee of the industrial worker).

Incidentally, there is a book by Kafka which enshrines that story in a very powerful way. It's called *The Castle*. Kafka himself was a European civil servant and bureaucrat; he wrote this very imaginative account of the loss of meaning, identity, and direction in the life of the civil service. By definition, a civil service is going nowhere, and anybody in the civil service is going nowhere. That isn't necessarily a bad thing. The idea of getting places, of going places, is a metaphor geared to the American vocabulary.

We should remember that a University is not going anywhere, and a city is not going anywhere, because the University's job is to be, not to go; and the city's job likewise is not to go somewhere, but to be a city. There is a huge gap between going places and being: one is role-playing and the other is job-holding. The job-holder may be trying to climb, climb, climb, to go somewhere; but the role-player is a person who gets deeply involved in his work and is completely satisfied by his work.

Electronically, we cannot specialize anymore. Electronically, information activity is at such high speed that the fragmented specialist will not hold up. The only hope of remaining inside the electronic situation is to become a role-player.

Medical deans are fond of saying on graduation day that "you people have been penned up here for five years and have lost complete touch with what is going on in the world, and there have been so many discoveries made since you began studying medicine that you are now obsolete!" They say this also to the engineers, and so on. But role-playing means involvement in depth. A school teacher doesn't think of herself as a job-holder, but as a role-player, because the commitment, the dedication to the activity of teaching young people, is not in any way, in any sense of the word, a job. That is to say, it isn't a 9-to-5 job. It isn't a fragmented specialist job. The satisfactions, therefore, that come from role-playing, whether as a medical man or a doctor or a teacher, are not the satisfactions of a job-holder. As a teacher, who has had lots of opportunities to live with job-holders, I know there is that huge gap between the two worlds. There's never a moment of boredom in role-playing. Well, Rex, if you have to play *Hamlet*, the same part 365 times or a whole year —

REX HAGON (actor):
It's a job.

MARSHALL:
Are you sure? It becomes merely a routine? I have heard it said by actors, who have had to play the same part over and over, and even relatively small parts, that the audience is never the same twice.

Role-playing does give an enormous amount back, if there is a détente going on, a dialogue going on all the time between the teacher and students; but the job-holder is not expected to inter-communicate. His activities are supposed to be relatively imper-sonal.

We should relate the dropout or the separatism thing to the hemispheres, and we will spend a little time doing this now. It's not a new subject for us. The two hemispheres, recognized by mod-ern neuro-surgeons, are called the left and the right cerebral hemi-spheres. They alternately control the left and the right hands, or sides of the body. The right hemisphere controls the left hand. If you are left-handed, it is possible that you are strongly influenced by the right hemisphere. The right hemisphere has completely dif-ferent characteristics from the left hemisphere, although in prac-tice they both manage to talk back and forth to each other through the *corpus callosum.*

Basically, the left hemisphere is the dominant one for right handed-people. The left hemisphere is characterized by, in the first place, lineality, sequentiality. It relates to people's habits of mak-ing logical connections. It relates to syntax and grammar, and to statements, propositions, and above all logical connectiveness: words coded in linear and grammatical form. This is a left hemi-sphere power.

The right hemisphere's dominant characteristic is the simulta-neous — pattern recognition and body language, rather than artic-ulate expression of the left hemisphere. The right hemisphere is the only hemisphere which enables you to recognize a human face. When the left hemisphere is left to itself, you are unable to recog-nize a human countenance; because there are so many components in a face, seeing them simultaneously is necessary to seeing them as affixed. So people who have had damage to their right hemi-sphere often lose their ability to recognize people. The left hemi-sphere is strongly marked by visual characteristics, visual order, visual space, visual connectiveness: Euclidean space. All the con-nective lineal space, whatever it tends to be, seems to be in the charge of the left hemisphere.

Acoustic space is space that we create by listening to all direc-tions at once; we hear from above and around, and below — all points at once. We hear from all directions simultaneously. That creates a space that is acoustic, auditory. The right hemisphere is the world of the figure on the ground — what is called gestalt, like the wheel and the axle. What made the wheel and the axle possi-ble is the interval between them. The dominant factor is interval, not connection. So the "wheel and axle" is a very powerful image of the *gestalt* world of figure and ground. The "rub," in dialogue between people, is figure/ground. There is encounter. There is interfacing. There is not necessarily logic in dialogue, but there is involvement; there is experience. Body language is characteristic of the right hemisphere: gesture, dance, and all forms of athleticism. A highly gifted athlete is a person with a strong right hemisphere.

One of the things that is happening today is that the environment that surrounds ordinary citizens of this planet is a simultaneous environment (we're talking about the electric environment). It has become the typical environment of everybody on the planet. This strongly favours the dominance of the right hemisphere, because what pushes one or the other hemisphere up into dominance is the kind of surround or ground in which they exist. For many centuries the left hemisphere has enjoyed dominance because of an environment of lineal characteristics, road systems, and the written word, the organization of speech in grammatical form.

The Chinese don't have these factors in their traditional world. Their ideograms, their forms of writing, do not require any syntax, any connectiveness, any lineality. They are icons that exist in their own right and they contain a whole world. The Chinese, naturally, are people with very high dominance of the right hemisphere.

Third World people all tend to have a dominant right hemisphere. That is a hemisphere in which things happen simultaneously or are recognized as happening in a pattern; it's a very musical world. The right hemisphere is musical and it is "group." Private identity tends to go with the left hemisphere. Group identity tends to go with the right hemisphere. The Third World does not stress private individual identity so much as group, corporate identity.

When something happens to the environment, which upsets the pattern of dominance and shifts the components of the experience around in different patterns, people tend to lose identity. Violent changes in the environment, such as industrialism, tend to upset existing identity patterns. In the Third World, when they learn our phonetic literacy, how to read and write in our patterns, they tend to lose their group identity. It is just as violent an experience for them to lose a group identity as it is for us to lose a private identity.

How about French Canada? Having long enjoyed a powerful group identity, it now confronts an industrial world which partly diminished that identity in favour of private identity, goal seeking, individual competition — things that the Third World deplores

50

and finds appalling.

One of the peculiarities of people who have lost identity is violence. When people have been robbed of their identities in some way, they become violent because, strangely enough, violence is a way of finding out who you are. If you want to know who you are, you have to discover where your boundaries are, what the limits are, what kinds of situations you are in; what kinds of people you are dealing with.

We accept the Western movie as a world of violence. Remember, when you are out on the Western frontier you are a nobody. Every day you have to prove who you are. So the Western frontiersman, John Wayne style, has to be tough. It's not a social environment. It is an environment where the individual has to prove who he is all the time. Just how this relates to French Canada I am going to ask Mr. Nevitt to comment, and you to comment. The separatist movement is a form of violence, it is a quest for identity. When a kid leaves home suddenly, it's an identity quest. He wants to know who he is. He doesn't think he'll find out as long as he is home. Nora Hellmer in the *Doll's House*, by the way, is a famous case of a mother who decided to leave home to find out who she was. Leaving home is just one form of violence, but it is obviously an identity quest. What sort of an identity quest are the French bent on?

BARRINGTON:

If we start with now, we'll see that this violence is a question of identity linked with something which is historical. The whole industrial establishment is identified in the French Canadian language as *Les Anglais*, the English speaking community. So that when they are feeling this transformation, from the communal world of the village to communities in the cities, occurring as it is in their society, they can very easily identify all their miseries as being associated with the industrial lords who run the industry down there. They are mostly, in their minds, English. It doesn't have to be so for this to feel true. If you look further back in their history, they were actually among the first to industrialize (in Canada), but it was always on a very small scale. Big scale industry and financing came first from England, for the staples. This was the early history of Canada, aligned with the fur trade, fish, and lumber. Great fortunes were built on this basis.

Although all these fortunes seemed to have originated with and to be controlled by the British, the French were not far behind. There was war between these two groups of rivals, who were vying to strip Canada of furs and other resources. It was finally won by the English at the expense of the Indians who were here. The people who became dominant were British. This situation settled down, with constant seeking by French Canadians to establish their own identity or dominance, yet never quite succeeding...

MARSHALL:

This is a good point to flip over to Levesque's talk in New York where he explained that he was now leading a country into the same course that the Americans had followed in leaving England. This is a bit of leg pulling.

BARRINGTON:

It is also a good example of a switch in figure/ground relationship that we are always talking about here — a typical demagogic trick. That is, take the present day situation, the figure that is visible as the French Canadian desire for separation, and put it in another context, a context of 200 years ago in the United States, as if those conditions still existed. But of course, they don't.

MARSHALL:

On the other hand, the conditions under which America left England are not unlike the conditions under which Québec is wishing to leave Canada.

BARRINGTON:

That is so far as the visible figures are concerned, but as far as the invisible ground is concerned we are living today in an electronic context.

MARSHALL:

Let's not skip too quickly over the visible figures.

BARRINGTON:

All right then, the visible figures appear very similar. This is where Levesque's story can have some attraction for the French Canadian. It is possible to say that this is unfinished business. This is the legal case, if you like, for the French Canadian who says: "we never did have the right to determine our own 'national' identity or our own 'national' future." The word "national" brings up a very special thing that Marshall has been talking about all along — that "nations" and "nationalism" arose only through phonetic literacy with Gutenberg technology. Before that, the dominant relationships were between families, and tribes, and clans.

In French Canada, you have all these things going on, and you also have the educated people being highly literate. They are closer to the people of 18th century France, that is, its Age of Reason, and the people who demanded logic in everything. Such is the elite of French Canada today. You notice it in the Cabinet Ministers that Levesque has chosen. Most of them have post graduate degrees, a sign of literary elitism, and, that with their academic French (which is more "purified" and specialized than English), further intensifies their "national" feelings. In this situation, these elites are still trying to complete the business of the 18th century by establishing a French "*nation*" (yet to be defined) in North America, which they hadn't succeeded in doing before, from the top.

From the bottom, you have the other situation — the tribal feeling of the country people who have always been French in another way, French in a non-literate, oral tradition.

MARSHALL:

You are covering an awful lot of ground, Barry! You covered the 18th century in about three seconds. Let's pause for a moment. Let's talk about it. The 18th century in France led to the 1789 blood bath.

BARRINGTON:

The logical outcome — getting rid of the *Ancien Régime*.

MARSHALL:

The kind of enlightenment that led to those blood baths is not exactly the kind that is happening today, is it?

BARRINGTON:

No. It's very different today.

MARSHALL:

However, if there are parallels there's no harm in looking at them. Mr. Nevitt's approach is to suggest that the French have a lot of unfinished 18th century business that they are trying to settle right now in Canada. It really doesn't have very much to do with us in English Canada, because, strangely enough, the British bypassed 1789 by having an Industrial Revolution much bloodier than 1789. The 1789, which the British bypassed by means of the Industrial Revolution, led straight to the world of the job, fragmented work, and the isolated individual by establishing a market in land, labour and capital. A market was set up in England whereby the work ability of anybody could be marketed for money. Nature, land, labour and capital all became purchasable...marketable.

BARRINGTON:

Nature became the market and the laws of the market became the laws of Nature, which is still being proclaimed.

MARSHALL:

That was a flip that wasn't a straight progress. But you see a pattern, the enlightenment marched toward the blood bath of 1789. The British veered off into the Industrial Revolution and let them have their blood bath. The British might have had a blood bath too, at that period, if they hadn't had the Industrial Revolution. They had much the same set of medieval backlog to manage or to liquidate; but French Canada today has been robbed of 1789. It did not happen in French Canada! One of the big gaps, I suppose, between French Canada and France is precisely the skipping of the French Revolution.

Now, I was giving it a moment to sink in. To skip the French Revolution is to have missed a great deal of experience and a great deal of identity quest; but French Canada, more or less blindly, went ahead, minus a Revolution. On the other hand, they were living a very violent life.

ANN GIRARD (French-Canadian TV journalist):

You must remember that the people who were living in French Canada had already been here for more than a 100 years. They were already Canadian.

MARSHALL:

Yes.

GIRARD:

That was a Revolution in its own way.

MARSHALL:

Yes, because they were leading very violent lives in the outdoors, and it was a tough, really rough life. They didn't need a revolution in order to be tough. However, the revolution had totally different consequences from being a fur trader in Calgary. It's difficult, for me at least, to decide which might have been the better fate. The Revolution opened careers to talents! (Napoleon)

Up to 1789, the channeling of human careers had been very much in the world of role-playing.

GIRARD:

Well that's exactly what I mean. The people who were already in Canada left France, because there was no place for them there. If they came to Canada, to the new land, they escaped all the role-playing. That is, they could become masters at their trade in two years, instead of having to go fifteen in France.

MARSHALL:

Yes. Why we called it a land of opportunity — the opportunity to become a job-holder rather than a role-player. But now we are flipping back into role-playing, in the First World, that is. The English industrial world is going back into role-playing. *Upstairs Downstairs* (BBC series) is not accidental. Its sudden popularity in North America is worth studying. It's a fascination with role-playing and fixed positions, where people "know their place," and that sort of thing. The world of this new series called Roots is a strange quest for "Who am I?" and "Where did I come from?": a desire to know one's limits, one's boundaries, one's identity. I've seen only one episode. It is a significant thing. The *Forsyth Saga* was an earlier gesture in the same direction. This 1910 English paternalistic family got tremendous attention and excitement in Russia.

BARRINGTON:

I think one can say that in Russia the classics, for the very same reason, have enormous audiences, just as the poets have — Pushkin, for example.

MARSHALL:

Well, nostalgia, which you notice in the world of our replays and revivals, is part of this questing for roots. This has something to do with French Canada and separatism. When a young person leaves home looking for identity, he severs. So we should know what sort of identity the French hope to find or want to find before they leave. Is it merely a repeat of the one they might have had if they stayed? Is it the desire to become what we are? The Third World in general is quite eager to assume the characteristics of the 19th century, the English 19th century, a world of big productions, big markets and big consumer goods. It seems odd to us who have been through it that anyone would want to do it again.

CARL SCHARFE:

Does the ground for that environment even exist anymore? A ground for a 19th century environment?

MARSHALL:

No. With the tremendous reality of electric power and electric information, the 19th century environment does not exist as a possibility.

CARL:

So where are they going?

MARSHALL:

They are obviously not going where they think they are going. They certainly are not. I'm not saying they shouldn't, if they could. It might be all right. However, the fact is they are breaking away. Don't worry about whether they do anymore; they already have broken away, probably as much as they ever will. Psychologically, the breakaway has been completed already. Some of the hardware links still remain; but, in spirit, the breakaway has taken place. On the other hand, that is also true of many situations in our world where separation or breakaway has also occurred within many institutions. It's true in religion, education, politics, and business. In all those situations massive breakaway or separatism has occurred. It's obviously not accidental, because it has taken place simultaneously at all levels, in all fields; and I suggest, at the moment, the dominant pushing up of the right hemisphere of the brain into dominance by the new electric environment is a very active cause, a very potent cause. If the left hemisphere enjoyed centuries of dominance from the 5th century BC until now, it was thanks to the lineality of the environment created by the services of literacy, which included industrialism and assembly line structures, and so on. These all date from the world of the alphabet, the world of the written word. Suddenly we move into a simultaneous world where the sequential written word is no longer dominant. It's still here, but it's dominance is certainly very, very much less and daily getting less and less.

To summarize, then, we are saying that this is, after all, speculative. This is not an attempt at a positive truth. We are saying that with the coming of the electric surround or environment of simultaneous information, the tendency for the right hemisphere to become dominant is the tendency to make First-World people into Third-World people. Our own children are going backwards into the Third World in tendency, and by wish. In reality, most of them are staying around doing much the same old thing. But the desire to break away from the industrial community and the highly pyramided, vertically structured, has been felt by all our young people today. It takes the form of looking for different kinds of entertainment, different sorts of costumes and communes, and various groups — grouping of themselves. Now, we are saying that French Canada is going through something like that on a big scale. But, because it was already Third World, it already had many of the advantages of the Third World, and its response to this new dominance of the right hemisphere is ambiguous. It's, in a sense, "coals to Newcastle." I mean they were already right hemisphere people, and to be suddenly handed an electronic package, which made them much more right hemisphere, is a strange fate. Remember, the right hemisphere tends to favour the ear, music, acoustic space, simultaneity. The French Canadian had this.

By the way, the world of Jimmy Carter — the Deep South — had it. He is the first president from the Deep South, the first ever. Only possible under electronic conditions. His image, from the Deep South — the voice, the rhythms, and so on — represents a real revolution in American life. But, for French Canada to be told that we envy you, "we really want to be like you," "we want to acquire your patterns of life," is a kind of treachery. In the very moment, when they want to be so different, they find themselves being admired for what they already were.

I was just thinking about the thing myself. I don't see the pattern very clearly. It's a funny pattern. It's not a logical pattern. There's a huge amount of illogicality in it. What could be more strangely illogical than the pronouncement of Davis (Ontario's premier) today? What is his theme? *What we must do with French Canada, For French Canada?*

VOICES:
Save it!

MARSHALL:
We must save it. From itself?

VOICES:
Save it from Canada! Save it from another conservative minority government?!

BARRINGTON:
I've heard it put the other way by the *Globe and Mail*: "French Canada should save us from ourselves."

MARSHALL:
This is what we have been saying, that with the Fourth World dominant, or rather, with the new electronic environment dominant, French Canada is in a position to save us from ourselves. It's in a position to go in the direction that our young people are going. Our young people want to get back to the farm. They want to get their bare feet on the ground again. They do this on the city streets as a token of their unrest. You see people walking around barefoot in the city street.

LADY (with Rex Hagon):

Excuse me, how do you explain the separation in Québec as being led by a group of men who are left-brained literates, who are very much grounded in that tradition. Yet they are leading a revolution, so to speak, of the right hemisphere.

MARSHALL:

Yes. French Canada is simultaneously enjoying this new electric service. That is, literacy fosters habits of careful ordering of things and putting things in their proper places. It is left hemisphere. So if you wish to maneuver or manipulate a world of strong left hemisphere characteristics, you have to acquire those qualities in order to rule, there is no question. This is a paradox: if you wish to change people from one state to another, you must, at first, come from the state from which they wish to leave. French Canada though is full of paradoxes, because it has lived through so many regimes. When you think that it took on the Olympic Games, the ultimate form of 19th century competition — nationalism and connection. The Olympic Games are the most extreme example of nationalistic competition in the history of the world and the French Canadians took on the Olympic Games this time. It may be the last time ever.

VOICE:

The Canadian government sold us down the river with the amount of money they got for all of that media coverage.

MARSHALL:

The Government was the recipient of payment for the showing of the Olympic Games?

VOICE:

No. The Canadian government was the laughing-stock of the world! All the major networks were amazed at how little we charged. Look at what the Russians are doing. They are charging for the next Olympic Games not only a shopping fee, but the American networks have to provide all the cameramen. CBC provided all cameramen in Montreal, and much more.

MARSHALL:

Well, what do you make of that in terms of the French Canadian situation? That they should have sponsored the Olympic Games is a paradox (because, as I say, this is an extreme form of 19th century nationalism), and may have been a challenge to these people.

I think there are a great many questions.

CARL:

It's Moscow that's holding the next games.

MARSHALL:

There again. Nationalism. There's not supposed to be any hint of that in the Soviet Republic is there?

Let's introduce some people here. Mr. John Muller from Holland, film maker — John just say a word about your work. He's come here to study at the Centre.

JOHN MULLER:

Well, I was just lucky enough to be sent by the Canada Council. Actually, my studies were started in California. That's when I first got in touch with some books by Professor McLuhan. Then, I ended up my film and television education in San Francisco, went back to Holland, and that's where I've worked since 1968. Glad to be back and see what had developed.

MARSHALL:

In the past year, you have made several films. How many did you say?

MULLER:

Twenty-five documentaries. That makes approximately two per month. So that's working too hard actually.

MARSHALL:

What kind of materials are you working with? What sort of documentaries?

MULLER:

16mm films, 75% of which were broadcast on television. Films, for instance, on some of the Dutch heritage in the United States, linked to the Bicentennial; some programmes on new school systems in Holland trying to get into a progressive way of integrating primary schools and secondary schools; and some documentaries, outside television, on pedestrian problems in so-called residential streets, which you might need here in Toronto too. I think it would be very interesting to see what has been developed in Holland on this matter. Some of these subjects I worked on last year, also some political specials.

MARSHALL:

What did you do about TV education on that documentary?

MULLER:

TV education, in that series on how to integrate the media in high schools, and the other documentary that I just told you about:

mainly, on what possibilities there are to integrate primary school without interruptions into a secondary school. That means how to build a Middle School — they call it in Europe now — to make schooling go more smoothly from one school into another.

MARSHALL:

At present, that tends to be quite a jolt?

MULLER:

It is. So I was very much interested in your last book.

MARSHALL:

You mean the one that hasn't been printed yet.

MULLER:

Yes. So that is actually what I have done.

MARSHALL:

Well, that's quite a lot. And beside Mr. Muller is Mr. Hickey from CBC. He's not here on any official mission. He's just sitting in. But you might mention a bit about your work too Mr. Hickey. What's your theme?

HICKEY:

I am working as a radio technician at CBC, primarily with the news department.

MARSHALL:

What's been happening there? What sort of new developments? New ways of gathering the news?

HICKEY:

Not since I've been there. I've only been working with them a couple of months. I am still more or less getting oriented.

MARSHALL:

We have some Sisters here from Kansas City hiding behind Mr. Furnette. Sisters, do introduce yourselves.

SR. JEANNE D'ARC:

I'm from Marymount College in Kansas. My background has been sculpture and art history. In the past three years I've been in adult education, which is the reason I'm here in Toronto. I'm studying at OISE [Ontario Institute for Studies in Education] studying in the adult education program.

MARSHALL:

And you have a colleague beside you?

SR. MARY SAVOY:

Yes. We're from the same place, Kansas; and I'm in Continuing Education at OISE. also. I'm interested in media as a form of education for adults.

MARSHALL:

For adults! There is a current issue of the *TV Guide* which contains a survey of convicts' attitudes towards TV. That is people really up for a long time, many of them for life, and how they regard television. All convicts are apparently now supplied with good TV sets. Such is the hardship of our prisons. They pass the word along: all the new gimmicks, all new twists they find in crimes; and these are passed along quickly to the boys who are on the way out, and are tried out quickly in the community. There really is an astonishing story of how much television has helped to improve the level of crime. But it's the first time I've ever seen a report from a penal colony of the effect of television on their activities. The effect is total and crosses the whole spectrum, whether they are in small time or big time crime. So TV has had a tremendous educational influence on our convicts. Nothing to do with violence, by the way. While they are getting panicky about violence on television, the convicts are quite quietly, calmly proceeding to improve their break-in techniques and so on.

HAGON:

You might wish to compare the fact that the private investigators recently were quite up in arms because, while the techniques displayed on television were indeed up-to-date electronically, the private investigators were getting the short end of the stick. They were not being fairly represented. Their life was not one of glamour. They had to follow the letter of the law and could not break into places. Indeed, the private investigator was going down and the criminal was getting a helping hand.

MARSHALL:

The gumshoe's lot is not a happy one.

HAGON:

No, definitely not.

MARSHALL:

This is Rex Hagon speaking, an old friend from St. Mary's St. days, when we lived over there. He is now in the field of TV, and acting. I think this is your first visit here isn't it, Rex?

HAGON:

I am getting more into literature. Surprisingly enough, I think television is having a very bad effect on our young, in spite of that being my livelihood.

MARSHALL:

You say you are tending to get a bit more into literature.

HAGON:

Yes. I think children's literature needs to have a far better shake. I've been visiting a lot of public schools and just been noticing that they can't read and are not speaking well. That's hurting and is going to hurt even more.

MARSHALL:

We have quite a number of visitors here tonight. I'm sure I haven't spotted them all. Oh yes, here's Mr. Mathias from the *London Free Press*. Could you say a word about what brought you here?

MATHIAS:

I'll be as brief as possible. I've lived in Toronto for a number of years. I worked for the now defunct *Toronto Telegram* and at the *London Free Press*. I'm doing a series of stories on "Downtown in our City of Toronto." It's not really a comparison because this is a major metropolitan city and ours a small community. The problem I'm interested in right now: I have been talking to the political officials, business people, street people; but I haven't heard anything on the inner scape: how the city affects the inner being — problems of human scale and grandiose concepts, compared to what a human being can handle. Things like that. One reason I came here tonight: I thought maybe the "carom effect" might give me some ideas.

MARSHALL:

The carom effect? Never hear of that.

MATHIAS:

Yes. Just by ideas bouncing off one another.

MARSHALL:

Well, we're bouncing. [People coming in, others moving to make space.] Mr. Fernette is an architect who studies exactly those things. You might wish to comment on Mr. Mathias's project; he is trying to get some idea of the impact of metropolitan inner city life on people.

FERNETTE:

Those kinds of concerns are being reflected now in the 40 foot limit, in construction, employing what is called low-rise, high-density techniques, based on a study that came out of New York; it addresses the kinds of issues you are talking about: scale, and impact of grandiose schemes. It's strange to note that you can get the same density that typical high rise buildings achieve — like 70 units per acre — with typical low rise construction, like walk-up apartments, things that people know how to use and can relate to. People don't seem to know how to use high rise apartments. They don't know what to do with the space that's left over. The park, whose space is it? It ends up being nobody's space. The issues you are talking about are being dealt with in some areas. You might look at St. Lawrence Housing Development and see how the concerns for human scale are being treated in a physical building.

MARSHALL:

We have Joe Keogh here, from York University. He teaches media up there. Do you have any thoughts you'd like to pass along?

JOE:

Those on page 22 of the current *Innis Herald* (Jan., 1977).

MARSHALL:

You have some observations on the habit of speaking aloud? Talking to oneself, he says...

JOE:

As a result of a couple of months of High School supply teaching. Being an old college teacher, suddenly discovering the drives of grade 9s, it occurred to me that the average student in today's elementary and secondary schools, when he is apparently thinking, is not doing the old literacy routine of sub-vocalizing. He's not talking to himself, which is the accepted critical, logical, post-renaissance method of thought. He is more frequently than not listening to himself. It's a form of meditation that is not liturgical or, at least, it's liturgical only in the sense that it comes from the new media.

MARSHALL:

A kind of inner trip?

JOE:

He is replaying all the radio and TV programmes he's heard in the last week, the last 24 hours.

MARSHALL:

When we go to sleep, is it not expected that we shall launder and scrub the imagery of the day? We purge the images of the day as we sleep. But you are saying that this activity consists of purging the past years of experience?

JOE:

It may account for the somnambulistic factor of a great many classrooms. The sleep may take place in our waking hours. Had you thought of it?

MARSHALL:

I'm thinking about it. We have some other visitors here tonight, Mrs. Bhatia from McMaster, actually Mohawk College. She is a personal friend of Mrs. Gandhi. Have you any kind words to say about Mrs. Gandhi tonight?

MRS. BHATIA:

Well, I'm not exactly in touch. I was there last year and that's about all. Things are very changed and erratic. I can't say very much because people tend to think in other ways. When I knew her, she was much younger and we sort of studied together, but she has gone a different way. I can't say what she is doing now.

MARSHALL:

It doesn't seem to carry much favour with the press.

MRS. BHATIA:

Yes.

MARSHALL:

Now, who else are visitors here tonight?

FR. CASEY:

I'm Michael Casey from Dublin, South of Ireland. As you might guess, I'm a priest in the Dublin Diocese, a Catholic priest, and am in Toronto studying Community Development. Many people ask why I came to Toronto, and Canada, to study community, coming from Ireland. There's a lot happening here at the moment.

MARSHALL:

How long have you been here?

FR. CASEY:

Just since August.

MARSHALL:

Have you had any luck in discovering the qualities of community in Canada, if any?

FR. CASEY:

Well, it's just a superficial look — a first impression. One thing the Canadian people don't appreciate about themselves, that's the fact that they are very reasonable people. They reason things out quite a lot. I'm not now comparing that to the sort of worst patterns of the Irish — fighting Irish — that we fight when we disagree. But I think that Canadians are quite reasonable in lots of differences they have. That's a first impression. They are all surprised when I say that. That's a useful attitude in a community.

MARSHALL:

Land of Rye and Caution. Canadians are a cautious people and this may come partly from the Scottish sector. But, no, I don't think we are exactly fiery people. Our encounters with the French Canadians will probably test us very much.

FR. CASEY:

Well, I'd that in mind, you know. Sort of reminds me of home. But I do think they may be cautious. It's a useful quality, which they shouldn't throw away quickly, being able to discuss things, and get on together as we should. The other thing that struck me about Canada, which again is superficial, the fact that friendships are rather transient here. Very nice people to meet, friendly people, but lasting friendships? — from my point of view, what I've seen so far, a pragmatic approach to friendship.

MARSHALL:

Do you see any reason why that might be so, that is, in the external world?

FR. CASEY:

I don't.

MARSHALL:

You know we have this incredible turnover of habitations Four years is the average maximum dwelling period. People are on the move all the time. There isn't much incentive to form lasting friendships, when you know you will be forming new friendships a few miles away very soon.

FR. CASEY:

Yes. There have been some suggestions. I've been trying to find out the reason. They were saying more mobility, etc. Besides (I worry about this) it is a fact that quite a lot of people say: "Well, I don't really need friends, you know, I can get on without friends," quite often; and I realize that really nobody can get on without friends.

MARSHALL:

You encounter that attitude quite a bit, do you?

FR. CASEY:

Quite a lot of people say more by their attitude really (implying, without actually saying: "I'll make friends, if I like them and they are useful, not to use them, but if they are useful to me here and now.") People like that are, maybe more often, the ones who need friends most of all, and are then surprised when they haven't got any.

MARSHALL:

What you say is very interesting. There is the two-car family, which is not exactly indicated as a place of friendship, but rapid turnover in acquaintances. The idea that we don't need friends is strange. It has maybe something to do with that much-earlier pioneer attitude. The pioneers came over here not expecting to have any friends; they felt sufficiently self-reliant to be able to make it without. The pioneers all tended to strike that attitude, at least, 200 years ago. They were very proud of their self-reliance, their capacity to make it without friends. So they would live miles and miles apart. That was one of the techniques by which the continent was opened up. Community in those towns was a very strange thing too.

There is a hangover from that period that you may, or may not, have noticed. North Americans go outside to be alone, and they go home to be social; whereas Europeans go outside to be social, and home to be alone. We reversed that attitude. It comes from that ancient period, when pioneers got along without friends. They came here to tame the wilderness. When they went outside, they went to fight with their axes and their weapons, their guns.

It's unconscious. Europeans are not aware that they go outside to be social. They take it for granted. But North Americans don't go outside to be social.

GIRARD:

Would you say that French Canadians are like that too?

MARSHALL:

Yes, to a large degree. I'm not as well acquainted with them; but the motor car is the symbol of that going outside to be alone. It is the supreme privilege of the American to be absolutely alone in his car, when he goes outside. That's why he doesn't like to have anybody else in his car, and doesn't like to use public transit. Privacy is something that you buy with your car. So traffic jams are very welcome to Americans. They love to sit in traffic jams. They've discovered this from questionnaires and interviews — that people held up in traffic jams, as long as they are alone, are very happy.

They do their thinking, their decision-making, their planning, while in the car. There is no privacy outside the car. That's why Americans do not mind commuting 20 or 30 miles a day. It doesn't bother them at all. So, in the sense of profound relation to community — what you've come to study — the motor car is really the antithesis of community. Yet it is the central fact of our lives.

QUESTIONER:

How would you explain the car pool then?

MARSHALL:

It doesn't work. It isn't used. It's a phrase honoured in the breach not the observance. Car pools never have worked. Often called upon in national emergencies and so on; but for daily use they don't work now, and they never have worked. Do you know any car pools yourself? I don't think there is such a thing except by dire necessity. Another aspect of that community thing is in order.

We take strangers home without a second thought. We bring strangers into our homes at the drop of a hat, because home is where we are friendly, kindly, and hospitable; but not outside the home.

FR. CASEY:

What really surprises me is that people here are very friendly, very sociable, when you meet them at work; but there is contradiction in following through of friendships, and I was rather surprised at that.

MARSHALL:

It's a kind of specialism, that of the job or the various areas in which you meet people. You don't give yourself. You specialize. Well, friendship, in your sense, is a kind of giving that requires a lot of time and devotion to achieve. It's alien, I think, to North Americans. Any more visitors here?

You wanted to comment on Fr. Casey's comments? Go ahead.

MULLER:

Well, we had the oil crisis in Europe. People tried to set up car pools. It didn't work very well. But what I think counts also for Europe is that somehow, real friendship starts only when you have gone through something together, a crisis maybe. I think the Canadians who went through the war — war veterans — are dependable friends, because they were friends during crisis times. Those are the ones they can count on. I think, at the same time, that, with alienation developing in our new town projects, we are coming back to what you call human scale.

We have the same kind of alienation (in Holland). Maybe in Ireland it is different, because you have some kind of tradition of pub life or social meeting places that the Dutch and, I think, the Scandinavians don't have. The English have this. I think we are also an alienated people. I don't think it's only the Americans.

MARSHALL:

Much of our literature is based on the idea of wandering forth to be very much alone, like Walden Pond. Thoreau at Walden Pond didn't want to meet anybody. I remember Herman Kahn saying (he grew up in California) that "when we went out for our Sunday walks, if we met anyone the day was ruined." And you can walk and walk in America without seeing a human being.

CHAPTER D

Teaching and Learning

We learn as we teach and vice versa. Wordsworth recognized this complementarity as: "The child is father to the man." The parents make their children just as the children remake their parents, and each other, in a continuing process. Marshall constantly demonstrated the essence of teaching: *provide shortcuts to old knowledge by organizing information, and explore means to discover new knowledge by organizing ignorance.* Like Samuel Coleridge, he also advised his students: "Start with the other man's ignorance, if you wish to gain his relevant knowledge quickly."

Mother St. Michael Guinan

Professor Emeritus, University of Western Ontario, founder of the Canadian Institute of Religion and Gerontology (now resident at Brescia College, London, Ontario).

I first met Marshall McLuhan when my brother, the Rev. Vincent Guinan (then President of Assumption College, now University of Windsor, Ontario), invited him to return to Canada from St. Louis, in the hope that his fame would revive attendance at the College.

That summer, I followed two of Marshall's courses: one on the development of the Humanities from the Roman Empire to the Renaissance; and the other, on what was really a preview of *The Mechanical Bride*. Marshall was very young at the time, very handsome, and he played upon the English language like Mozart played upon the piano. It was a wonderful experience.

The implication that society of the late 1940s was married to the bride of technology was rather startling. But the way Marshall developed it was hilariously funny, and we began to realize what a gross error we were making in putting all our developmental eggs in the technological basket.

In the Humanities course, Marshall pointed out that there was not just one Renaissance, but several before the 16th century. Otherwise, there would have been a lack of manuscripts on which to base the new learning.

I can remember one exercise in which Marshall gave us several poems of about eight lines, but without the names of their authors. He asked us to evaluate them. Many of us threw classical poets into the Dead Sea (including Shakespeare and Shelley), while placing some of the moderns high on the pedestal of fame. There were many red faces when he later read out the authors' names. While evaluating these poems himself, Marshall could speak with respect of any poet displaying mystical knowledge, although, at this time, the word "mystic" was greeted with pitying glances.

After Marshall became Director of the Centre for Culture and Technology at the University of Toronto, I visited him from time to time. When he was engaged in writing a book on Work and Leisure, I dropped in to ask him for his definition of "leisure." After thinking for a moment, he said: "To be at leisure means that all the human faculties are developed to their utmost, running at full tilt with ease. We are most at leisure, when we are completely involved."

When Marshall said "The medium is the message," I am convinced that half the faculty, and at least three-quarters of the students failed to understand what he was talking about; but, for the ones who did, he opened up vast new territories in every field.

When I visited him, Marshall always had at least three books in progress, and I would meet three representatives from three different publishing houses. Yet, he somehow managed to find some time for me along the way.

JOSEPH KEOGH

Media and Educational Consultant, a long-standing friend, responded to our questions by letter, cited below. "Joe" has generously suggested much more by telephone.

A more appropriate question for me might be: "What haven't I learned from McLuhan!" I was a sophomore when I first encountered him, in September 1955, as my teacher in Renaissance English. Right from the start, my world was transformed. He had me reading Ezra Pound and Wyndham Lewis, as well as sitting in on his fourth year Modern Poetry course. Knowing I aspired to be a writer, he allowed me to come to his campus home and share in a fourth year reception for Roy Campbell (South African poet).

It is the perceptive and probing question which leads to discovery, a dialogue between student and teacher in which they learn from each other. Marshall McLuhan was this rare kind of teacher, in whom discovery and teaching (*inventio* and *dispositio*) could be found united — much to the consternation of the sort of student, who simply wanted to be told what to memorize for the exam.

Marshall taught me to work, when I was his Secretary and Research Assistant in 1960. What didn't I learn from Marshall McLuhan! How to read, how to study, how to discover things, how to survive! Eventually, in 1962, "Mac" made it possible for me to get a teaching fellowship at Buffalo, and to be accepted into Summer School at Oxford in 1965.

Was I satisfied? Never! I continue to ask Marshall for things as our presumed heavenly intercessor. Perhaps, I'll come to my senses and start giving thanks for a change.

PHILIP MARCHAND

During the academic year 1968-69, Philip studied with McLuhan, as an undergraduate student, and graduated from the University of Toronto in 1970 with a Master's degree in English. He subsequently embarked upon a career in journalism that led him to write, on his own initiative, a first unofficial biography of Marshall McLuhan.

Philip, who interviewed Maurice and me for background material to his biography of Marshall, gives us a detailed account of what learning from Marshall meant to him.

Some of the most important messages McLuhan transmitted were nonverbal. They were transmitted by his sheer nervous energy, his penetrating voice, the vigour of his walk — the physical as well as mental alertness that confronted students when he walked into a classroom. Such alertness, more than anything else, made it clear he was enjoying his probes. The combination of his physical and mental vitality, moreover, suggested that the intellectual life, as lived by a spirit as adventurous and passionate as his, was an affair of both mind and body, senses and intellect.

He refused to become a tired, disillusioned, unhappy academic — the very notion of McLuhan accepting such a defeat is absurd, although he worked in an institution full of men and women who had done just that. By not accepting that defeat I suppose it could be said McLuhan taught one simple and overwhelmingly valuable lesson, especially to those of his students contemplating a career in the university. To state the case in its simplest terms, he taught that a teacher did not ever have to lose enthusiasm for intellectual discovery.

But to point to McLuhan's attitude as the most valuable lesson he ever conveyed is to ignore the rather large question of whether or not the things he actually *said* justified McLuhan's particular kind of exhilaration. His more outraged critics, after all, maintained that McLuhan's high-energy excitement of discovery was at least partly due to his living in a fool's paradise.

McLuhan's exhilaration in launching his probes and the sureness of his touch in pursuing them are, in fact, inseparable qualities. He was excited because he really was discovering valuable things; and he discovered valuable things at least partly because he never lost that excitement. His mental and physical vitality is really an inescapable dimension of the words he uttered — a dimension which was always present in one's recollection of those words and which helped to give them force and meaning. And the words, ultimately, were what one came for, when one sat down in an uncomfortable chair at the Coach House for the start of each McLuhan class.

The class I took was an undergraduate course in modern poetry, held in St. Michael's College in the academic year 1968-69. The appreciation of the poets on the course was something he (McLuhan) cared about more deeply than any other intellectual pursuit. And yet he said surprisingly little about the poems on the course. I think now, in retrospect, that he was more interested in helping orient us to the world these poets created than in "analyzing" their poems. (Although he could analyze as well as, or better than, conventional critics or teachers.) As a means of so orienting us, he would occasionally prod us with statements meant to wake us up, to stimulate fresh thinking on these poets.

The statement I remember most clearly, in this respect — and the statement I consider his most valuable teaching legacy — was a flat copulative formula: "Modern poetry is resonance." That pregnant sentence was uttered in his characteristic offhand mode, like a man saying: "Yes, I climbed the Eiffel Tower once — it's in Paris, you know." For those who are sure the Eiffel Tower is in the Rocky Mountains, such a remark can well puzzle and irritate. It has remained for me, the single most clarifying remark on the subject I have ever encountered.

Not that I fully grasped its import at the time. If I had been better versed in McLuhan's own techniques for penetrating the heart of a word or phrase, I would have gone to the O.E.D. for the definition and derivations of resonance. "The reinforcement or prolongation of sound by reflection, or *spec*, by synchronous vibration." The word is derived, we are told by the O.E.D., from the Latin word *resonantia*, meaning "echo."

O.E.D. examples of the use of the word through history include William Caxton, 1495: "Merueyllcus howlynges and wailinges ...whereof the resonnaunce or sonne was soo horryble that it semyd it wente uppe to heuen." Also, Burney's *History of Music*, 1789: "Resonance is but an aggregate of echoes or of quick repetitions and returns of the same sound."

From this entry, from the definition and from Caxton and Burney, McLuhan might have established first the simple fact that the heart of resonance is "sonne," as Caxton printed it. (What puns McLuhan might have discerned in that spelling, as in Sonne = Son = Divine Word, are also relevant to his statement about modern poetry.) This fact, that modern poetry is more intimately related to sound than to meaning, imagery, or what have you, may be a commonplace (although not such a commonplace that students still don't trouble understanding modern poetry because they fail to read it out loud, carefully and deliberately). It is a fact, regardless, which is still the shortest route to understanding modern poetry.

It brings us immediately to Hopkin's statement that once his poetry is listened to, it comes out all right; to Yeats's statement that he has learned ruthlessly to cut out words in his verse meant for the eye instead of the ear; and to Eliot's classic formulation of "auditory imagination," and his stated preference for an audience that can neither read nor write (and hence an audience that *has* to listen to poetry).

The other essential of the word is equally important: resonance is sound as echo, as repetition and prolongation. Again, this formulation is the shortest route to understanding Pound and Eliot, those two overwhelming figures of twentieth century poetry. What are lines such as "Why then Ile fit you. Hieronymo's mad againe" in Eliot's *The Waste Land*, or the constantly recurring phrases in Greek, Latin and twelfth century Provençal in Pound's *Cantos*, but precisely echo? Not simply "allusion," or hoicking the meaning of centuries old poetry into the meaning of the twentieth century poem, so that commentators can be kept busy comparing Elizabeth and Leicester with Eliot's typist and the young man carbuncular, but echo. The prolongation and repetition of "sonne," of spoken words, of "merueyllous howlynges and waylinges," linking the listener, even as these sounds are enunciated in the present, with the most remote ages and understandings.

All this leads, as well, to McLuhan's distinction between acoustic space and visual space, and the key, perhaps, to the understanding of his own work. One did not have to pursue the lead, however, to understand the statement in class in order for one to understand it. In a sense, he did elaborate on it, negatively — he refused to treat the poetry on the course as if it were an intellectual puzzle, for example.

73

He did not treat us to speculation on whether or not the Dog in *The Waste Land*, "that's friend to men," stood for Liberal Humanism, or any other abstraction. He liked, most of all, to read the poetry out loud or to hear it read out loud.

It was not necessary for him to elaborate on the statement in other ways. The statement was simply a helpful hint — not unlike the helpful hint he himself received, when he heard a professor at Cambridge, another great teacher, I.A. Richards, compare *The Waste Land* to the "music of ideas." That hint, McLuhan later recalled, was sufficient to point the students in his class the right way. No longer did they have to "figure out" what the poem meant. They were freed to understand the poem in an entirely different fashion than the way they had been taught to understand poetry.

In much the same way, McLuhan, with his own comparison of poetry and resonance, freed us to understand Eliot, Pound and others in a different way than our previous literary training had prepared us for. The juxtaposition of Richard's classroom statement with McLuhan's statement constitutes, in fact, an example of resonance almost as satisfying as some of the echoes sounding in modern poetry.

In our work, we constantly stress not only resonant response that keeps in tune with another's action, but resonant action of our own that fosters participant interaction. We deliberately avoid rigid connections; and highlight multisensory metaphors that replay the process patterns of today's global electric theatre, rather than visual models that display yesterday's "wired city."

TOM COOPER

Professor of Communication at Emerson College, Boston, studied for his Ph.D. at the Centre, during the 1970s. He also wrote his doctoral thesis on McLuhan, and became a good friend to Marshall and his family.

What did I learn from McLuhan that I did not know already?

The noted nineteenth century orator/thinker Elbert Hubbard wrote that "Fences do not exist for those who fly." McLuhan taught me to fly from field to field, century to century, culture to culture, thinker to thinker without a passport. The artificial boundaries erected across disciplines and fields had always seemed bogus to me, but various parts of my academic training taught me the necessary protocol of learning each field's basic literature before quoting or borrowing from it. For Marshall such context-building was a waste of time: one could pole vault from idea to idea based upon the fit between the ideas independent of their historical rooting within disciplines. Such an approach was ideal for brainstorming and discovering new patterns. I'll always be eternally grateful to him for teaching me to have no fear of flying — after all, some of the most successful inventions and perceptions were based on what seemed to be a wild or far-out suggestion. Having no fear of the absurd or outlandish juxtaposition of thoughts greatly enlarges one's ability to see possibilities. Often great scientific discoveries, works of art, or inspiring breakthroughs come because the offbeat idea was given full consideration. From this standpoint, Marshall was never discriminatory — in welcoming new ideas, he was an equal-opportunity employer.

What anecdotes best illustrate McLuhan's humanity?

Most people never realized how generous Marshall was. I was a U.S. graduate student in Canada at Thanksgiving, alone and away from my family. Although I had friends to celebrate with, and although Marshall trained me as an assistant (not just another of his grad students), I was nevertheless touched when he invited me to share Thanksgiving dinner with his family, a time often reserved only for family. He, in effect, was making me an honorary member of his family...which he often did with others by inviting them for a meal or an evening. Sometimes he even invited his entire class for a session in his home: a lovely atmosphere of comfort and relaxation surrounded them. When Marshall did invite me over for Thanksgiving, I was treated to Marshall the grandfather — who was being exceptionally kind to his daughter Mary and her daughter.

As was often the case, I had borrowed some special media for Marshall to see — in this case FIDDLE DE DEE, an animated experimental short by Norman McLaren, featuring authentic fiddle-playing of Canadian folk origin. Marshall almost cried with joy when watching the film — as his own father had been a fiddler. Marshall summoned Corinne and the whole family who were there into the screening room during FIDDLE DE DEE and sang along with the fiddler. He then exuberantly encouraged them to sing along as well. This deeply humane side of Marshall — a man moved by music, by nostalgia, by the authentic, and by family communion and fellowship — was not known to the general public and indeed to many of his associates. His giant mind, as imagined by colleagues and the media, was actually no larger than his enormous heart. For those who really knew Marshall, his spirit actually outdistanced his letter.

NELSON THALL

President of the Marshall McLuhan Centre on Global Communications, Nelson completed his MBA at York University and was preparing to earn a degree with Marshall. Now a senior consultant for Torstar Corporation, he also spearheaded the "McLuhan Funfare" at the Coach House for a brief period after Marshall's death.

Marshall didn't want people to take him too seriously. But he gave me a good "do-it-yourself kit." He saved me tremendous amounts of time. He forced me out of my old mode of thinking that was lineal and logical — looking at figures rather than looking for patterns — classifying everything without considering the effects of the new environment. Marshall exposed this environment for me.

I began to "read between the lines," as I read the news, not taking things at face value as before. I also recognized that "news" had to have certain characteristics to sell "ads" that aren't just facts. (Marshall always began by exploring the sensory effects of any process of communication upon its audience.) And I began to look at the newspaper as more of a story book than a science text.

I became obsessed with studying Marshall's works from *Counterblast* to *Take Today*, but it took me years to grasp their meaning. It is impossible to describe in words the change Marshall brought about in my thinking.

KATHY HUTCHON-KAWASAKI

A teacher by profession, collaborated with Marshall and his son Eric in writing the *City as Classroom: Understanding Language and Media.*[21] This unique book is devoted to training perception — today's most urgent need. The authors conduct an exploration of the CLASSROOM as a FIGURE in relation to the CITY as GROUND to *make sense,* in a process of learning and teaching that goes beyond conventional bounds.

I met Marshall as an undergrad. This was before his Fordham experience (1967-68). He was still teaching one undergraduate as well as graduate courses. I had him for fourth-year Modern Poetry. It was my last year in English Literature. Marshall set his own exam, because we would have flunked the one set by other English

Departments of the University of Toronto. Everyone at the University thought this a big joke.

As Marshall talked, the students in the class would groan and, looking at each other, would ask: "What's he saying?" I remember one St. Valentine's Day, when he walked into class, looked around, and said: "Contrary to popular opinion, birds don't sing for joy." The whole class went: "Aaaaag!" Then he went on to discuss Robert Ardrey's *Territorial Imperative*, and the question of clashing metaphors. That was typical of him.

What did I learn? Well, the next year I went into the Centre for Medieval Studies. I was studying Anglo-Saxon which uses such metaphorical techniques. Suddenly, I realized that I understood Marshall McLuhan.

In a flash, what Marshall had taught the year before made sense. Looking for structural relationships in Anglo-Saxon poetry, I realized that his discussion of two and three-dimensional relationships gave me a handle on all academic disciplines. One could organize the history of Art or Literature that way. In fact, one could organize everything that way, by the resonance of the ear and the perspective of the eye. [see page 145]

Until graduate school, I didn't recognize the difference between visual-space and acoustic-space structures. Marshall had already revealed this in Shakespeare's poetry when I was in fourth year. At the time, however, we just sat there like zombies. Now, it all came together.

When I began teaching, I would combine poetry and painting from the same period (as McLuhan and Parker did in *Through the Vanishing Point* [22]). It was easier for the students to understand the visual presentation of a painting than a poem. I would show them a Renaissance painting and its single point of view.

I could now distinguish between three-dimensional Art with its single point of view, and two-dimensional Art which has no single, but multiple points of view. This distinction enabled me to collect a whole range of data for retrieval in that framework.

I never thought logically, but analogically. Born in 1945, I was brought up on TV. After learning about the influence of that medium from Marshall, when I was around 30 years old I began to understand why I didn't have any identity. I just hopped from one role to another. I got married when I was 34, but still had to find out who I was.

From Marshall, I learned that you make your own identity. I had to struggle for years to develop it. With the children, I fell back into the role of "mother" and away from my own identity. I am still struggling to achieve it.

The tendency in our society is simply to disappear into the "ground" to become part of some corporate identity. Formerly, children were to be "seen but not heard" (until they had secretly formed a private identity).

BARRINGTON:

The "crisis of identity" is a central theme of *Take Today*[23] that you, Kathy, helped Marshall and me to put together. We had already recognized that this crisis was a consequence of electric information speedup, especially of TV (not merely its programs, but the medium itself) that deprived the young of both identity and goals. This "electronic drug" created the "unperson" in constant quest of identity. And that led not only to more drug addiction, but also to more violence in search of new "tribal identities."

KATHY:

Let me tell you of my students who benefited from Marshall's re-creation of their world. When I began teaching, many of them were on drugs. I taught in a suburban High School in an area where all the houses were alike — a cultural desert. A lot of the students I taught, in grades 12 and 13, were on drugs. There were students in my class whose arms looked like pincushions.

I was really worried about one particular girl. I thought she was on the verge of dying. I took her, with other kids, down to one of Marshall's Monday-night seminars. Perhaps, because he knew they were present, he began talking about the drug culture — why it had grown up in suburbia, with its lack of any sensory input that would help them see meaning in their lives. There was nothing to hang on to. As he talked about this, the kids got more and more excited.

When we left at about 10 o'clock to drive home, the little girl I was concerned about started turning cartwheels all around the parking lot. She began screaming: "Hey, I know why I take drugs. I know why I do it."

Next day, she came to me and said: "Do you know what I did last night? I got all my needles, put them in a bag and got rid of them. I know why I was taking drugs, and I don't have to do it any more."

A couple of weeks after, her friends at school began to tempt her again. She went and told the community cop, who had her put into a hospital (to complete the cure).

The best thing that had ever happened to her — meeting Marshall.

Let us digress here to share a parallel concern with

MURRAY KOFFLER

Renowned Canadian entrepreneur, who came to our 1970 Bahamas Seminar, as Chairman of the recently founded Council on Drug Abuse, in the hope of finding answers. He feared that, like opium smoking in nineteenth-century China, drug abuse in North America was now leading to its destruction. Whereas Mao's Red Youth had rescued China and reversed the process by killing the culprits, North America had not yet learned how to cope with this problem.

MURRAY:

Other people looking for "answers" also came to that forum. The highest concern for black people was recognition of their professional and other educational qualifications. Catholic Nuns, however, were concerned that, because their habit hadn't changed with changing times, they had lost credibility. So what I believed was the crisis, I found was just one of many.

I made a presentation at the conference, and we talked about it in depth. I had hoped to come back with some earth-shattering news on how we might combat the problem of drug abuse, but they didn't have answers.

I came away with the realization that mine was just one of many urgent problems of our day. Marshall took my question seriously and introduced me to "pattern recognition of process."

BARRINGTON:

In other words, there are no fixed answers to such questions, but there are ways of discovering patterns that can serve as guides to action in the constantly changing human situation.

The problem is to find or design the relevant questions that can reveal the nature of the dynamic process from which these problems arise. Yesterday's answers are rarely valid for today's questions.

Marshall sought patterns that would lead to understanding of constantly changing processes rather than to "frozen" categories, like "good" or "bad," that lead merely to judgments based on past experience. His approach never relied upon any theory, perforce expressed in terms of concepts derived indirectly from attempts to understand the past, rather than understanding the present

79

directly in its own terms.

Today, by making an inventory of the effects of any problem in any field of human endeavour, we can recognize what they all have in common: a new world of electric information speedup, where the old logical ways of sequential thinking can no longer keep pace with the new "eco-logical" action of our simultaneous being via media.

Our seminar was trying to show how everybody can now learn to make inventories of the effects of any problems that concern them, and to recognize process patterns that can serve as guides for broader understanding and relevant action.

MURRAY:

The conference lasted three days. Marshall and other speakers played interlocutor roles, responding to each of the addresses made on the various crises. It wasn't one-to-one.

My summation of the conference is similar to the one Barrington has just given. Twenty years later, we are just beginning to see the results of it. I observe that drug abuse has been contained, for example, in Toronto and other Ontario cities, to a better degree than, say, New York and Chicago.

BARRINGTON:

Besides the very effective way of sponsoring student groups to dramatize the causes and prevention of drug abuse, through "service clubs" (that you so kindly invited us to witness), what other means have you found useful to deal with this problem in your community?

MURRAY:

We have had to use 10 to 15 approaches (too many to discuss in detail here).

Kathy and Murray demonstrate the essential difference between Argument based on confrontation and Dialogue based on mutual trust. (Whereas Argument organizes specialist knowledge to put down all opposition, Dialogue explores shared ignorance to discover new knowledge for everybody.) Dialogue also exemplifies the future of learning — the shift from book-learning (with visual bias) and TV-learning (with audile-tactile bias) — to replay ancient rhapsodic-learning that uses all wits and senses with rhythm, rime, and reason.

Back to Kathy Hutchon:

One day, Marshall asked me if I had any ideas that might help his daughter, Mary, provide her students with an understanding of TV. He then added: We should write a book about it for all students. By the way, since you are not doing anything this year, write down all the ideas that come to you. Eric is returning home and will do the same. Then we'll put them together." That's how we started to write the *City as Classroom*.

For the next three or four months, I recorded everything I had done with my students. Eric did likewise. And we talked as his secretary Marg Stewart took dictation, then typed it. After that, we sent it off to the editor, whose sister, a retired school teacher, edited it. Another publisher handled the American edition. The book was also published in Italian.

One of the interesting things about Marshall was that many people thought of him as forbidding. Some even maintained that he was terribly proud. However, I found him to be quite the contrary, always willing to learn from others.

But he wasn't interested in people simply repeating to him what he had said. I noticed, for example, with his grad students, if they asked questions merely to impress the professor, while cutting out everyone else, Marshall wouldn't hesitate to cut them down to size. He knew what they were doing. Our impression was that only the cleverest students could say anything in his seminars.

On the other hand, when I brought my students to the Centre, Marshall would take an hour out of his afternoon to talk to them. Even if they asked the stupidest questions, he would not only be gentle, but he would explain in the old logical way, beginning with point one.

Although he was so patient with my students, with adults he gave the impression that, if he had taken a lifetime to figure things out, why should he hand it to them on a silver platter? He expected them to think for themselves.

I recall a Sister [of St. Joseph's Convent] who used to phone Marshall and say: "You know, so-and-so needs an operation (or some other urgent need), but can't afford it." I would overhear Marshall ask: "How much will it be? $5,000? Right. I'll just send a cheque. Don't say who sent it."

Something like this would happen every couple of months, but it was always: "Don't tell them." He didn't want anyone to know. But when it came to himself, Marshall was a penny-pincher.

MARY JANE SHOULTZ

Now a mother, hails from Ann Arbor, Michigan, is a teacher and a "woman's lib" pioneer.

There is not a day goes by that I don't think of Marshall McLuhan. There is not a magazine that doesn't quote him. There is not a present-day problem that couldn't be solved, if we understood his insights.

In 1962, as a teacher and mother in Wayne, Michigan, I was in despair over the plight of the younger generation unable to master the "3Rs." I could teach anyone anything one-to-one. But I could see that the huge classes then being integrated made competition hopeless for those at the "F" end of the grading curve. It seemed that the black children were being bussed in to get the "Fs" that formerly went to white children, when kept in their groups.

I was in despair, feeling hopeless, almost suicidal. I wondered what could there be for the illiterate majority, but drugs and disaster. Then lightening struck — an article by Marshall McLuhan, in the morning mail.

McLuhan wrote: "Our young people are not illiterate, they are post-literate. Today's students want immediate roles, not far-off goals" (regardless of ideology: Left, Right, or Centre — Russia, USA, or Canada). That opened my eyes! It gave me hope and insight into the problems of today's education. From then until retirement, I remained a teacher, and a professor of educational reform, never in despair again, only waiting for all the others to see Marshall McLuhan's insights recognized. ...

For the next ten years, off and on, I attended his fascinating classes with international students and gurus of "futures" and media. I remember that to promote conversation, he preferred the glow of lamplight — the intimacy of a dimly lit restaurant — instead of the harsh glare of fluorescent lighting.

I think that I helped McLuhan as well. We all felt that we helped; that was part of his charm. We'd bring clippings, sayings, rumours, and jokes to mingle with his, and we'd all be enriched.

I was into "women's lib" at the time. I proceeded to introduce Marshall to some of those ideas. He laughed and listened. Strange for a man! I insisted that male literacy, male mathematics, and male logic had been on the decline, since the advent of the electric age.

Of course, this reflected my major concern — the smothering of generations of children with the now useless "literacy" — and I tended to see the death of those visual, linear straight-jackets as a plus. McLuhan explained why schools were so boring to TV-oriented children. Due to television itself, they even focused their eyes differently.

Personally, I love television. McLuhan rarely watched TV. He underlined the point that the TV child is constitutionally different from the literate child. He emphasized that it was not what they read or watched, but that they read or watch. The medium makes the difference between my generation and theirs.

People seem to make much of the fact that McLuhan, though completely literate, emphasized the explosive changes inherent in the electric media. If we disagreed on any point, McLuhan would not argue. He'd just keep filling in facts, ideas, and one-liners until we understood. I pointed out to him how feminine were his ideas, like his Mom, his wife, his daughters, of even the Virgin Mary.

In 1970, during the Bahamas conference, I was astonished to see him cross himself at breakfast. It surprised me. I didn't know then that he was a devout Roman Catholic, also a Marian, who never tried to foist his faith on anyone.

He also warned me of the noise level to expect from the slaves in the kitchen, who could express their rage and frustration only by dropping and clanging things. This they did in decibels! Bless them! Bless him!

When I was on staff at the University of Brandon in Manitoba, McLuhan visited us at home, and took us all out to breakfast. He told my sons about the guy who protested at having to go to school one day. "You must," said his mother. "But Mom, ..." "First, you're all dressed. Second, I've made your lunch. And, you're the principal!"

Next day, after lectures, he came over to my place for a huge whipped-cream-strawberry-shortcake party. We had four TVs, four Radios, and four Record Players for accompaniment. By means of cereal, we buried the alphabet, reading chapter and verse from the Bible (the *TV Guide*).

A Professor of Religion, who attended, was affronted. "What if someone wants to read?" "That's OK too." McLuhan got a kick out of that. The Professor thought we were serious and said so. "We are," I said.

When the Brandon newspaper called for an account of this mysterious ceremony, I hesitated to explain for fear no one would understand. I did. They didn't!

In Toronto, through the years, McLuhan held both formal classes and informal meetings and lunches on campus, as well as at home, where his gracious wife was always so present and aware — not afloat and aflit, like many wives. I remember their familial conferences about refreshments and arrangements. We watched while McLuhan brought up logs from the woods to the fireplace — a scene so homey, generous and safe, so hopeful for us all.

McLuhan's birthday and mine fell on the same day, July 21st. I thought it more than coincidence. One year, my students phoned Marshall on "our day." They all shouted: "Happy birthday! Whatcha doin' Marshall McLuhan?" He answered each in turn, and shared with them new thoughts and discoveries. My students were shy, but they didn't want to say "good-bye."

In my classes, we saw all his movies, read all his books; rather, I read the books and shared them with my students. McLuhan's writings are acoustic, not visual. His magic is personal and involved, not stand-offish and stiff. He was never abstract or "in the clouds." I always found him precise and concrete in his observations concerning the drug scene, ads, music, art, demonstrations, and communes. ("They always break up over one question," he observed, "Who'll do the dishes?")

Long before we became aware of Sushi and Zen, McLuhan saw that the West was going East, just as the East was going West; and this, before the Japanese began turning out cars and appliances (of high quality).

He further pointed out that multi-national corporations have no boundaries, and can, at any moment, instantly transfer their assets to any part of the globe. We rode the acoustic wave of new knowledge, and, of course, never thought it would end.

Though I saw McLuhan only a few times each year after this more frequent association, each day he kept me alive with his shared insights and observations, and his hope. Funny stories, calls, letters were forthcoming, and I knew that I could always call and he would answer. I still pretend it possible.

TOM LANGAN

Professor of Philosophy, a colleague and friend, recalls what Marshall said about TV during the 1970s, while stretched out on a couch at home watching one of his favourite programs:

Do you want to know what I really think about these machines? If we want to save a trace of Graeco-Roman-Christian civilization, we'll have to smash all of them!

That was one of Marshall's "probes" to be taken seriously, but not literally! Marshall was insisting upon the urgent need to ration an "electronic drug" that substitutes instant analogical imaging for logical sequential thinking. (Electric media, like "liquor," shift our sensory responses from visual to audile-tactile, whether we know it or not.)

Tom recognized that Marshall was the first to grasp the meaning of electric media, backed up by empirical evidence; and Marshall advised all of us to "become infallible prophets by being among the first to see what has already happened!" But that requires perceptual, rather than conceptual training. Percepts, not concepts, created the "marvel" of Marshall's prophecies!

Tom wittily describes another form of Marshall's "probing" that other close friends also experienced whenever Marshall, who was no respecter of time, had a breakthrough.

One Easter morning, in the mid-1970s, Marshall called Tom to announce,

I've discovered the answer to the Greeks.

TOM:
What's the question?

MARSHALL:
This is serious. It's the key to the whole Greek way of thinking!

TOM:
It's Easter morning, Marshall. It'll have to wait.

MARSHALL:
So, let's have lunch together, Tom.

YOUSUF KARSH

Replying to our questions by letter on 5 December, 1988, master photographer Karsh affirmed:

I always thought of Marshall, despite his 21st century reputation, as basically a courtly, classical, exquisitly mannered man; he seemed to be more suited to the previous century than ours. What I learned from him, as a human being, was what we should all learn from each other, since he was the essense of consideration. His sense of humour was delicious. After a streaker had disrupted a surprised Academy Awards television presentation, he wryly remarked: "Streaking is but a passing fanny."

ELWY YOST

Well known to TVOntario fans for his friendly comments on its "movie" programs.

His dictum, "the medium is the message," and its underlying revelation, if you like, of the influence of media upon the freight they carry, is awesome in its implications. It has profoundly affected the way in which I perceive all forms of communications.

Before encountering Marshall McLuhan, I was most fortunate to have studied economics under Harold Innis at the University of Toronto in the late 1940s. I absorbed his theories of "hard" and "soft" media, from clay tablets of ancient times to corner-drugstore paperbacks of the 20th century.

Thus, when Arthur Knowles (Executive Director of The Metropolitan Television Association of Toronto) first introduced me to Professor McLuhan in 1964, and we set out to produce a program together on English Poetry, I was at least prepared to some degree. He was one of the true "originals" of this planet. But he was also enormous fun.

I have tried to make his observation "that which pleases, teaches" basic to everything I have done over TVOntario Network during the past fifteen years — a mosaic of subjects.

DERRICK DE KERKHOVE

We remember not only Derrick's persistence as a student, but also his skill in translating *From Cliché to Archetype* into French. Derrick is now director of the McLuhan Program for Culture and Technology at the University of Toronto.

It's impossible for me to think about Marshall without experiencing first a warm and strong feeling of sympathy. Marshall was fun. He taught me that enjoyment, not discretion was the better part of valour. The first time I noticed him was when, during a class, to make a point nobody understood he proposed a preposterous etymology for the word violence which he claimed came from the Latin "via". Any Canadian railway user knows that via means "way," "path." He said that violence meant "crossing somebody's way." His point, not that different from Jean-Jacques Rousseau's or Robert Ardrey's was that violence originated from one's excessive identification with property limits. I am not an expert etymologist but, after seven years of Latin and at least an acquaintance with several romance languages, I knew for a fact that violence comes from "vis" which means strength. I said so. I don't think he cared one way or the other.

He had made his point and Marshall was of the opinion that one should never let a fact stand in the way of an intuitively exciting perception. He went on blissfully ahead to the next point, and the next, and the next, never bothering to stand corrected.

The first time he noticed me was when, upon receiving a letter from Paris containing a translation of an essay on education he had written for *Le Monde*, he turned to me, mostly because I happened to be there, to ask me to read the text over to see whether it was well translated. How he remembered my name, let alone the fact that I spoke fluent French, is still a source of surprise to me even though I had spent a year and a bit in his class. I read the translation. I was not provided with the original English version but I believed I spotted three mistakes or at least misinterpretations of what might be Marshall's thinking. He asked me to explain why I thought these were mistakes. I blushed and I mumbled a few words that I am not sure I fully understood myself. He looked at me with uncharacteristic surprise and pronounced: "Why! you know my stuff!" I answered something like: "Oh, I wouldn't be so bold," blushing even more. Then Marshall turned to Barrington Nevitt who was standing next to him and declared, king-like: "From now on, he shall be my translator." I couldn't fully take in what had just happened, hardly believe that it had happened, only that I was about to enter into a rather special relationship with the only person I had ever met who I really believed to be a genius.

Translating Marshall's work was not easy. I had first to understand what he meant. Many people unkindly asked me whether I was translating his work in English. And in a way that is what I have been doing too, in my own words. But translating Marshall's work was fun. I learned a lot about English and French, of course, but I learned even more about how language can be used as a shovel to penetrate the stuff of thought, to see the back of the words, to float in the space of meaning. I guess Marshall enjoyed that too, at least on occasion, probably when he couldn't sleep. He would call me at 2 a.m., and wake me up to suggest this or that amendment to his collaborative effort with Wilfred Watson, *From Cliché to Archetype*, a book that he seemed to be rewriting as much as I was myself. He was quite proud of the result and he would say that the French book was far better than the original, but I don't know where he got this impression because he never really read the French version — nor the

English one for that matter.

Marshall's influence on me was considerable. Although I do not at present feel that I have achieved anything of note, I can at least measure the difference he made between an exceedingly Belgian youth quite haplessly caught in the undemanding mesh of the Canadian academic life of the sixties — a time when you could get a job simply by showing that you could speak French *à peu près convenablement* — and the passionate observer of the present that I have become. I can still remember how little by little, half-guessing things more than knowing them, skimming the surface of books and life, I began to see sharp edges for the first time through the fog of my own past education. Still, it did take forever. I registered in Marshall's "Culture and Technology" seminar during the year 1968-69. I was desperately bored in the French department. Marnie, who was soon to become my wife, had recommended that I sample the best and the brightest that the Arts and Sciences had to offer, Robertson Davies, Northrop Frye and McLuhan. I stayed with McLuhan because I couldn't figure him out. The year after, in spite of getting one of the lowest marks in the class, I came back for more. Even after translating the first book, I felt that I was hardly *au fait*. Sometime the fog was so thick that I thought my head was filled with white cheese.

One day, early in the spring of 1974, I was sitting gloomily by myself at the large table in the Centre for Culture and Technology. I was very depressed at the thought that I was in my seventh — and last admissible — year of the time allotted to write one's Ph.D. dissertation, and still no further advanced than the introduction and the first chapter, both so blatantly awful that I couldn't bear to reread them. Nor could I bear the thought of reading once more the dull tragedies of Voltaire which I was supposed to write about. Nor could I bear the thought of reading, period.

I was looking once more for an escape, when Marshall came in, full of energy and ready to chomp on the first available insight. He looked at me, saw that I was not in my usual deferently high spirits and began to talk to me personally, something he was not prone to do. I explained. He pulled back in irony and suggested that reading was indeed a crashing bore unless you knew what you were after. "To enjoy reading, you must know what you are looking for." I was almost thirty then, and I tried to remember the last time when I enjoyed reading. When I was in high school? No, at that time, I wasn't looking for anything special, I just enjoyed reading novels and plays, the great classics, and some moderns too.

He asked me to remind him of my thesis topic. I mumbled that it had something to do with the "sense of the tragic — or the lack there-

of — in the early tragedies of Voltaire." He asked me for my definition of tragedy. I began to quote Aristotle and Hegel. He cut me short
and asked me if I knew that tragedy was not an art form. "What is it
then?" I said, feeling reluctant. "Tragedy is a technology of communication. Theatre was invented by the Greeks to help them recover
from the invention of the alphabet. I call it 'quid', that is 'quest for
identity'".

I didn't get it right away. The conversation ended almost there.
Marshall added no less cryptically that the Greek alphabet had pre-
cipitated society into a deep crisis of identity, and that it took something as powerful and original as the invention of theatre to help the
Athenians to reorder their shattered perceptions of reality. Then he
got up and went to work with Marg Stewart, his secretary. The whole
exchange had lasted less than five minutes, but after a full week of
bewilderment and four months of feverish work, my thesis was done,
all 450 pages of it. Marshall surprised me by coming to the defence.
He could be extremely kind and attentive even though on a day-to-
day basis, he was strangely impersonal.

What happened during these five minutes? I am not sure. At first,
what he said did not seem to be more important than so many other
exciting or mysterious and challenging things he would say in class
or in conversation. But I never looked back. From before the time my
thesis was finished, I had already embarked on another one, this
time on Greek tragedy and the alphabet, to see whether this hypothesis that the alphabet had made us what we are was true or not. I now
believe very strongly that it is and that it may be one of the most
important and the richest clues to understanding not only ourselves
but other cultures and much of the development of history. In those
five minutes of a single conversation with someone I could see every
day, I found enough to unlock 3000 years of time and mankind.

EARLE BEATTIE

Our friend Earle (formerly at York University, Toronto, and
founder of the *Canadian Journal of Communication*) discusses teaching McLuhan and what he learned from Marshall.

As a professor of communication, I used to be in a quandary
whether to study and teach "McLuhanism" or not. My knowledge of
"McLuhanism" grew and changed with the years. There were many
and separate clues along the way. One was in his changing of titles:
from the medium is the "message" to "massage" to mean the medium

always works us over.

Finally, I taught as a section of one course: "Twelve Concepts of McLuhan" that discussed his ideas on sensory interplay and participation, sensory ratios and sensory bias, the extensions of man (closed systems), the "global village," linearity versus simultaneity, "the medium is the message," professionalism as environmental, the "rear-view mirror," "hot" and "cool" media, tribalization and re-tribalization, "figure and ground."

I particularly liked two of his ideas: "professionalism is following the leader" and "history can be changed."

The idea of history as changeable struck me like a thunderbolt, since we regard history as immutable. It is not: it is a VIA Railway that traverses the territory, or does not, according to the government of the day, or the perception of the people. Other concepts that we have in mind as immutable are equally likely to be changed or to die out altogether.

These twelve insights of McLuhan did not prove to be particularly popular elsewhere, but were of high interest to the class. Like so many of his insights, there were always spin-offs, or almost always. And there was controversy, much controversy.

Sensory ratios, of course, could apply directly to newspaper work, as could sensory bias. The "closed system" of headlines, likewise. In teaching TV, the concept of global village" was very apt, and McLuhan's central theme — "the medium is the message" — was naturally very apropos. The "rear-view mirror" analogy always provoked glee and enlightenment. And "figure and ground" were straight out of psychology.

It all applied to the current events of the day, whether it was a senseless shooting in Montreal or a "big bang" theory of the creation of the universe.

For more than two thousand years, Western philosophers have equated statements about abstract Greek Nature with the nature of existence itself. As Alfred North Whitehead once said, "We think in generalities, but we live in detail."

BHATIA & BHATIA

Professor of Education, Kamala Bhatia, was a much appreciated friend of Marshall McLuhan in Canada, where she has long served as a talented multi-cultural teacher with her husband, Baldev, while bringing up their own family. Mrs.

Bhatia also had the privilege of receiving much of her early education through close association with Mahatma Gandhi in India.[79] Kamala kindly granted Maurice and me an interview.

McLuhan's Impact Abroad

MAURICE:

What was the resistance at McMaster University to your proposed Ph.D. thesis on Marshall?

MRS. BHATIA:

In the 1970s, they shrugged their shoulders. They wanted someone more established. Milton would have been more in their line. I returned to Buffalo, considered Thoreau, but he hadn't anything to do with education as such.

Of course, there were Mahatma Gandhi and Aurobindo Ghosh (who is a philosopher, educator and founder of a university, and a writer of many works, whom I refer to in my book[79]). But I could not find anyone as exciting and as novel as Marshall McLuhan. The Department of Education of the State University of New York at Buffalo, accepted my proposal.

BARRINGTON:

What was new to you in what Marshall McLuhan was saying?

MRS. BHATIA:

The explanation of "reality." Mahatma Gandhi, for example, explored reality in terms of the old Indian cultures, superstitions, religions, industrializations — Western thought backed by British rule. He tried to find out where we are going and what truth is in terms of those things.

BARRINGTON:

How did that differ from the conventional Western understanding of reality?

MRS. BHATIA:

The Greek philosophers have done the same thing and tried to probe behind it. Then McLuhan comes along as a new person who examines truth and reality in terms of what is going on. That's what Gandhi did. That's what Socrates did in trying to find out "what is truth?" And McLuhan found it in things like advertising in his *Mechanical Bride*. In *Understanding Media*, he traces the history of the media — the telegraph, the telephone, the photograph, the radio, and so on, — trying to discover how we get to reality when we hear all these noises coming out: War and Peace,

TV and Satellites.

BARRINGTON:

And what did he present to you that you hadn't known before?

MRS. BHATIA:

Well, I never learned to explore truth and reality in terms of modern civilization as Marshall McLuhan did. He undertook to explore the industrial world of the machine, the railway, the bicycle, the car, and he went beyond that into the electronic era.

MAURICE:

When working on your Ph.D. thesis did you come in regularly to visit Marshall?

KAMALA:

I used to come in during the daytime to sit down and talk to him. I attended his daytime graduate seminars on Eliot and Joyce for about a year, and was a regular participant in his Monday night seminars, even after I had obtained my Ph.D. degree from the State University of New York at Buffalo. Although my Ph.D. thesis was on the perceptions of Dr. McLuhan as they related to education, I felt I had to learn much more from the great Guru; hence, I continued attending the Monday night seminars for over seven years.

BARRINGTON:

Around that time, we began with friends and colleagues to organize these effects into "Grammars or Laws of the Media." We considered including at least some of them in *Take Today*, but it had already grown too large. However, we did write articles on these "laws": "Causality in the Electric World," published in *Technology and Culture* in January 1973; and "The Future of 'New' Media," commissioned and completed in December 1973 for an Encyclopedia of Futures that was never published.

KAMALA:

I had studied Thoreau, before meeting McLuhan, and I would say that my interest in Thoreau led to my interest in both Gandhi and McLuhan.

BARRINGTON:

Like Thoreau and the Romantics, the Eastern philosophers believe that we can return to nature as in times past — to become merely an extension of nature. But this is impossible once man begins to make a new Nature, which is not necessarily something we like, but something that we are responsible for.

KAMALA:

Marshall calls it the *City as Classroom*. The student can imbibe a great deal from the environment directly, by studying the effects of various artifacts on people in the ways they are used. I think that was a great breakthrough in the tradition of John Dewey.

BARRINGTON:

But Dewey didn't know where his own thinking came from — the man-made Nature that was remaking him. McLuhan, on the other hand, recognized that his own process of thinking, as well as that of others, had a history that depended upon the sensory bias engendered by currently dominant media that he studied by using all his wits and senses.

KAMALA:

Gandhi based his scheme of education on the thinking of Dewey, but "found it a very philosophical matter."

BARRINGTON:

One might speak of Marshall as a philosopher in the same sense as the Zen-man who rejects all philosophy. Marshall said to me once that the nearest his approach came to philosophy was Structural Phenomenology, but of *percepts*, not *concepts*. He said the same about his search for an "epistemology of human experience."

In short, Marshall rejected the possibility of describing any human experience in abstract scientific, philosophical, or mathematical terms that could evoke this experience for other human beings. That is a task of the poet who can discover *le mot juste:* "the exact word which brings the effect of that object before the reader as it presented itself to the poet's mind at the time of writing the poem."[60]

KAMALA:

Marshall had the ability to provoke and to disturb the minds of people so that they might start questioning. Very often his questions were probes — sometimes they revealed to you your own ignorance, and sometimes they made you think way beyond the obvious. To some extent his questions appeared to be Socratic in nature.

McLUHAN'S PERSONALITY

MAURICE:

How did you find Marshall as a person? Did you find him abrasive, threatening, warm?

KAMALA:

He expected you to understand what he was saying. Unless you had the necessary knowledge, you couldn't appreciate him.

MAURICE:

How did Marshall respond to those who didn't understand him?

KAMALA:

He would become a little impatient.

BARRINGTON:

I think "impatient" is the proper word, because he wanted fellow explorers. He welcomed them from wherever they came, and he found more outside than inside the walls of his institution.

KAMALA:

Exactly. That is what he wrote on a book he gave to me.

BARRINGTON:

He didn't want anyone hanging on his coat-tails.

KAMALA:

I have a Master's degree in English, and I'm familiar with Eliot and Joyce — the things he liked. When I came to his class I was comfortable and could relate to what he was saying.

When we were late, after lectures at his home, he would say to Corinne, "Let us take Mrs. Bhatia to the bus stop." When I came to the office in the daytime, he would also often say, "I'll walk you to the bus on Bay Street." He was a very thoughtful person toward me and very stimulating, but he was very impatient with those who could not tune in on his wavelength.

McLUHAN'S TEACHING

KAMALA:

His thinking was very quick, by leaps and bounds, but I could follow it. I found *Take Today* a very provocative book. There is an element of philosophy in it.

BARRINGTON:

Take Today exposes the interplay between Eastern and Western thinking. *Finnegans Wake* is its subplot. It explores the processes of management historically and mythically to discover what works and what doesn't, both WHY and WHY NOT.

The discoveries are written "in Aphorism," rather than "in Method." Each page can be expanded into a book by Comprehensivists who don't need to, but not by Specialists who do. Our admonition: "Take today directly on its own terms" is now more relevant than ever. But alas that book is still ahead of the readers who need it most!

KAMALA:

I presented a copy of it to Indira Gandhi, which you also auto-graphed. She wrote a letter of thanks to Dr. McLuhan.

Many Westerners have preconceived notions of India and the East as being uncivilized, unsophisticated — all sorts of put-downs. My interest in multi-culturalism stems from Marshall's works. When Trudeau gave his address on multi-culturalism, which only reflected on ethnic groups, I went a step further. It gave me a vision of people who think alike.

Here I am from faraway India, and yet I feel so much at home in the little classroom of Dr. McLuhan. There must be a way in which human beings are related, rather than merely by colour, or creed, or facial form, or language. That was my distant vision of multi-culturalism. Although it comes down to something political, it was a broader vision.

BARRINGTON:

We were looking behind and beyond the political structures in our work toward the cultural interplay and complementary develop-ment of ear-and-eye peoples everywhere. In considering "Causality in the Electric World,"[80] we also went beyond the historical and sequential to the mythical and simultaneous — the timeless, beyond time and "under the aspect of eternity."

Unable to recognize the boundless Multi-verse in its own terms, Western philosophers and scientists alike have been striving to reduce the "reality of eternity" to their "concepts of history" that demand an absolute beginning to their limited Universe, rather than an end to their limited thinking. Even the "computer at wits end leads to process pattern recognition."[19]

W.G. MITCHELL

Manager, Planning and Implementation, Computers in Education Centre, Ontario Ministry of Education.

Marshall McLuhan was in his lifetime many things, a philosopher, a humanist, a media communicator, a father, a humourist, and a man with a firm sense of the Divine.

My strongest impression of Dr. McLuhan was, however, as a teacher. I hope the following anecdote illustrates this. It certainly illustrated it to me at the time, and gave me one of the severest intel-lectual jolts I have ever received.

The time was the early Seventies; the place, University of Toronto. I had been reasonably successful in both undergraduate and graduate studies in a university milieu. Indeed, I had somewhat arrogantly gone so far as "to figure the system out." I would simply pay attention to what the professors were saying, diligently review the required reading (with particular concentration upon the professors' own work) and shoot the material back in the form of appropriate essays and examinations.

Then I enrolled in one of Dr. McLuhan's courses, and the roof fell in on my tidy system.

The panic began when Dr. McLuhan made it all too clear that what he was interested in was your own thinking, your own thoughts, your own way of reasoning a thing out to a logical and workable conclusion. Moreover, he was emphatic that texts and publications written by him would probably mislead and obfuscate, and should therefore be rarely if ever be relied on.

Ye Gods, what was one to do?

Up until my first assignment was due, a seminar paper on the Shakespearean critic A.C. Bradley, I wrestled with the most difficult thing I had ever encountered to this point in my mini-academic career: to argue a position making use of minimal sources, and without a clue as to how Dr. McLuhan would receive it.

The day arrived. Three papers were scheduled for presentation, mine among them. The first two were received politely, and politely commented upon. (I thought they were brilliant analyses.) Dr. McLuhan, however, indicated that in each case the content contained in the papers had been discussed extensively in this text or that journal — the man's knowledge of who said what and when was nothing short of encyclopaedic. Then it was my turn.

I had decided to gamble, and take the man at his word, I had read Bradley, but no one else. My thesis was that Bradley's treatment of Shakespeare resembled that of film going through a movie projector at so many frames per second. Bradley's review of play after play, one following hard upon another, to me resembled a projected film, difficult to deal with until over and a pattern had emerged.

I went on to describe the nature of that pattern, its major features, and the conclusion I had reached: that both figure (the plays) and ground (a definite pattern) existed in the Shakespearean canon, and that Bradley was one of the first to explore that line of criticism; that is, analysis done in terms of pattern rather than analysis restricted to a specific play or group of plays.

Silence greeted all this.

"Well," asked Marshall, "Comments?"

No one volunteered anything. I had by this time gone into a semi-catatonic state, waiting for the inevitable cutting remark that would smash a budding academic ego into a thousand pieces. But Marshall McLuhan was not given to making cutting remarks to his students (colleagues and critics, I learned later, were a different matter).

The silence — now distinctly uneasy — was finally broken by Dr. McLuhan himself.

"Your response to Mr. Mitchell's paper," he began, "is interesting, and typical of any group confronted with the new, the novel, the original." He then turned to me.

"Took some gall," he said, — was there a twinkle in his eye? — "took some gall to see old Bradley as a movie projector. Not a bad analogy at all, rather think he would have appreciated it."

This reaction — the words are a recollection, but their gist is accurate — has remained with me since then, and to the extent possible, I have tried to base my own teaching on the model of McLuhan's, a model which encourages students to think on their own, and to gain confidence in their own reasoning ability. For that, Marshall, my gratitude. What you taught was not a subject, not a course, but yourself.

CHAPTER E

MAKING MOVIES AND VIDEOS

DAVID MACKAY

A pioneer in graphics and film production (former Supervisor of the CBC's Graphic Design Department, and later a Producer of IMAX films), David was also Producer of the celebrated Expo '67 Ontario film "A Place to Stand" that pioneered multi-imaging on film. David found its title, and the refrain for its musical accompaniment, from re-reading McLuhan's *Understanding Media*, rather than from reading the declaration of Archimedes: "Give me a place to stand, and I will move the world!"

Early in 1968, David came across the monograph *Problems of Communicating with People through Media*,[17] which he adopted as a training manual for his staff. That led him to me, its author. My office was in the same building, and I introduced him to Marshall. And Marshall invited David to teach him how to use a movie camera to record the antics of some new-born kittens.

DAVID:
   I was thrilled at the opportunity of meeting and talking to Marshall, just as he was by the kittens' behaviour. They start, knowing absolutely nothing, then learn to play and do all kinds of marvelous things by themselves. Marshall wanted to explore their learning process in slow motion.

   Pat Watson (a moving force at CBC) was Marshall's guest at the time. We asked him how to slow down the motion of the kittens, and he said, "All you do is slow down the camera." So we loaded a 16mm camera, slowed it down, and sent the film out to be processed.

   Of course, slowing down the camera speeded up the action. So instead of slow motion, the kittens were jumping around like crazy! Marshall went absolutely bananas! He blamed us. He blamed the camera. That was the first thing we did together.

   But, soon after, Marshall began calling me to share the latest jokes, such as, "Message to deep-sea diver: 'Surface at once. Ship sinking.'"

We recorded a lot of things that are stored away somewhere.

BARRINGTON:

I remember both a tape recording and an unfinished film that you made of Marshall and me discussing *Take Today*; and I shall never forget what must be the only "contract" of its kind in existence that Marshall wrote for us about them. It ended: "We hereby agree to share the proceeds fifty-fifty," signed by all three of us! That was the end of it, for we received no financing, and there were no proceeds.

DAVID:

We did complete one film "A Burning Would." (Eric McLuhan explains that the title originated in *Finnegans Wake* [24]: it refers to the "fires of technology" that replay "the burning wood" of Shakespeare's *Macbeth*. It also replays the "wold" or "would" of old English, with a reversed meaning.)

This 12-minute film was intended to support growing public opposition to a Spadina Expressway for Autokind that would cut across some of Toronto's best residential districts for Humankind.

In the early 1970s, conscience-stricken Frank Sorbara visited Marshall at the Centre not only to confess, but to make amends for some of the disservices that his high-rise developments had created in Toronto.

Sorbara had once asked a crowd of rowdy youngsters in his own high-rise neighbourhood, why they couldn't play more quietly. They had retorted: "There's nowhere to sit!" Suddenly his eyes were opened, and his purse — $10,000 that he generously put at Marshall's disposal to make that film.

It was barely enough to pay for the cost of processing and putting the thing together, not counting the time and effort. I still have that film. It seems to be getting better and better all the time.

It shows two beautiful scenes of the ravines that were going to be ploughed up, and turned into highways. Here we see children playing, cycling, walking with dogs and other things. But, instead of hearing the beautiful sounds of birds and babbling brooks and children laughing, we juxtapose the sounds of ambulances, bulldozers, jackhammers, and traffic congestion that we shot on the Don Valley Expressway.

JANE JACOBS

City-planner and environmentalist, who was also involved in this "resistance movement," recounts that architect and journalist Colin Vaughan, a neighbour of Marshall's in Wychwood Park, had introduced her to him.[25]

In his wonderful energetic and optimistic way, he said: "We need a movie about Spadina Expressway! You and I can do the script."

But I don't know a thing about scriptwriting. I won't be any use.

"Oh, I've never written one either," he said, "but we can easily do it together. Come on down to my office and we'll get to work."

I was dubious about this, but I was carried away by his enthusiasm. We really did need a movie about the issues involved. It was a good idea, so I went to his office in the Coach House, and McLuhan called in his secretary, introduced her (Margaret Stewart), and said: "She'll take down what we say."

So we talked. Both of us were enthusiastic and much of our conversation consisted of: "Hey, what about this?" followed by some notion, and: "Hey, what about this?" followed by another. After we had talked for about an hour, Marshall asked the secretary: "Have you got it all down?" Then he turned to me and said: "Well, that's it. We've got the script."

No, we don't! It's all just "Hey, what about this?" I said.

"Oh, that's immaterial," he replied.

He made a date for us to see the filmmaker, who was David Mackay — the man who made "A Place to Stand." When we arrived at his studio I was handed a typed copy of the script. I started looking through it, and it was even more garbled and unreadable than I expected. It was not the secretary who had garbled it — she had done an excellent job — it was just that what Marshall and I said was so garbled. All the "Hey, what about this's" were in there. The thing jumped around, without beginning or end. This did not bother Marshall, but it did bother me. I thought we needed a thread.

Mackay also had a copy of the script in his hand, but to my mingled relief and alarm he didn't seem exactly to read it. He flipped through it, back and forth, and said congenially that it was fine; it was something to go on. He asked us a lot of questions about the issues. Marshall went off and I remained a while longer to answer some more questions. That's all I did.

Once in a while Marshall phoned, and said everything was going fine, and in due course invited me to a viewing. I couldn't have been more astonished that there was a film. ... There was shape to it. It had music. It did have a thread, and raised a lot of important issues. Colin Vaughan provided an excellent narration. It was a good movie; furthermore, it was shown a lot, especially in the United States. However, the final product bore no relationship at all to our original script.

That was my experience of writing a script with Marshall McLuhan. I'm still as bewildered about scriptwriting as I was when I began. ... He was at peace with those dazzling sparks and fragments. He was not a disintegrated man, but the opposite. I saw that his brilliance swiftly opened up whole avenues of thought even if you had some suspicions about them. Like our movie, Marshall really got somewhere.

David MacKay emphasized what we are now doing. Our greatest problem in composing this book has been the structuring of such resonant cuts and juxtapositions by editing and balancing the many contributions and digressions required to present "Marshall" and "McLuhan" as a vibrant mosaic. Now, back to David.

The fun we really had was in editing. Marshall never wanted to finish the film. He enjoyed the process of editing — of trying out this and that, on and on. If I asked, "Is that sequence all right?" he would say, "It will depend on the next sequence." We both learned that way.

Marshall kept saying to me: "Well, you know, the action is in the interval. It has nothing to do with what is on the screen. It's the energy created between the two sequences — their resonance."

So I began to think of this more and more. Over the years, people couldn't understand why my montage worked, while theirs didn't. It isn't just a matter of stringing things in a row like beads. What kinds of things do we juxtapose? How do we select them? I think that is Marshall's greatest contribution to movie-making.

At the Ontario College of Art, I had learned the Principle of Dominance: If you wish to portray a group of objects, always choose an odd number; if they are of various sizes, choose more small than large ones; and if they are of different colours, show more red than yellow. Where does this dominance arise in colour? Is it culturally determined? (You can extend this principle into music also.) I play it by eye and ear. I don't really know. It's a mystery and I'd rather keep it that way. (I don't want to spoil the experience by having some explanation at the back of my mind.) With Marshall we could never nail anything down.

I became very conscious of the "cut" in the film — the stuff would explode in my eyes when I made a cut. In making a film "Quik Cut" for Nestles' Quick, I learned that (at 24 frames per second) the audience could still see the electronic image easily with only three frames. (It reminded me of my aircraft recognition training as a pilot during the war, before the TV age.) Marshall was quite conversant with this process, and asked, "What was the difference between black and white, and colour?" I didn't know, because it was all done in black and white. But, even in our casual conversations, Marshall was always interested in hearing whatever we might have learned about sensory responses.

I also took Marshall to Ontario Place to see "Catch the Sun," on IMAX with six-track stereo sound [David's production]. Whenever it got loud he stuck his fingers in his ears, for he was very sensitive to sound.

Many people have made mistakes in trying to "shoot" IMAX, because they haven't understood that "the medium is the message" — its size, its shape, its wraparound effect when sitting in the middle of its curved 80-foot screen. It switches from the non-involvement of a flat screen to total multi-sensory involvement.

MATIE MOLINARO

Although Marshall had been involved in several movies and videos, none gave him more pleasure than Woody Allen's invitation to "play himself" in "Annie Hall." Marshall said that he arrived early at the site and kept the crowd laughing until "shooting" started.

Matie Molinaro, Marshall's publicist and literary agent, gives a more complete account, excerpted with her permission from "Marshalling McLuhan," in *Marshall McLuhan the Man and his Message*.[4]

In late summer of 1976 Woody Allen, a McLuhan favorite, asked Marshall to appear in a cameo role in *Annie Hall*. (This incidentally was the name of one of Marshall's forebears in the early nineteenth century.) Marshall wanted to do this, subject to the requirements of the film, as we had been told at the outset that Marshall would be playing himself. On arriving in New York, I found Marshall's "script" in my letter box at the hotel. A quick perusal indicated Marshall could not say those lines. When Corinne and Marshall arrived, we discussed the difficulties but had to wait to see Allen on the set the next morning. The "set" was the New Yorker Theatre at Broadway and 85th. Street, and the sidewalk in front of it. On arrival, we were ushered into a large Winnebago parked on Broadway and were soon joined by Woody Allen and assistants. Allen said the lines were not unchangeable and that Marshall could say whatever he felt comfortable with as long as it emphasized how little a character in the film (a so-called communications professor from Columbia University) really knew about Marshall's theories. In a little run-through, Marshall listened to the Columbia Professor's lines, followed by Woody Allen's lines and then said something we'd all heard many times before, "You mean my fallacy is all wrong?"

The crowd of extras fell apart, and the laughter was spontaneous, genuine and sustained. Allen looked very surprised. A further discussion with Allen indicated that he did not want the word fallacy used. He said he'd prefer focus or something they could lip-sync into the fallacy frame. I immediately said that fallacy was funny, focus was not. How ridiculous for Marshall to say his focus was all wrong. It would have been academically unsound and stupid . . . and not true. It was not funny. New York suffered a hurricane that afternoon and evening but we were ordered to wait so that Allen could see the rushes of Marshall's scene. On the third day, Marshall had to re-record sound and neither Corinne nor I was allowed to go with him. We kept reminding him, up to the very last minute, not to say *focus* at any cost. When the film was released the scene was as Marshall played it, with one notable omission — the spontaneous laughter had been erased.

Some weeks after "Annie Hall" reached Toronto, Corinne and Marshall invited my wife and me to go and see it; we were all delighted to hear the spontaneous outbursts of laughter from the theatre audience that greeted Marshall's "acting." Maurice and his wife had already seen it, where the audience burst out clapping. We heard afterwards that Woody was happy too.

TERI MCLUHAN

During 1980, Marshall's daughter Teri, author of *The Way of the Earth*, and film maker, celebrated a preview of "The Third Walker" with family and friends in Sidney, Nova Scotia.

First and foremost, "The Third Walker" explores with archetypal force the mystery of identity through the prism of family tragedy. As an identity quest, the drama of the film is focused on divisions and losses derived from a complex tangle of identities among three brothers, who wrestle over who they are, as they come face to face with one another and their real mothers for the first time in twenty years.

A sub-plot throughout the film is the question of motherhood and the multiple meanings this role has, and has come to represent. As an allegorical drama, "The Third Walker" explores three men's spiritual and family ties. ... The "twinship angle" is not the peg of the film, but is rather a dramatic and supportive element more than anything else.

Dad does not appear in the film. He has a small (less than a minute) voice-over role of a Scottish judge in which he renders the verdict of the court (that concerns the results of a skin graft — the indisputable test of identical twinship). That's really it.

Alas, Marshall had never heard of Twinsburg, Ohio, where, by August 1989, over a thousand twins were already celebrating their 14th annual meeting.

There were several attempts to make movies or videos of Marshall that never came to fruition. One was a proposal by the National Film Board of Canada to record his Monday-night seminars at the Centre for a year. Another, by producers John Muller and David Nostbakken, proposed much more in a joint venture with McLuhan, just before he was afflicted with aphasia. Only a few remain as art films and videotapes in university archives and private collections. Many of these remnants are now being gathered for a CD-ROM on McLuhan.

CHAPTER F

OUT FOR LUNCH

Before Marshall left for New York (1967), going out to lunch with him required advance confirmation. My office was then too far for quick noonday visits, and Maurice was still living in Vancouver.

By the end of 1965, I began inviting Marshall to lunch at the Carleton Club, which was then on Hayden Street (about halfway between the Centre and my office at the Ontario Development Corporation, which was then on Yonge Street).

We often met midway and walked to the Club. On one such occasion, I asked Marshall playfully: "What has the world's greatest communicator failed to communicate today?" He retorted with good humour: "Most people assume that anyone who can speak or write clearly can communicate. But communicating anything really new is always a miracle — very rare, but not impossible!"

At lunch, Marshall and I more than once discussed the desirability of testing (under proper medical control) the effects of LSD upon ourselves. Like J.B. Priestley and mescaline, Marshall wanted (in T.S. Eliot's words) "to have the experience with the meaning." But I dissuaded him, because, at that time, he was already suffering occasional blackouts (due to the undiscovered tumor growing under his brain) that would make such experiments much too risky. Neither of us ever did.

At such lunches, I also introduced Marshall to "Jim" Davey (through "Joe" Kates, then President of KCS, and Chairman of the Science Council of Canada, whose pioneering work in computer science I had first encountered through his branch office in Sao Paulo, during my long residence in Brazil). Jim had been associated with KCS as a consultant to Premier Jean Lesage during Québec's "quiet revolution." He subsequently joined Prime Minister Pierre Trudeau's group of advisers in Ottawa. This led initially to our correspondence with the Prime Minister through Jim, and later to Marshall's personal friendship with Pierre Elliott.

After Marshall's return to Toronto from New York (1968),

we were more often "out for lunch" at the Centre than else-where. Its refrigerator was usually stocked with bread and cheese, and occasionally beer and wine, to take care of unexpected guests. We often brought our own lunches to share with each other. Sometimes visitors would drop in with a treat for everybody. But the treat of stimulating conversation was never lacking.

Those of us who worked most closely with Marshall knew that he normally attended midday Mass at St. Basil's church on the campus, and would often invite one of us to lunch with the Basilian fathers afterwards. Otherwise, we might buy our own, and share a table with him and his students, or other faculty members, in the cafeteria next door. But the dialogue never ceased.

After joining the Centre in Toronto, Maurice also recollects:

In the early 1970s, Marshall (who was then often branded as a mere "guru" for "hippies") invited a local leader of the "student revolution" to lunch at the Centre; he intended to make this leader "see reason" through verbal castigation (that was not his wont). During the course of their meeting, however, Marshall couldn't refrain from exploring the "ground" of the students' grievances. He then reverted to dialogue that led both "leaders" to a better understanding not only of their conflicting assumptions, but also of their complementary purposes.

In the 1920s, Mary Parker Follett had called this recognizing the "law of the situation" — a main theme of *Take Today*.[8]

Marshall had much more difficulty with some of his best friends and brightest students, who were constantly trying "to straighten him out" — to transform his art into their science.

PETER NEWMAN

We are indebted to Peter (well-known Canadian author) for his account of a light-hearted lunch with his friend Marshall at La Scala Restaurant (near the Centre) on Bay Street.

Marshall McLuhan slumps through the doors of the restaurant

with an oddly rolling motion, like that of a shorebound sailor, squinting into the half-light, testing his senses against the glum plasticity of the dining room. At 59 (this was in the spring of 1971), white-haired, full of honors, McLuhan has grown a little weary of watching the world through his famous rearview mirror. His delphic ideas, which once made him sound like a distant interplanetary intelligence trying to tell us something, have become the dominant ideology of the 20th-century life, so that even the girls who enhance the mystery of their sexuality with tinted stockings and dark glasses are subconsciously responding to his message.

"I heard a story the other day," McLuhan says, as we begin a long, relaxed lunch together at Toronto's La Scala Restaurant, "about a Scot who comes on the scene of a motor crash. The injured are lying around, and poking one of the survivors in the stomach with his walking stick he asks: 'Has the insurance adjuster been here yet?' When the guy replies: 'Not yet,' the Scotsman asks: 'Do you mind if I lie down beside you?'"

When I was a University of Toronto student in the Fifties, McLuhan used to be pointed out on the campus as that kooky author of *The Mechanical Bride* and in those days he always seemed punishingly intense.

Now there is a playful new aura about him; he has become a freelance intellectual minstrel, coining apocryphal slogans for an apocalyptic age. As a fellow diner gets up and pays for his meal, McLuhan winks at me and says: "Money is the poor man's credit card." Seconds later, he tells a story about a man who went out on a date with Siamese twins. "The next day a friend wanted to know if he'd had a good time, and his answer was: 'Well, yes and no.'"

Canadian critics were inordinately harsh when McLuhan's two books were published last year, and I ask him why he stays in Canada instead of moving permanently to the U.S., where several universities have offered amenable surroundings, amiable colleagues, large salaries and the respect of his peers. "Well," he says, "I experience a great deal of liberty here in Toronto that I wouldn't get in the States, because I'm taken quite seriously there. The fact that Canadians don't take me seriously is a huge advantage. It makes me a free man."

The pop culture we've adopted from the U.S. discards its gurus with alarming haste, and McLuhan is no longer listened to quite as attentively as he once was. Yet his intuitive leaps, the quality of his probes into a dim future, where not only facts but the very dimensions that contain them are changing, remain as brilliant as ever — becoming even more relevant as the world he envisioned a decade ago moves closer and closer to reality.

Here is a sampling from his table talk from that day, more than a decade-and-a-half ago —

Pierre Trudeau is an actor, he's both emperor and clown. The clown is really the emperor's P.R. man who keeps him in touch with the world that the emperor cannot reach himself. The clown in turn interprets the emperor to his court or the public and indicates their mood. He tests the emperor's mood by teasing him, and in turn interpreting the whims of the crowd to the emperor. I've never heard of a politician who could fill both roles. Trudeau is unique.

Poor old Richard Nixon hasn't got a chance. He has no mask. He just has his bare face hanging out, just private, tricky Dickie Nixon. The public are dying to see themselves there. They don't want to see Nixon; they want him to put them on. If he would even grow sideburns, if he would do anything, they would be transformed in their attitude to Nixon.

The new human occupation of the electronic age has become surveillance, CIA-style. Espionage is now the total human activity — whether you call it audience rating, consumer surveys, and so on — all men are now engaged as hunters of information. So, women are completely free to take over the dominant role in society. Women's liberation represents demand for absolute mobility, not just physical and political freedom to change roles, jobs and attitudes, but total mobility.

Trudeau is able to wear this corporate image which is not private or personal. He gets it, as far as I know, from his Indian heritage. He must be 40% Indian, like many French Canadians, and I think this corporate tribal mask is his greatest asset. Nobody can penetrate it. He has no personal point of view on anything.

Québec is being pushed out of Canada by the simple knowledge of what's going on in Québec. The more they know about the decision-making processes, the less they want to stay in Canada. Secession has already occurred in Québec. Physically it may or may not happen but psychically secession has already taken place. They're dropouts, absolutely. You can't put them back in by legalism, there's no technology to enforce it.

I wondered during the debate on the War Measures Act if it would be possible to turn radios off in Québec and just leave on the TV. Radio is hot stuff for such people as the French Canadians. It appeals to the ear, which for tribal cultures is their keenest sense, so it's like firewater to an Indian. It literally has the same effect on these people as booze. It drives them mad. English Canadians are not nearly as prone to getting excited by radio because they have a much bigger backlog of literacy and visual culture to protect them and immunize them against the ear.

Canadian politicians are faced with a serious "dropout" problem. They're still talking, but fewer people are bothering to listen. The successor to politics will be propaganda. Propaganda, not in the sense of a message or ideology, but as the impact of the whole culture and technology of the times [See Jacques Ellul's classic *Propaganda*]. So politics will eventually be replaced by imagery. The politician will be only too happy to abdicate in favor of his image, because the image will be so much more powerful than he could ever be.

Trudeau is aware of more than himself; he's not just trying to project an image. He is interpreting a whole process that he's involved in. So that when he slides down a banister or hops off a camel, it's not really a way of expressing what it feels like to be Trudeau; it's trying to express what sort of a hell of a hang-up he's in. He'll do anything to snap the tension.

What do I feel about my critics? Well, it's a normal pattern. Anybody can have a career as a promising young man, but the moment any signs of accomplishment occur bitterness sets in. Exile, physical or psychic, seems to be a necessary feature of the writer's existence. My interest in popular culture as an art form arouses uneasiness in many quarters. Manipulators of these arts seem to panic whenever their efforts are regarded seriously.

It's a nuisance having my books criticized. It's like being caught with your fly open. It confuses my students. But I don't think I've ever had more than half-a-dozen students who read anything I've written. They're not interested in my stuff and they know very well that if they use it anywhere in their essays it's going to be held against them. I warn them never to quote me. Some of my fellow academics are very hostile, but I sympathize with them. They've been asleep for five hundred years and they don't like anybody who comes along and stirs them up.

What is Canada? Obviously, BC regards the Prairies as a foreign country. The Prairies regard Toronto as enemy territory and so do Québec and the Maritimes. All the decisions are made there on everything, and their miseries are invented there — that, plus the opulent and rather self-pretentious image that Ontario political and business figures present to the Westerner. They look like something out of a Mac Sennett comedy. I personally can't take them seriously either.

But Canada as an entity still has value as the DEW Line for the rest of the world, we have the situation of relatively small involvement in the big headaches. The Canadian has freedom of comment, a kind of playful awareness of issues, that is unknown in, say, Paris or

London or New York. They take themselves too damn seriously; they have no choice. Here you have a little time to breathe, to think and to feel. It's because Canadians are protected from encountering themselves by layers of colonialism. I'm trying to alert them to the dangers of the 20th century, so they can duck out.

Other regular haunts, especially for inviting outsiders, were: "Stop 33" on the top floor of Sutton Place Hotel, at the East end of a lane leading from the Centre to Bay Street; and, in contrast, the Members' Dining Room (open to the general public) on the bottom floor of Ontario's Parliament, at the West end of a tunnel leading to Queen's Park.

WALTER PITTMAN

A past Director of the Ontario Institute for Studies in Education, recalls a luncheon during which Marshall demonstrated his playful, but direct, approach to converting breakdowns into breakthroughs for dealing with Toronto's ethnic problems.

I met Marshall McLuhan only once — but that single encounter is one I have never forgotten.

At the invitation of Paul Godfrey, Chairman of Metropolitan Toronto, I had agreed to study the problem of racial tension in Toronto. To be more specific, East Indians were facing abuse and violence particularly on the city's subway system. The situation culminated in dozens of incidents on New Year's Eve, 1977, and it was clear that people who had come from Pakistan and the Asian sub-continent were becoming the objects of the mindless anger of more established groups in the city and somehow this nasty and potentially volatile situation had to be turned around.

One of the most obvious factors was that these quiet and hardworking recent immigrants were being ridiculed and humiliated by a form of humour which emphasized their fragility and their vulnerability — the Paki joke. These vicious stories seemed to flood the community, imported like exotic fruits from other climes and other places. It took about four days for a new joke to travel from London, England, to Scarborough or North York.

The "Paki" joke inevitably focused on violent and horrible death and disfiguration for masses of unfortunate East Indians in the guise of a funny story that was expected to set off an entire roomful of non-Asians on a binge of hysterical laughter.

It was Russel Jurianez, himself an East Indian, a lawyer who was to distinguish himself as a colleague of Gordon Fairweather on the federal Human Rights Commission who suggested that we should talk to McLuhan. After all, here was the ultimate theorist of communication. Part of the reason for the negative reactions of Toronto citizens to East Indians was the obvious failure of each to communicate with each other. If McLuhan could help us to understand the complex problem of this breakdown in human relations, we would be enormously advantaged.

McLuhan agreed to meet us, in, of all places, the restaurant in the basement of the Ontario Legislative Assembly buildings. This eating facility though bereft of any reputation for culinary delight, was but a few paces from McLuhan's now famous coach-house off University Avenue. Moreover, the food, though somewhat tasteless, was modestly subsidized by the people of Ontario and the ambiance was one in which talk, not taste, was the dominant activity.

We explained our problem. McLuhan's response was immediate. It was not a scholarly discourse about prejudice and violence. It was a simple message of advice.

"You want to help these people? Forget reports and commissions...you have to change peoples' attitudes...and do it quickly. You say these awful Paki jokes are poisoning the minds of people, young and old. Then, replace those terrible stories with positive humour. Hire a public relations firm to make up wholesome jokes about East Indians, jokes which emphasize the colour of their lives and the quality of the characters. That's how the Jewish people have become accepted, yes, loved and respected in North America. The Jack Bennys, Eddie Cantors that veritable host of Jewish comedians have helped us laugh with other Jews at Jewish traits and predilections."

A simple message — too simple for a report to a Metropolitan Council. Too uncomplicated for a problem so serious and so broad in its implications. We are realizing that joy and laughter can initiate and sustain relationships, can bring us health and a sense of well-being, can enhance learning and spiritual development. And it can banish stupid racial intolerance and nasty-minded prejudice towards those who speak differently, eat different foods, pray to different gods or inhabit a different coloured body.

Marshall McLuhan knew this simple truth and unashamedly expressed it!

Our use of this approach is further exemplified in "Leave 'Em Alone and They'll Come Home: Can the Bottom Line Hold Québec?"[26]

FRANK ZINGRONE

Professor of Communication at York University, Toronto, reveals the human drama of a lunch with his colleague and close friend Marshall, near the end of his university tenure.

The last afternoon I spent with McLuhan, in early August 1979, just prior to his stroke in September, is a myth of remembrance now. All the time (22 years of sporadic contact) and space (I was in the U.S.A. teaching at MIT, a job his strong endorsement helped me to secure) collapsed into an imploded afternoon that was resonant with finality.

When I returned to Toronto from Boston in 1970 I maintained my prodigal stance and did not join his coterie. He was adequately surrounded by concentric circles of support: a circuit of cognoscenti, a ring of aware admirers, and a periphery of proselytes, some of them poseurs, content to bask in the ersatz illumination of his fading fame. (He complained to me once that many of these hangers-on could not read.) I invented instead a game of contact in which I sent outstanding people from York University down to his Monday-night seminars and we interacted by these catalysts, the "finely filiated platinum wires" of a personal network.

After a special visit to a coach-house session one Monday evening in 1972, when I tried but failed to bring him and William Irwin Thompson together (Mac took an instant dislike to Bill) there began a series of late night telephone calls. Perhaps I had caught his interest by the style of my countering his looser assertions — adverse when necessary but usually productive of breakthroughs. That night he was saying that the West lacks a theory of change and that we are therefore completely vulnerable to change and devastated by its electric speedup.

I remarked that we once had such a defense but gave it up, in fact, expurgated it: alchemy. I'll never forget the look he gave me when I offered that. There followed a guarded discussion of the function of the Hermetic Tradition. His solid knowledge of the subject intrigued me. But he was backing off Thompson, uncharacteristically hostile. Talk faltered. I had stumbled onto intimate ground. Bad timing. It wasn't until I'd read his Cambridge dissertation that I learned the connection between the Grammarians and the Hermetic Tradition.

During one of the eleventh hour calls McLuhan invited me to come down to the Centre and lunch. He had heard unofficially that the University of Toronto was going to cut off his funding and wanted to wind down his Centre for Culture and Technology since McLuhan was two years past retirement and they saw the Centre simply as his personal stage of operation. Having spent a good deal of his valuable time helping other people, he now was in need of help. There was no one there.

I felt flattered to be considered for a role in saving the Centre, but in truth that was a measure of his desperation. In its fashion, Toronto was giving McLuhan what Dublin gave Joyce: paralyzed indifference. Only in Canada could a personal friend of the Prime Minister have nowhere to turn for support. Shutting the Centre down was to shut him down, a special kind of death, and he knew it. The official announcement would come next Spring but the ghost as lethal rumour was afoot. I had mentioned the possibility of funding from IRPP in Montreal where I knew the deputy director, and apparently that had caught his interest. So down I went to St. Michael's, naively expecting a typical lunch of fissionable repartee.

When I arrived, he was in the coach house, in the semi-dark on a brilliantly lit August day. He was straightening up some papers, waiting, alone. We'd last met for lunch that spring; now he looked older, the fragile lineation of terminal age was creeping into his face. He seemed to have turned the fateful corner in the labyrinth of time and his body had begun to broadcast the news.

Irrepressible, however, his tone rose to upbeat with the challenging and paradoxical banter that was characteristic of him at his best. He was always such fun to be with. I was feeling badly at not having been a more faithful colleague over the years.

"How about the Courtyard Cafe?" I suggested.

"Anywhere's fine," I think he said.

He was as underdressed as I'd ever seen him — sloppy sport shirt and light inexpensive summer pants — incognito? — not with that face. We were off at a brisk pace, a sense of fun enveloping us as we strode up to Bloor under a lucid blue sky. Our talk centred on the short-sighted frugality of the University and what he regarded as a treacherous reversal of promises dating back to Claude Bissell's original mandate for the Centre. In truth the Centre had never been meant as anything more than a device for setting McLuhan's mind loose. In spite of his fame, many U. of T. bureaucrats (and more than a few of his colleagues) still regarded him as a flash in the panacea of mass culture, the charge of media "guru" was enough for them. (To be fair, their blatant willfulness to misunderstand him may have had something to do with the fact that he often told them they were obsolescent.)

We arrived at the portal of The Windsor Arms. A swift convergence at the doors brought us into collision with Donald Sutherland and his film entourage. Sutherland recognized McLuhan and jovially jostled Mac making to enter first, which he did in a stagy fashion. McLuhan didn't get it. When I explained who Sutherland was, Marshall made some Hitchcockian remark about actors being over-paid nobodies.

Usually a chat with McLuhan involved getting caught up in a galaxy of enlightening insights. This day he was fixated on the funding problem. We were a shade early for our reservation, and the place was festooned with gaudy media people who were taking their time over their parsleyed Brie and white wine; we headed to the bar for a drink.

Sitting on stools, like scribes manqué, we scripted scenarios for the salvation of the Centre. I wanted to get off the subject, but he was tenacious. I was buying lunch so he bought drinks. The barman put a handful of change in front of Marshall and went about his business noisily. Marshall withdrew a coin from the pile. More noise. Another withdrawal.

"I'm diminishing his tip because of the noise," he said.

"You're joking?" I queried.

"I only joke when I'm serious," he explained, unnecessarily.

McLuhan had a notorious sense of humour. Jokes, he said, are a cover for hidden grievance. He used them as examples of figure/ground relationship in communication theory. The meaning of a joke lies in its interpretive context. We had changed the subject, I thought. Our table was ready; the seating tight. Several people recognized him and were clearly eavesdropping. What they overheard might have surprised them.

"Most jokes are on the subject of elimination," I pressed, "what's the hidden grievance in scatological humour?"

"He had no quick response. Unusual. He was waiting for me.

"Since 'merde' is a symbol for gold, the hidden grievance must be economic, not having the alchemist's know-how for making gold. Lack of money, that is, filthy lucre, is the underlying meaning of offal jokes," I assayed.

"Yes, we still have the expression for it: King Shit," he took me up and we were off, but on the same subject. We discussed the relations between the basest and the highest in alchemy, the sun, the monarch, the uses of urine in alchemy and wine making, the steps of transformation on the way to spiritual gold. We hit on Joyce's use of the Hermetic, and I reminded Marshall of Freud's peculiar admission in a letter to Fliess that he saw himself as "a new Midas" who turns things into — "excrement."

"Alchemy flipped into its opposite," he offered.

"Psychoanalysis as outhouse?" I joked.

"Freud also says that art is playing with crap, so he must have believed himself to be an artist," and we both raised our eyebrows.

As we probed on, animated, I realized that he was dilating on a subject that he never talked about publicly, or privately as far as I knew. It was the intimate subject, antithetical to orthodox Catholicism, that he had cut short during the ill-fated Thompson visit years earlier. I queried him on the commitment of Aquinas to the alchemical view (Was he the author of the *Aurora Consurgens?* Why did he make a distinction in the *Summa* between alchemist's gold and true gold?) after his training under the public Hermeticist, Albertus Magnus. That wasn't Mac's approach.

He made it clear why he was focused on such arcane matters. Renaissance Humanism, he reminded me, which began with Petrarch, was at base a return to the great Grammarian Tradition, an attempt to supplant the "barbaric dialectics" of the Schoolmen of the middle ages. He had gotten into this material when he was doing his dissertation at Cambridge on Nashe and the history of the Trivium. The great alchemists, the Paracelsans from Raymond Lully to Cornelius Agrippa (who Joyce invokes in *A Portrait)* were Grammarians!

Grammarians from Augustine to Bacon viewed Nature as a Book, but one for which the language had been lost. This language (mythic consciousness) was analogous to human speech, alive and Protean in its evolving etymologies and stood adversarial to the streamlined, logical prose of Dialectics. McLuhan regarded dialecticians as obsolescent now that electric process had retrieved paradox and uncertainty by its effects on thought and perception. For me, the difference was between opposite visions of life, one of being or one of having. Only in the Hermetic sphere of thought had both co-existed in harmony.

I forget what we had for lunch but afterwards we roamed Bloor Street, still dialoguing at high speed. We popped into a shop in Yorkville where my wife and sister were selling ladies' fashions. They were charmed by the eminent distraction. Marshall always held that clothing was a medium of communication, but I discovered that he knew almost nothing about clothing and cared less. "This is the only business in the world where the figure is the hidden ground," I teased. "Not if you've got a good figure," he shot back. But as we left the shop I could see that he was taking me for being one of the faithful who also understood business.

As though to offset the alien surround of the dress shop, he headed straight for the Bob Miller underground bookstore, where I prevailed on Marshall to buy a copy of De Santillana's *Hamlet's Mill*. "The most important book since the Bible," I touted. He bought it. I wanted him to discover the book, to make it a benchmark work like Havelock, or Chaytor, or Lewis.

McLuhan wound down, with the long afternoon. On the street the traffic rose around us. We crossed Bloor ineptly. A close call. His trot was tottery. The second oar of the 1935 Cambridge light eight was pooped. It was with a spent cataract of dialogue that I returned quietly to the coach house and my car. McLuhan had fallen pensive and I felt good that he didn't need to be unrelentingly "on" with me. During those silent, unstressed moments walking together I thought, yes, my spiritual father and I'm going to lose him soon.

Before I drove him home to Wychwood Park he wanted to go into the Centre for a moment. He gave me a copy of a draft of *The Laws of Media* and then began to look around the coach house, nostalgically referring to this or that artifact as though to impress me with its significance, perhaps to spur me to action. I don't know what came over me but I asked him how it felt to know that he would leave one book of permanent value. I meant *The Gutenberg Galaxy*, of course. He turned to me with that penetrating look, the eyes of genius *en garde*, "Oh," he said slowly, in absolute seriousness, "I'm not very proud of my books."

Two or three evenings later, I got my last call from him, in which he offered the highest praise for *Hamlet's Mill*, "full of insights" he allowed. When he hung up I was seized with the memory of a poignant chat I had with Giorgio de Santillana, at MIT when he and Hertha von Dechend, a few doors from my office, were locked in the desperate struggle to finish *Hamlet's Mill* before Giorgio, who was extremely ill, could not go on with the work, or worse. He just made it, producing the most important book on science and technology I have ever encountered. Together with *The Galaxy*, they are a complete education.

Both Marshall and Giorgio were archaic thinkers, who "thought rather in terms of what we might call a fugue, in which all the notes cannot be constrained into a single melodic scale, in which one is plunged directly into the midst of things and must follow the temporal order created by their thoughts." When I put the phone down that night, I never heard his voice again, though in my ear's memory it dialogues away.

Here Frank reveals the depth of Marshall's medieval awareness which is evident in this dialogue dominated by the metaphor of transmutation — ennobling the "base" through the operations of art on matter and the soul.

CHAPTER G

COMPLEMENTARY COLLEAGUES

Many contributors to this book, are, in some respects, complementaries of Marshall McLuhan. This chapter reports from some who were his contemporaries, and others who were his former students — not only collaborators, but also critical critics.

M.B. McNAMEE, S.J.

Professor Emeritus of English Literature and Art History, St. Louis University, illuminates, in his "Analysis of Verbal Fibre," the background of McLuhan's approach to literary criticism, when they were colleagues.

I can honestly say that Marshall McLuhan was one of the most important influences in my whole academic career. He and I came to St. Louis University at about the same time, he as a professor of English and I as a student completing the work for my doctorate in English. I had already finished all my course work and the comprehensive examinations; I had only the dissertation left to do. I had intended to do my doctoral work at Cambridge but the war intervened and I was prevented from doing so. Marshall came to St. Louis University from Cambridge at this time. He came full of enthusiasm about the work of Frank Leavis and I.A. Richards in the then new modern criticism. I was somewhat acquainted with it from the *Scrutiny* magazine, its chief organ, so I decided to sit in on Marshall's class in Practical Criticism to get a better idea of the much touted modern criticism "hot from Cambridge." It was a very revealing experience, and what it revealed was that, at this late stage of my academic career, I didn't know how to read. All my course work had been heavily laden with historical and biographical background of the periods and authors studied, and with a plethora of secondary comment. But I had never been made to dig into the actual verbal fiber of literary texts and learn the precise way in which diction, imagery, and rhythm work together to make the rich communication of a given theme.

I signed up for every course that Marshall taught, and the insight I gained from his courses on how language actually works in a given piece of literature, whether prose or poetry, became the foundation of my own teaching (and I later received the Nancy McNeir Ring Outstanding Faculty Award). When I became Chairman of the English Department at St. Louis University I made the close study of the verbal fiber of the text an integral part of the teaching on all levels in the whole Department. Every new teacher took the course in Practical Criticism that I designed before teaching in the Department. This was all the result of what I myself had learned about taking the challenge of the text in Marshall's classes. This close textual scrutiny became one of the central emphases in the teaching in the English Department of St. Louis University. It influenced the teaching of the countless teachers who were trained there.

The learning experience, however, was not all in one direction. Marshall himself learned a great deal about medieval history and philosophy in the years he spent at St. Louis University, especially from his contact with Dr. Bernard Muller-Thym in the Philosophy Department. Marshall was still working on his own doctoral dissertation (on the prose style of Thomas Nashe) for his degree from Cambridge. He came to see, more clearly than most of his contemporaries, the distinction between the two cultural strains in the Middle Ages — one oriented around the grammatico-rhetorical approach centered in the Cathedral schools of Chartres and Orleans and the other oriented around the exaggeratedly dialectical scholastic approach centered in the Universities, especially the University of Paris. Marshall saw the results of this dichotomy and was applying it to the multiple stylistic modes of Thomas Nashe. In this, as in other areas, he had the ability to almost intuit relationships in matters of thought and literary style. At the time, he did not have the command of Latin to justify some of the generalizations that the Latin sources alone would substantiate. But when one dug into the original sources you often found that Marshall had intuited relationships derived from secondary sources and commentaries that the original texts bore out. At this late stage in his own development he sat himself down and learned Latin so he could go to the original sources themselves. And he learned it well.

His insight into the grammatico-rhetorical tradition, as opposed to the dialectical scholastic tradition and method and the influence of this dichotomy on prose style, fascinated me. I persuaded Marshall to direct my dissertation on the thought and style of Francis Bacon in that context — which he happily did. His direction consisted largely of his coming to my room in the Jesuit quarters, throwing himself on my bed, and discoursing endlessly about his own dissertation on Nashe which he was completing for Cambridge at the time. But what he was doing on Nashe was so parallel to what I was doing on Bacon that his long disquisitions were immensely helpful in putting my own project into proper perspective. My work on the influence of the grammatico-rhetorical tradition on Bacon's theory of induction and on his own prose style was ultimately published with favorable comments from Bacon scholars. Much of what I had done was an extrapolation of what I had learned from Marshall. My work on Bacon's thought and style became the basis of my later graduate teaching on the history of prose and several doctoral dissertations which I directed and which were also published.

So I repeat what I said at the outset of these comments: Marshall McLuhan had a very substantial influence on my thinking and academic career. I am glad that on a couple of occasions I had the opportunity of telling him that in person. His sweeping and quasi-pontifical pronouncements sometimes irritated his students and readers, but often, when they looked into the sources for some of his generalizations, sources which Marshall himself may not have explored thoroughly at the time, they found that he had intuited something close to the truth. That is what lay at the heart of his ability to irritate and inspire at the same time.

Tom Easterbrook

Successor to Harold Innis in Toronto, was also Marshall's lifelong sparring-partner. During his undergraduate years at the University of Manitoba, Maurice knew Tom as Marshall's friend. In the summer of 1932, Tom and Marshall crossed the Atlantic together by cattle-boat to go cycling in Britain, and to go to Cambridge.

I remember first meeting Tom through Marshall, and then several times afterwards through Corinne's friendly invitations to parties at home in Wychwood Park. The last time I saw him was there, in the early 1980s (just before his death). Tom told me then that his greatest regret was his own incorrigible habit of arguing with Marshall about everything they ever discussed.

Tom recounted that, during his last visit, instead of trying to begin a dialogue on what Marshall set before him to read, he had started to argue about it vigorously. And Marshall, bereft of speech, had turned on the radio full blast to end the argument! Tom never saw him again.

Keeping in mind Marshall's hypersensitivity to sound, this event is the antithesis to the auditory parable that developed at the 1970 Bahamas Seminar. I sat between Buckminster Fuller and Marshall during plenary sessions. Even with a powerful hearing-aid of his own design, Bucky had great difficulty keeping track of the proceedings, except through scribbled notes. As a young naval officer, he had ignored advice to protect his own ears during gunnery practice.

I also sat a row in front of Marshall (at his insistence, for my own hearing is poor) to share the pleasure of watching Bucky replay his famous three-hour lecture on the gyroscope. Nobody seemed to tire and everybody roared with delight, as Bucky twirled, while blowing a stream of peas from a peashooter, to show how it felt to be a gyroscope!

At breakfast on the following morning, I heard Marshall try valiantly to explain to Bucky that his high-speed performance of the gyroscope had compressed sequent action in visual space into simultaneous interaction in multi-sensory space, but all in vain. Bucky insisted that he didn't understand a word of what Marshall was trying to tell him!

PETER DRUCKER

Renowned author and management consultant, a long-time friend of Marshall, kindly gave us permission to republish excerpts from his "Modern Prophets" that compares McLuhan with our mutual friend Bucky Fuller.[28]

Bucky Fuller and Marshall McLuhan had been friends of mine long before they became celebrities. I had met both first around 1940. For long years I was one of the few who listened to them. But even I doubted for long years that their voices would ever be heard, let alone that either man could attract a following. They were prophets in the wilderness — and far, far away, it seemed, even from an oasis, let alone their Promised Land.

Suddenly, in the 1960s, technology was seen as a human activity; formerly it was always a "technical" activity, Technology moved from the wings of the stage of history to which the "humanist" had always consigned it, and began to mingle freely with the actors and even, at times, to steal the spotlight. ...

And so Bucky Fuller and Marshall McLuhan suddenly became visible and important. To a generation which realized that technology had to be integrated with metaphysics and culture, aesthetics and human anthropology — that indeed it was at the core of human anthropology and of the self-knowledge of man — these two prophets offered a glimpse of a new reality. That their landscape was fog-shrouded and their utterances oracular only added to their appeal. ...

Technology, in other words, was not quite as simple as the traditional view that both "humanists" and "technologists" had assumed. It somehow defined to people who they were, or at least how they saw themselves, in addition to its impact on what they produced.

So I sought out McLuhan and asked him to come to visit. And he soon got into the habit of dropping by whenever he was near us ... He usually came with a minimum of warning or no warning at all. Once, in New Jersey, in a tremendous midsummer storm with tropical downpours and Doomsday thunderclaps, our doorbell rang about one in the morning. There was McLuhan, sopping wet but grinning from ear to ear. "I had some business in Upper Montclair," he said (it was three miles from where we lived), "and thought I'd walk over." "Why didn't you telephone, Marshall?" I asked. "What would you have done in this weather if we hadn't been home?" "But Peter," he said, "you and Doris are much too sensible to be anyplace else in weather like this." With this he dismissed the weather, sat down in his wet clothes, and talked about his ideas until breakfast time

It was as the prophet of television that McLuhan became a figure in the intellectual "jet set" of the sixties. This also explains, I believe, why McLuhan has not really become much more than that. To be sure, television — and the "media" altogether — have been changing what is communicated, and not merely how. They have been changing our perception of the outside world, but also how we see ourselves and what we see in ourselves. Yet not one of McLuhan's specific predictions has come true and not one of them is likely to come true. Printing is not being made obsolete by television. There are more books and magazines being published today than there were before the "tube" invaded the living room, just as drama and poetry did not disappear once "storytelling" became "writing" and "writing" became "printing." ... And the Xerox copier makes every man his own Gutenberg.

The interaction between the "medium" and the "message" is more profound than McLuhan's aphorism has it; neither determines the other, but each shapes the other. McLuhan knows all this, I am sure. But because his moment of enlightenment came to him over television, he has become known — and may even see himself — as the pop culture's Thoreau. This however is grossly unfair to the man and to his insight. McLuhan's most important insight is not "the medium is the message." It is that technology is an extension of man rather than "just a tool." It is not "man's Master." But it changes man and his personality and what man is — or perceives himself to be — just as much as it changes what he can do.

While still "famous for being famous" and constantly misunderstood, Marshall never ceased to appreciate Peter Drucker's friendship, as well as his work.

Drucker seems to stress McLuhan's ignorance of Alfred Russel Wallace's view that "man alone is capable of purposeful non-organic evolution; he makes tools;" and he appears to have missed our quotation in 1972 of Wallace's contemporary, Ralph Waldo Emerson, who wrote: "The human body is the magazine of inventions. ... All the tools and engines on earth are only extensions of its limbs and senses" *(Take Today*, p. 86). Nor have we yet found any reference in Drucker's works to James Joyce's modern parable of *Finnegans Wake* (which extends Wallace's insight by replaying its material, psychological, and social consequences from ancient to modern times) that Marshall and his collaborators continued to extend in their own works.

Much confusion has also arisen from the failure to distinguish between the differing sensory and social effects engendered by Gutenberg's moveable type of "alphabetic" symbols ("phonemes" having neither acoustic nor visual semantic meaning), and Korea's earlier block-printing of "syllabic" symbols ("morphemes" having either, or both, visual and acoustic semantic meaning). But their differing effects, as media, was actually of prime concern to Marshall (see Chapters K and L).

Further misunderstandings have, no doubt, resulted from McLuhan's rhetorical use of the word "obsolete" as a "probe" (before the 1970s) instead of "obsolescent," to provoke discussion. Since then, however, he has emphasized their difference. Surely, Drucker's insistence that "not one of McLuhan's specific predictions has come true" (p. 253) arises from taking this rhetorical paradox too literally.

In *Take Today* (1972), we stressed what Drucker himself aptly points out: printing, like writing, was obsolesced (not obsoleted) by new media. More generally, "prominence is the harbinger of obsolescence:" not disappearance, but proliferation of old clichés in new forms with new meaning. Likewise, in "The Man Who Came to Listen" (1970), dedicated to Peter Drucker, we highlighted the continuing shift from "hardware" to "software" production, from "centralized" to "decentralized" organization, and from "jobs" to "roles" in the new "global theatre" created by electric communication speedup.[29] Also,

> The growing clamor for more jobs and more pay heralds the obsolescence of job classifications and pay scales alike. The main action is now shifting beyond production for market to global role playing. In this new situation the market itself has returned to theatre — a place to haggle rather than a place to stand (as Cyrus the Great remarked more than two millennia ago).[30]

Today, we can predict with certainty that *the future of economics is politics, and of politics show business.* Who can now fail to see that it has already happened? We also foresee that Peter Drucker's human wisdom will continue to provide clues that can reveal hidden patterns of the Next Industrial Revolution.[31]

McLuhan, however, described this relationship in terms of the ebb and flow in relative dominance of two radically opposed intellectual traditions in which the meaning of ancient and modern reversed as dominant media shifted sensory stress from EAR to EYE and vice versa: beginning with the original "ancients" (EAR-people, rhetoricians and grammarians) and followed by the moderns (EYE-people and dialecticians), in which the Graeco-Roman phonetic literacy created and established the trivium of dialectic (subsequently logic), grammar, and rhetoric in the schools of Western civilization.

> Socrates turned from rhetoric to dialectics, from forensics to speculation and definition, raising the issue which pitted Plato and Aristotle against their formidable rival Isocrates, and which pitted the forensic Cicero against Carneades and the Stoics. The same quarrel as to whether grammar and rhetoric, on the one hand, or dialectics, on the other, should have precedence in organizing the hierarchy of knowledge is

the key to an understanding of the Renaissance from the twelfth to the seventeenth centuries.[32]

These conflicting, but complementary, traditions were recognized by Francis Bacon in his *Advancement of Learning*[33] in terms of "aphorisms" and "methods;" and he also replayed this insight aphoristically: "Aphorisms, representing a knowledge broken, do invite men to inquire farther; whereas Methods, carrying the show of a total, do secure men, as if they were at farthest."

As a modern "ancient" with Baconian insight, McLuhan favoured aphorisms to stimulate fresh discovery rather than methods to consolidate old knowledge. Aphorisms, like myths, encapsulate, instead of merely describe, human experience; they can embrace volumes of reading and writing rather than merely spelling it out, as the old "ancients" knew.

NORTHROP FRYE

A professor of English and renowned literary critic replied to our questions by repeating from memory the essence of what he had most generously said at a celebration, organized by Mary McLuhan on December 14, 1988, to honour her father as a great teacher among great teachers.

Marshall was an extraordinary improviser in conversation; he could take fire instantly from a chance remark, and I have never known anyone to equal him on that score. I also feel, whether I said it or not, that he was celebrated for the wrong reasons in the sixties, and then neglected for the wrong reasons later, so that a reassessment of his work and its value is badly needed.

I think what I chiefly learned from him, as an influence on me, was the role of discontinuity in communication, which he was one of the first people to understand the significance of.

JOHN ROBERT COLOMBO

Canadian encyclopedist, considers his contemporary teachers, Marshall McLuhan and Northrop Frye, as "Cultural Generators."

There were two enormously powerful generators of literary and cultural thought in operation on the campus of the University of Toronto in the late 1950s. Every student of the humanities knew that the currents of thought were of two kinds — DC and AC. The Direct Current emanated steadily from the office of Northrop Frye at Victoria College; the Alternating Current came in waves from the Coach House of Marshall McLuhan at St. Michael's College. If one was an undergraduate with an interest in the literary and cultural matters of the day, one could not help but be affected by one or both of these generators. Certainly I benefited from both the DC and AC currents.

In later years I expressed it otherwise. Northrop Frye was the Plato of Canada: divining the Pure Forms, assuring us of their existence. Marshall McLuhan was the country's Aristotle, taking inventory of material causes and immaterial effects, assuring us of their interconnectedness.

It was more than thirty years ago that I first heard the names "Northrop Frye" and "Marshall McLuhan." I attended their lectures and addresses and I read their essays in journals like the *University of Toronto Quarterly* and *Explorations*. Since then hardly a day has gone by that I have not pondered an insight or formulation, a phrase or thought, of one or the other of these two great contemporary thinkers. I selfishly believe that fate ordained it that they would come to Toronto at the appropriate time to wield an influence over my mental development. Indeed, one of them traveled from Eastern Canada, the other from Western Canada; one emerged from Protestantism, the other from Catholicism. In my mind's eye they are entwined, so entwined as to be a single, double-faced figure, like Janus. They function as my mental bookends. It is easy to visualize Frye and McLuhan as polar opposite figures, easier to see them as complementary figures, and easiest of all to benefit from their sense of what constitutes tradition and transformation.

Marshall McLuhan was a joker, but he was never a practical joker. If a practical joker is someone who does silly, impractical things purely for effect; McLuhan was an impractical joker for he did serious, practical things to upset the processes of thought and feeling. Anyway, he loved a good joke, and I love this one, which was once told at his expense.

It concerns the parking space reserved for his automobile in the tiny lot beside the Coach House which housed so memorably the Centre for Culture and Technology. One morning he drove into the tiny lot and tried to park his car in the reserved space, only to find it occupied by another vehicle. He succeeded in parking his car elsewhere, but he decided for future benefit to leave a note on the windshield of the illegally parked vehicle. On a scrap of paper he scribbled a warning and fastened it under the windshield wiper. The note read: "Dear Driver: Do not park here. This parking spot is reserved for the undersigned, Marshall McLuhan."

In the late afternoon he returned to his car. He was pleased to see that the offending vehicle was gone, but surprised to find a scrap of paper on his windshield. It read: "Dear Dr. McLuhan: I have copies of your books. Your warning about parking in the space reserved for your car is the first thing of yours that I have ever read and understood." There was no signature.

The joke is amusing in a way. But it is pure invention. It seems McLuhan, the guru of the electronic age, never did learn to drive an automobile.

Marshall McLuhan possessed the aphoristic style or was possessed by it. So many and so varied are his aphorisms that it should be possible to compile an entire "quote book" drawing exclusively from the well of McLuhan's published and unpublished observations. His most familiar aphorisms and formulations served me in good stead when I compiled *Colombo's Canadian Quotations* (1974).

Collecting "quotable quotes" is easily done. What is more difficult is documenting them, running them to ground, tracing them back to their first appearances in print. For instance, I had a problem with McLuhan's most familiar formulation: "The medium is the message." This celebrated aphorism is the most famous formulation of any Canadian anywhere at any time. It explains or at least seems to explain the relationship between form and content in media. What date should I give it?

It first appeared in *Understanding Media*. That book was published in 1964. But the sentence was a lot older than that. I had heard it during my student days at the University of Toronto and I did not leave the campus until 1960. So the expression preceded its appearance in book form. It did not appear to be in any of McLuhan's published articles or essays. Nor was it in any of the interviews I had seen published before 1964.

I took the direct approach and wrote to its originator. McLuhan telephoned to say that he could not remember when and where he had first said the five famous words. [See Alan Thomas, Chapter B.] He added that if I cared to attend one of the Monday evening seminars that he conducted at the Centre for Culture and Technology, I would be most welcome and he would raise the issue there. Perhaps someone would remember. I accepted the invitation and attended a couple of sessions. I found the discussions at the seminars to be at one and the same time irritating and exhilarating.

At these seminars McLuhan acted like Aristotle — that is, when he was not acting like Socrates. He schematized and systematized, as did Aristotle, bending words at will and wending his way around them whenever they resisted. When he encountered resistance — from a persistent critic or a specialist in a discipline about which he was not knowledgeable — he turned into the interrogator. Socrates-like he forced the person to define his terms. He would scrutinize the definitions and squeeze the words dry of any meaning they may once have had. Subjected to such scrutiny, a word would yield an unexpected confirmation, or better yet it would fly off on a crazy tangent.

I remember one memorable exchange. A graduate student of English, disagreeing with some point or other that McLuhan was making, refused to be silenced. It was apparent that the student knew more about the subject at hand — the language of John Donne's poetry — than did McLuhan. That did not prevent Socrates from pressing on. In desperation the student blurted out, "That may be so from your point of view..."

McLuhan cut him off before he could even complete his sentence: "There is no point of view! There is no such thing as a point of view in acoustical space or in the electronic age." The student, rattled, managed to begin one more sentence, albeit with a mangled word. "That may be so," the student bravely continued, "but when you say that what you do is cagetorize all the arguments..." Realizing his mistake, the student paused the way a radio announcer does when he senses that he has mispronounced a word. Before the student could correct himself, McLuhan blurted out: "There is some subtle sense here! To categorize is to *cagetorize*, cage-to-rise, to cage-too-rise!" Done with was the language of John Donne. McLuhan was off on a new tangent; the student was off the hook; and everyone was elated! ...

I am prepared to argue that the intellectual climate of contemporary Canada, while the product of innumerable factors and forces, was created by two "little magazines." The word "highbrow" was used to characterize the two journals in their day. That word may no longer be in vogue but it does describe the form and content of the two publications. Both journals were written, edited, and published with a coterie in mind — a highly intelligent and influential one, to be sure.

One of the little magazines was *Cité Libre*, which was issued from Montreal from 1950 to 1968. It was edited by Pierre Elliott Trudeau and others. The other was *Explorations*, first issued from Toronto between 1953 and 1960. It was edited by Marshall McLuhan and others. The country's problems and possibilities are writ large in the print of these publications.

Cité Libre and *Explorations* did more to define and thus determine the intellectual climate of contemporary Canada than any other publications. Thus the greatest contribution to the cultural concerns of contemporary Canadians were made by Pierre Elliot Trudeau and Marshall McLuhan.

JOHN WAIN

English scholar and poet, was not only a good friend of Marshall and his family, but also a complementary colleague. He answered our questions by very kindly inviting us to choose selections from *Dear Shadows* his many-sided portrait of Marshall and McLuhan.[34]

Marshall at the wheel of his car, driving through the busy streets of Toronto with a nervous impatience that expressed itself in rapid changes of pace, now jamming the brakes full on, now trampling on the accelerator so that the car sprang forward like a greyhound that sees the electric hare receding in the distance... Marshall coming in out of the night in Brooklyn Heights, masculine and companionable, a cigar fuming at the corner of his mouth and that burly Irish priest [Fr, John Culkin] in tow... Marshall sitting on a bar stool in Washington DC, burping with indigestion, discussing with one of the local habitués various remedies for 'gas on the stomach'... and always Marshall talking, talking, pouring out the continuous stream of notions that issued from his ceaselessly active mind like an unstoppable flow of ticker tape. ..."Incidentally, John, that was the moment when the Ivory Tower became the Control Tower", "Incidentally, John, the view of the world as global village," "Incidentally, John, it's no accident that after 1850 English prose becomes a p.a. system," ..."Incidentally, John, some of the new material brought into the focus of poetry by Laforgue and Corbière was intentionally hilarious." Everything seemed to be thrown off incidentally, as if to one or other side of the main thoroughfare of his thinking, but what it was incidental to I never could tell. ...

Herbert Marshall McLuhan, as he tended to sign himself, was not quite the ordinary New Critic. He wrote what I used to think of as "brain-teeming" criticism. Where the traditional scholar rarely ventured outside his "field", and the conventional New Critic applied what were becoming well-worn techniques to the text in front of him (the sacred phrase was "the words on the page"), McLuhan worked by sending up a shower of comparisons, analogies, wisecracks, sudden satire jabs at people and attitudes he disliked, and equally sudden excursions into scholastic philosophy or modern advertising practice (both these last were subjects he had studied attentively), all in the service of illuminating, or preparing for illumination, whatever book or writer he was discussing. It was like riding on a roller-coaster; it also reminded me of Johnson's description of the practice of the Metaphysical poets: "the most heterogeneous ideas are yoked by violence together." In McLuhan's case the violence had nothing sullen or offensive about it; it was the natural outcrop of a geniality, an impatience with conventional categories, and a willingness to have a go and try anything for size. Most critics make an *aperçu* serve them as theme for a whole essay or even a whole book; McLuhan provided an *aperçu* in virtually every line, and if they were not all equally good, if indeed some of them were unconvincing to the point of absurdity, well, there was always the interest of seeing what the man would say next; and there was a large, gusty breeze of fresh air blowing through the whole enterprise.

I remember feeling more than once if the title of any of McLuhan's essays were to get lost, no one would be able to say, from reading the essay, what it had actually been about. In the 1950s he began to contribute to English periodicals; I believe the first British editor to use him was Cyril Connolly, who included an essay on "American Advertising" in the number of *Horizon*, in 1950s, that dealt specifically with the American scene. You could at any rate tell what that one was about; but when Marshall moved to the Oxford periodical *Essays in Criticism* a little later, he contributed an essay on "Tennyson and Picturesque Poetry" (I, iii, 1951) which gave me the impression, on reading it, of having to keep my seat-belt fastened. Here is a specimen paragraph.

> It might be suggested that landscape offered several attractive advantages to the poets of the mid-eighteenth century. It meant for one thing an extension of the Baroque interest in *la peinture de la pensée*, which the study of Seneca had suggested to Montaigne and Bacon and Browne — an interest which reached a maximal development, so far as the technique of direct statement permitted, in Pascal, Racine, and Alexander Pope. Pope especially deserves study from this point of view since he first developed the couplet to do the complex work of the double plot of the Elizabethans. He discovered how to make a couplet achieve a symbolic vision. That is, to effect an instant of inclusive conscious-

WHO WAS MARSHALL McLUHAN?

ness by the juxtaposition without copula of diverse and even paradoxical situations or states of mind:

> The hungry judges soon the sentence sign,
> And wretches hang that jurymen may dine.

> The judges are hungry but not for justice; yet there is no suggestion that they would be better judges if they had dined. The stark confrontation of this human condition is enforced by the second line or "sub-plot" which is parallel but inferior. The suggestion that meat must hang before it is edible, and that jurymen are merely promoting the proper business of society by seeing that it gets hung is analogous to the vision of society in Swift's *Modest Proposal* and to Lear's vision on the heath. The couplet in Pope's hands escaped from the conditions imposed by univocal discourse which had developed in the Cartesian milieu.

Let no one imagine that I am quoting such a paragraph satirically, to show Marshall as a quaint or clownish figure. On the contrary, I admired it then and I admire it now. I like the sweep and audacity, the impression he gives of having so much to say about so many subjects that one thought can scarcely be brought in without three or four others which have a bearing on it, a bearing often hitherto unsuspected. The incidentals are as important as the main line, the digressions as essential as the ratiocinative thread. In that respect Marshall was very like Sterne (who had an Irish mother); and when you add his veneration for James Joyce and the fact that during the war years he had been in close contact with Wyndham Lewis, another adventurous polymath and controversialist, the lineage becomes a little clearer. ...

But where the New Criticism slightly bored me, and the tradition of "contributing to knowledge" seemed to me a dead hand, McLuhan's essays galvanized me into a new awareness of the diversity and richness of the field there was to be cultivated. I also liked his watchful, ironic eye on the social scene: no ivory-tower scholar he; his chief claim for literary study, indeed, was that it sharpened one's response to experience and helped one to stand out from what he called the "zombie-horde" or urban consumers.

When, in 1951, his first foray into social criticism appeared — *The Mechanical Bride*, a study of advertising techniques — I was ready for it. The blend of learning, speculation, satire, and comic-strip presentation seemed to me an idiom that only McLuhan could have developed; and now, thirty-odd years later, I am sure I was right. ...

I think indeed that I had struck him at a moment of immense

fecundity, when a mass of apparently random ideas had begun to form into a whole in his mind. He must have been putting the finishing touches to *The Gutenberg Galaxy* and getting ready for the most speculative flights of social criticism that were to take him to the peak of his reputation with *Understanding Media*. Perhaps, by listening so attentively through so many hours — and it was certainly no trouble — I played a small part in helping to ready him for his most spectacular burst of ideation.

I found Marshall intellectually persuasive at this period more than later. Indeed, I look back on the years from 1962 to about 1965 as those in which some traces of influence from his ideas filtered into my own. ...

The Oxford visit of 1965 is also useful to look back on because it helps to date Marshall's spectacular rise to fame. That came with *Understanding Media* in 1964. *The Gutenberg Galaxy* had been much talked about but it was still the book of a literary historian. Marshall had not yet become taken up as a propounder of solutions to social questions. Once he was taken up, he became — for a time — a world celebrity, a sought-after oracle, besieged by publishers and TV networks, and inevitably he tended to disappear from our ordinary life. We were still friends, but my life was never again as close to his as it was during those first seven years. ...

Beyond Exposition to Exploration

Civilized, rationally educated people expect and prefer to have problems described and analyzed sequentially. They try to follow your argument to a conclusion. They expect the conclusion to be your point of view, illustrative of your values. In contrast to the method of exposition is the method of exploration. This begins by the admission of ignorance and difficulties. Such statement will tend to be a tentative groping. The blind man's cane picks up the relation of things in his environment by the quality of resonance. His tapping tells him what objects are adjacent to his stick. If his stick were connected to any of these objects, he would be helpless so far as orientation is concerned. This is always the plight of the logical method. It is useless for exploration. Its very strength makes it irrelevant. "Proof" of sanity is available only to those discharged from mental institutions.[35]

In our explorations of "inner" space, we constantly sought to raise the subconscious to conscious levels of awareness to create a new form of "comprehension" that would bridge the

EYE/EAR worlds and foster human diversity without loss of identity. However, too much suspended judgment can also suspend conversion of breakdowns into breakthroughs.

ERIC KOCH

Began his career at the CBC in Montreal in 1944. Eric was a producer in Public Affairs and Network-head of programs on the arts and sciences. In Toronto he was involved in launching "This Hour Has Seven Days," a controversial Public Affairs show that appeared weekly over two years. And Eric survived its May 6th, 1966 demise. Marshall McLuhan was the last guest on the last show. For a complete account of this interview see Eric's *Inside Seven Days*.[85] He provides the following note, then Patrick Watson introduces McLuhan and sets up his interview with Robert Fulford.

In the fifties and sixties I was a program organiser at CBC Public Affairs — for better or worse the intellectual centre of the Corporation. We thought of ourselves as dedicated to the noble task of defending the ancient virtues against the onslaught of vulgar commercialization. What was therefore more natural than to take a bleary-eyed view of a professor who seemed to be by no means appalled by — of all things — **advertising**?

We shuddered. But we were fascinated, especially since he took special delight in talking — and writing — about our work in a language which was to our language what twelve-tone music was to traditional tonality, i.e. familiar and adventurous but, alas, not always intelligible. However, there was the suggestion that we were wasting our time and that we were fighting a losing battle. To which he seemed to add "And a good thing, too!"

Naturally, in self-defence, we jumped to the obvious conclusion that he was not to be taken seriously. He was clearly "anti-intellectual." Did he not say that the content mattered no more than the message [medium]?

The brightest and most articulate of our producers who most emphatically begged to differ was Patrick Watson. To him McLuhan was never a crusader for the phenomena he was examining. It was therefore particularly fitting that in the spring of 1966 McLuhan put the record straight in the last program of Watson's and Leiterman's *This Hour Has Seven Days*.

PATRICK WATSON:

Tonight we can report that our national image is changing. After years of exporting wheat and aluminum and newsprint and Lorne Greene and Raymond Massey we've finally come of age, and now we're exporting ideas. The man responsible is a tall, gangly ego who is professor of English and director of the Centre for Culture and Technology at the University of Toronto. In the past year his name has become a password for the world of real and pseudo intellectuals. From New York to San Francisco, from Chicago to Atlanta, our own Herbert Marshall McLuhan has been labeled poet, philosopher, prophet. *Life* magazine has called him "the oracle of the electric age." His critics are almost as lively as his admirers. They call him a gadfly, a spellbinder, a word-merchant. But almost everyone agrees: no one can make sense out of more than ten percent of what the professor is saying, and that seems to include even the professor himself. Tonight he tells Robert Fulford — and you — how the world is going out of style, or maybe how it's coming back into style. Well, try and figure it out for yourself.

ROBERT FULFORD:

You've been writing about the mass media for a good many years and now are an object of the mass media. ...

McLUHAN:

Let me explain why this has happened. It's because people have suddenly become obsessed with the consequences of things. They used to be obsessed with mere products and packages and with launching these things out into the markets and into the public. Now they've suddenly become concerned with what happens when these things go out on the highway — what happens if this kind of program gets on the air. They want safety air, safety cigarettes, safety cars and safety programming. This need for safety is a sudden awareness that things have effects. Now, my writing has for years been concerned with the effects of things, not their impact, but their consequences, after impact. TV, unlike the fantasy escape world of the movies, creates an enormously serious and realistically-minded kind of person, almost oriental in his inward meditativeness.

FULFORD:

... And changed because of television?

McLUHAN:

Television gave the old electric circuitry that's already here a huge extra push in this direction of involvement and inwardness. You see, the circuit doesn't simply push things out for inspection, it pushes you in. It involves you. When you put a new medium into play, people's sensory life shifts a bit, sometimes shifts a lot. This changes their outlook, their attitudes, changes their feelings about studies, about school, about politics. Since TV, Canadian, British and American politics have cooled off almost to the point of rigor mortis...

FULFORD:

What kind of world would you rather live in? Is there a period in the past, or possible period in the future ... ?

McLUHAN:

No. So, the only alternative is to understand everything that's going on, and then try to neutralize it, turn off as many buttons as you can, and frustrate them as much as you can. I'm resolutely opposed to all innovation, all change. But I'm determined to understand what's happening because I don't choose just to sit and let the juggernaut roll over me. Many people seem to think that because you talk about something recent you're in favour of it. The exact opposite is true in my case. Anything I talk about is almost certainly something I'm resolutely against and it seems to me that the best way of opposing it is to understand it. Then you know where to turn off the button.

The program ends with a nostalgic review of *Seven Days* highlights.

NOTE: Robert Fulford, well-known and respected broadcaster, TV commentator, and former editor of *Saturday Night*, has spoken for himself as "an intellectual among journalists and a journalist among intellectuals" in his *Best Seat in the House*.[36]

Fulford, who was both a friend of Marshall and critic of McLuhan, observed what, for him, seemed to be the main lesson of "The McLuhan Age": "television leaves us with feelings and impressions rather than with facts and arguments — though facts and arguments must be there as well," which our own experience also confirms.

However, Fulford also insinuated that, aside from Christianity, McLuhan's religion is "technological determinism." But that is the exact opposite of "comprehensive awareness" as the foundation of human wisdom, fostered by Marshall and his fellow explorers from the mid-1950s onward, to bypass hitherto inevitable fate. In other words, as Marshall often said, "as long as we are willing to think, nothing is inevitable."

What Fulford had witnessed, as we did, were differing aspects of the transformation of McLuhan's approach: from humanistic concepts and value judgments (exhibited in *The Mechanical Bride)* to "suspended judgment" and process pattern recognition by making inventories of effects. McLuhan represented his discoveries in Aphorism rather than in Method throughout his works, savouring multi-sensory Joycean language.

Our book is concerned with how Marshall and his friends extended this "new" approach not only in harmony with old ancients from Cicero to the Elizabethans, but also in tune with new ancients from Edgar Allen Poe to James Joyce, whose genius, like McLuhan's, was first recognized outside their native lands.

During his life, as Fulford reports, McLuhan never stood still, never held a fixed point-of-view, nor did he hold high regard for mere consistency (pilloried by Ralph Waldo Emerson who proclaimed: "With consistency a great soul has simply nothing to do."). Like Socrates, McLuhan never ceased to examine dearly-held assumptions (including his own); he had no fear of changing his mind or his identity, for he never ceased to grow.

B.W. POWE

A controversial "angry" young voice in Canadian letters, was in Marshall McLuhan's last Graduate Seminar (1979) at the University of Toronto. Bruce replied to our questions by "A Measure of Light."

The last time I saw Marshall McLuhan was before Christmas in 1979. A group of former students and colleagues — among them Derrick de Kerckhove, R.A. Paskauskas, and George Thompson — took McLuhan for lunch at a Hungarian restaurant on Bloor Street. McLuhan's speech was handicapped; he only had an often exasperated repertoire of shrugs, grimaces, grunts, ums, uhs, yes's, and no's. Yet without uttering a full sentence, McLuhan dominated our conversations, and he clearly delighted in our opinions and mild questions. I had been reluctant to disturb his rest and recovery; on the contrary, though, I found that he loved talk, relished response, needed our contact, welcomed our touch of holiday cheer. Almost silenced, he had become a model listener. ...

More and more I am convinced that McLuhan was an original. He may or may not be Canada's Vico or Bacon, as his apologists claim; however, I'm not certain we know how to approach his eclectic method, his cultivation of chaos, his wild wit, and his profound understanding that the literary sensibility initiated by the print medium was transformed by TV and computers.

I know now that McLuhan's message to me was meant to go beyond the adolescent angers I often still nurse. So long as art, science, literature, social observation, metaphysics, and politics are separated through specialization, any attempt to heal the world, make things whole, will be frustrated.

Radically, he asked if the literary establishment courted obsolescence by imposing single points-of-view, an automatic allegiance to categories based on a visual bias. When literary people impose systems, the old continuous modes of expression, and stated them with dialectical self-righteousness, they blinded themselves to possibilities in the electronic world. Isolation, sterility, and totalitarian judgment are the only results of such an imposed bias.

With the passion of one quickened by vision (itself a term that betrays a literate bias), McLuhan dared to suggest that only a reconstitution of the *sensus communis* — a common sense of arts and sciences, united in a poetic wisdom — could save us from entrancement with our technologies. Above all, there must be dialogue between forms of media. The Book was one medium among others, and the true value of a medium was ensured by the insight that medium brought to its user. His humane faith was based on the belief that we could read, scan, or compute our situation, no matter what.

Some say McLuhan never stood for anything. "Standing for something" implies a fixed point-of-view, with a mechanical answer for all received data. McLuhan knew that staying static was the way to obsolescence; so he probed the currents, often urgently, often foolishly, as he tried to grasp the flux, our fluid state. He'll be remembered for multiple views — his cubist approach to perceiving change. The one constant in his eclectic body of work was a willingness to admit transformation.

I remember that McLuhan was kindly, otherworldly, odd, monomaniacal. For one who generated so much uncertainty, who fired probes in every direction, and who despised holding a settled position on any subject, there was a mysterious centre of gravity in him. Others say his probes were a failure. But if you measure success by the measures of light in a person's eyes, McLuhan's eyes were perpet-

the measures of light in a person's eyes, McLuhan's eyes were perpetually bright. He lent to others, like myself, that need for illumination — a search that always brings failure of a kind, the expression of confusion, and the saying of absurd things. Breakdown was McLuhan's great obsession. Yet for him, all breakdown was a prelude to a greater breakthrough.

Powe thus highlights the problem of literate communication in an increasingly non-literate electronic world, where the audience for writers has become totally fragmented.

Two decades ago, American playwright Arthur Miller had already recognized the end of unified theatre audiences. He had also observed: "We are killing ourselves with abstractions," and asked his audience: "Why can't we ever get below the issues?" Doesn't this also account for the fall in "ratings" of many kinds of literary work since the 1970s?

Eric McLuhan who, among other things, teaches speed-reading, writing and editing to executives, also throws light on the future of literacy as a retrieval of Baconian writing "in Aphorism" with fresh meaning, rather than a further extension of writing "in Method." In a recent article on "Postliteracy," Eric quips that electrocution has supplanted elocution as a mode of sensibility.

> Like all other media, the alphabet acts like a drug: it is addictive, as TV is addictive or the telephone is addictive. ... Anything "read" off a TV screen has the form of TV and produces (as best it can) the satisfactions of TV. Sesame Street has not produced a generation of Matthew Arnolds or Samuel Johnsons — nor could it. Nor will the word-processor — another form of television.[38]

Thus, Eric reinforces Marshall's most famous aphorism; for no program can ever exceed the power of its medium to create the effects that are its "message." The narrow context of computer programming unavoidably imposes literate visual assumptions (with Yes-or-No Logic) upon its progammers, who may "become what they behold." But computer users are ineluctably the "content" of our much wider electric information environment, a multi-sensory structure (with Yes-and-No Dialectic) that is extended and intensified by electric speedup of every kind.

SAMUEL D. NEILL

Professor of Library and Information Science, University of Western Ontario, is a former student of McLuhan. Marshall regarded his staunch literacy as highly as their long friendship. He has kindly given us permission to choose excerpts from his unpublished "McLuhan Remembered."

After reading Bruce Powe's article on his experience in McLuhan's course Media and Society in 1978, I realized how different was my time in the same course ten years before. ...

The class met Tuesday evenings at 8:00. If there were twelve members in the class it was hard to tell, for the room in the Coach House where it was held was always crowded. There were nineteen folding metal chairs and it was necessary to arrive early to get one, which I did, since I found it extremely uncomfortable to sit on the floor with no room to stretch. On any night there could be forty or fifty in the room, all ages and all kinds, including one young woman with flowing black hair and long loose garments. She might have come straight in from the desert of Omar Khayyam.

McLuhan, whom I had known casually for many years, passed out the famous reading list and introduced Harley Parker, the artist. The first two classes were conducted by Parker, showing the slides which became the illustrations for *Through the Vanishing Point*.

My relationship with Marshall was always warm and friendly. I had taken one of my first year courses from him in 1946-47. It was called "Seven Shakespeares" and all I remember was some reference to Hamlet, Johnny Ray and Frank Sinatra. During the next four years, while I was studying history, he was going around campus giving the lecture which would become *The Mechanical Bride* (1951).

After I graduated from the University of Toronto Library School in 1951, I went to work in the Long Branch Public Library. Long Branch was on the far reaches of what became Metro Toronto and was then one and a half hours by street car from St. Michael's. I sat in on McLuhan's course in Modern Poetry in 1951-52. It was very enjoyable and one could make references and comparisons to current popular culture such as advertisements and comics.

It was after one of these classes that Marshall invited me home for supper. We stopped first at the Baybloor for a beer, then took a street car to 27 Wells Hill Avenue. His wife Corinne was not expecting anyone and had to set another place at the table. I have always been easy around little childrenand it is just as well, for all six of the McLuhan brood were still very young. You can imagine the hectic

140

time Mrs. McLuhan was having if you have ever been in a large family of small children. I sensed the difficulty, ate, bided my time, and said farewell. Not before, however, I had been shown one, or was it two, small paintings by Wyndham Lewis. ...

Once, in the '70s, I don't remember when, I was in Toronto and dropped in to the Coach House. McLuhan was dictating to his secretary, Mrs. Stewart. He was standing in the small entrance "foyer" that led into the larger meeting room (which was decorated with posters and a large mural by René Cera).

He interrupted himself and took me upstairs to his office for a chat. There was a couch or narrow bed and one chair. On the floor were piles of books, perhaps ten piles of two to four books each. These were the chapters of something he was working on. "The way to write a book today," he said, "is to get yourself some file folders, fill them with relevant clippings, and then comment on them." His comments, at that stage of his career, were made conversationally to his secretary, Mrs. Stewart. The result of the file folder was *From Cliché to Archetype* — the mosaic idea in practice, the chapters in alphabetical order. ...

I have always assumed that he was thinking of himself as much as of every other famous person when he wrote in *Explorations* (4 -1955, p.56): "For it has always been an advantage to have direct contact with eminent men, if only because proof positive of their essential mediocrity spurs younger talent." He knew he had the broadcast media by the tail and he knew why and how he had them by the tail and he enjoyed it enormously.

McLuhan once said "man should maintain a constant, nonstop dialogue with his Creator. And for that kind of dialogue you don't need even to be verbal, let alone grammatical."

WILLIAM KUHNS

Author, broadcaster, and dramatist, already overloaded with compiling material for an "authorized" biography of Marshall McLuhan, Bill Kuhns replied to our questions with kind permission to cite from *The Post-Industrial Prophets*,[37] where he examines the relationship between McLuhan's work and the work of Harold Innis.

The work of Harold Innis raised more questions than Innis ever answered. Are the time and space biases the only criteria by which we can judge the effects of media in society, or are they the only two

Innis had chosen to explore? As media involve more and different kinds of technologies, do their modes of influence change accordingly? Would electronic media create such an overt spatial bias that no new medium offset its effects?

McLuhan's work appears as more of a departure from Innis than an attempt to resolve its questions. Indeed, McLuhan drew from Innis little more than a fundamental way of approaching media and Innis's dense, elliptical method for dealing with the subject. Innis's most important theories — the time-space tension in history, the function of media in usurping or supporting various kinds of authority, the relationship between media and organizations — do not appear in McLuhan's work except in the most tangential way. *The Gutenberg Galaxy*, the book by McLuhan that is closest to Innis's thought, and that McLuhan himself considers a footnote to Innis, carries a premise that Innis would have approved — the printing press as the focal event in recent history — into areas that might have surprised Innis as much as anyone else, for example, the notion of linearity and "linear thought" as a fundamental feature of post-print culture.

There can be no question that McLuhan owes a great deal to Innis. The two were good friends for several years, and McLuhan never hesitates to point to Innis as *the* pioneer in these questions, but apart from certain similarities and parallel developments, ... the two men have followed different courses and have reached different conclusions.

Hitherto, some of McLuhan's critics seem to have missed the many shifts of emphasis in his work: from considering the effects of conventional communication media upon their users to *reconsidering the effects of our study process on its users, as a communication medium.* In what follows, we shall try to elucidate the nature of these changes and their unlimited consequences, as we experienced and explored them with him. And, subsequently in his spirit, with our own limited wits and senses, we shall explore the grounds that give meaning to our thoughts and feelings and exert their powers over each of us by remaining hidden.

CHAPTER H

VISUAL AND OTHER WORLDS

McLuhan's basic quest: "What effects does any medium, as such, have upon our sensory lives?" raises other profound questions: "What kinds of world are presented to us by our senses?" "Are such worlds identical?" "If not the same, in what way do they differ?" "What is their 'real' nature?" "How do the senses relate to each other and to their total environment?" "Which senses dominate differing cultures in different stages of their historical development, and why?"

CARLETON WILLIAMS

Former President of the University of Western Ontario, and previously Professor of Psychology at the University of Toronto was one of Marshall's close friends. "Carl" was also one of the original explorers to whom Marshall attributed the discovery of acoustic space.

Carl explains:

I learned that there are many ways — not one way — of viewing reality; that even if the medium is not the entire message, few if any before McLuhan really explained and exploited the enormous, often unconscious, impact that the medium has in shaping the said message. A little experiment that we did in the Culture and Communications Seminar demonstrated that students' scores in remembering the points made in a lecture, varied significantly with the medium through which the lecture was delivered. (For example, the best students scored highest on TV, while no one did outstandingly well by reading the lecture.) Such an experiment was unthinkable prior to Marshall.

I learned too, to think of contemporary technologies as extensions of man's senses and behaviour, and so it went for the two busy, hectic years of the Ford Foundation grant (1953-5).

Incidentally, at that time, this experiment did not demonstrate that TV was the most effective medium for education. It was only a beginning which required further testing that did not materialize through lack of funding. Also, educational "experts" were concerned only with the effects of their programs, while assuming all "media as such" to be neutral.

In reply to our second question on anecdotes about Marshall, Carl recalled:

While I learned much from him, I also taught him about auditory space. He, by the way, always — and wrongly — called it "acoustic" space. (I say "wrongly," because acoustics pertain to the physical properties of the room, auditorium or whatnot, in which human auditory capacity is called into play).

At one of our earlier sessions we were wrestling with *Space, Time and Architecture*, a major work by the architect Siegfried Giedion. He made the point that one could, and indeed had to, consider space in various ways: it was not a simple "given." There was, he said, "hollowed out" space, as in a cave; "enclosed" space, as in a stadium; and "infinite" space, as in the heavens.

This put me in mind of a comment of Herman von Helmholtz, a major figure in German psychology and physics at the turn of the century. Helmholtz used the phrase, "auditory space" to describe the notion of space experienced by a blind person, or a seeing person wearing a blindfold. Such persons are at the centre of an n-dimensional sphere, in that they may detect a sound from any angle. The ability to locate the sound stimulus (right-left, front-back, above-below, etc.) depends on the differential impact of sound waves on the two ears. One has trouble distinguishing sounds directly above from directly below the body and even more difficulty distinguishing directly in front from directly behind the head, and so on. ...

The notion of auditory space struck Marshall with great force and I was thereafter bombarded with telephone calls, (usually after midnight), as he presented his latest insights sparked by this idea. This was characteristic of Marshall: that he appropriated ideas from others, developing and expanding them beyond anything contemplated by the original proposal. An excellent example of his extraordinary ability to make such gigantic intuitive leaps was the lecture in which he dazzled and baffled a Cornell audience, titled: "Acoustic Space in the Poetry of Ezra Pound."

This illustrates the effect of electric process retrieving auditory sensibilities. For this reason Marshall often cited what T.S. Eliot called the *auditory imagination*,

... the feeling for syllable and rhythm, penetrating far below the conscious levels of thought and feeling, invigorating every word; sinking to the most primitive and forgotten, returning to the origin and bringing something back, seeking the beginning and the end. It works through meanings, certainly, or not without meanings in the ordinary sense, and fuses the old and obliterated and trite, the current, and the new and surprising, the most ancient and the most civilized mentality.[39]

The discoveries, stimulated by Carl's first articulation of what Marshall later called "audile-tactile space," are nowhere better illustrated than in articles subsequently published in *Explorations in Communication:*[40] for example, "Ted" Carpenter and Marshall McLuhan's "Acoustic Space," followed by Siegfried Giedion's "Space Conception in Prehistoric Art." These led to still wider discoveries reported by Carpenter in *Oh, What a Blow that Phantom Gave Me!*[41] and also to "rediscoveries" of space in poetry and painting *Through the Vanishing Point*[42] by Marshall McLuhan and Harley Parker, that retrieved with new meaning Andrew Marvell's old clashing metaphor of eye and ear — "stereophonic perspective."

> But at my back I alwais hear
> Time's winged Charriot hurrying near:
> And yonder all before us lye
> Desarts of vast Eternity.
> (Andrew Marvell, "To His Coy Mistress")

Most of us have already noted with admiration how the deaf learn to use the eye and kinesthesia as an EAR through sign languages, but we often remain unaware of the effects of deafness upon their sensory lives.

INSIGHT GAINED THROUGH EYESIGHT LOST

At the Centre, we were particularly interested in hearing from the blind about their more mysterious sensory world that uses the ear, tactile interval and kinesthesia as an EYE. French author, Jacques Lusseyran, from his classic *And There Was Light,*[43] illuminates the vast enrichment of his sensory life through accidental blindness. For example, Lusseyran describes the conflict between the eye-world and the other sensory worlds:

When I came upon the myth of objectivity in certain modern

145

thinkers, it made me angry. So there was only one world for these people, the same for everyone. And all the other worlds were to be counted as illusions left over from the past. Or why not call them by their name — hallucinations? I had learned to my cost how wrong they were.

From my own experience I knew very well that it was enough to take from a man a memory here, an association there, to deprive him of hearing or sight, for the world to undergo immediate transformation, and for another world, entirely different but entirely coherent, to be born. Another world? Not really. The same world rather, but seen from a different angle, and counted in entirely new measures. When this happened, all the hierarchies they called objective were turned upside down, scattered to the four winds, not even like theories but like whims.

How do the sightless organize their perception? From notes translated for a magazine article by one of our editors, Lusseyran describes his own experience of non-visual space.[44]

I don't have to attribute an object or a person to a particular place in the world. ...reality is no longer enclosed in space. Things are present without my having to attribute to them a particular place. All I need to do is take a new direction within myself to notice them.

Pressure is the common ground of the senses. All the objects that make up our world, even those that we consider immobile or dead, produce a sound. Gates, walls, the shade of a tree, sand, and even silence, produce a trembling, a gentle sensation, repeating endlessly. I eventually noticed that most sensations, even hearing and even smell, always were in essence pressure. The universe has weight, and weighs on me forever. Perception, then, means entering into an equilibrium of pressure, into a force field. The oneness of the world is then experienced as a physical event, not a mystical one.

Objects exert pressure on us. We exert another pressure on them. The real images in our experience are produced suddenly at the meeting place of these two movements. When one knows this, the proportions of the universe change with new resonance. There are echoes and presences everywhere; hollows, voids, bursts, and responses. Armed with these "new" proportions, with this force field, I no longer need to touch all the statue to know it completely.

When I place my hand on one brick of a house, I can know the house entirely. In the very first glance, in the first brick that my hand falls on, or the first tone of a melody, I find a progression in which all the elements are predictable. A brick makes the whole house, the first step into the vestibule creates the living room, the first sound of the voice makes the man. The part equals the whole. The body announces the actions past, present, and future of he who is the body.

In contrast to Jacques Lusseyran, whose blindness enriched his sensory life in a dominantly seeing culture, Richard Wolkomir's brief history of *American Sign Language* [44] discusses enrichment of sensory life achieved by deaf students when liberated from assumptions imposed by dominantly hearing teachers.

But every human artifact is a communication medium with its own distinctive effects, which reshape its content of human users, physically and psychologically and socially. This is its often hidden message, regardless of any program or other human intent.

Meaning is always a relationship between a consciously chosen figure and some visible or hidden ground; for these are in constantly changing "figure/figure" relations with each other, both historically and under the aspect of eternity. The ultimate ground — the mystery of boundless existence — is made manifest by human experience and affirmed in religious faith.

Once upon a time, reality meant *matching the old*. McLuhan and his collaborators were among the first to recognize that reality is not something outside of our skins that we match inside of our heads. Today, "reality" means *making the new*. Like truth itself, it is something we make in an unending process of remaking our world as that world remakes us. It is a process not only of discovery, but of retrieval with new meaning in each new situation that involves everything else, both past and present, visible and invisible.

Third-World people, learning to cope with modern technology, now recognize that all "fixing" is provisional. The invisible Fourth World — a modern "Globe Theatre" via electronic media — has revived the resonant non-visual structure of the ancient Tribal Village and the blind seer's vision alike, with new meaning.

EDWARD T. HALL

In two classic studies of sensory perception,[45] this renowned cultural anthropologist examines "Culture as Communication and Communication as Culture." With Carpenter and McLuhan, Hall explored "The Language of Art" and "Art as a History of Perception," and pointed out that "only on rare occasions do art and science merge." These explorers observed how *each sense makes its own space* in differing cultural contexts.

Long before public relations packaged McLuhan for public consumption the two of us knew and appreciated each other in a variety of contexts. I have been asked: "What did you learn from Marshall McLuhan?" The question is not as simple as it might appear, which I will go into in a moment. I am not even sure that is an appropriate question. First, it has been my observation that human beings "learn" very little from each other. The term learning is used much too loosely particularly in the present context. In fact, what we think of as learning in the sense that the question has been put to me may involve quite different processes. Before continuing I should comment on what the question implies. To ask thirty or forty people what they "learned" from so-and-so is like building a house without plans or design. One is inevitably left with a hodgepodge of bits and pieces — parts that are assembled by some mysterious process which could not possibly reflect the man from whom these others presumably "learned." This is particularly applicable to McLuhan.

The conventional use of the term learning in this culture is a process that occurs from the "outside-in," a laying on approach. Whereas what I am talking about is the other way around and is particularly characteristic of McLuhan — an inside-out approach. The two are irreconcilably different.

I am not making this point to be difficult but because there is an imbedded error in our thinking and one which Marshall would have appreciated. The error is of course one in which our educational institutions are mired and one of the reasons they do not serve us as they should.

Therefore, if I were to rephrase the question it would be somewhat as follows: (and I am not at all certain that this is the way to go.) Anyway, I might ask: What new perspectives or ways of looking at things did his writings suggest to you? In what ways did Marshall's work help you to make more appropriate statements? Did he call attention to anything in yourself that made you aware that you were not exploiting some talent of your own, or even a feature of the environment as much as you should? What insights or concepts did he or his work provide that enabled you to organize the data in your head in a more satisfactory manner.

To illustrate what I mean I am going to turn the situation around. In the early days Marshall was struggling with two processes which he called "innering" and "outering." The trouble was that the metaphors were not ones which people could relate to or grasp easily. However, on reading my book *The Silent Language* [45] he found something that expressed this innering and outering process but in a way that could be readily understood by others. The term I had used described a process found in a number of living organisms but is the one on which all culture rests, and one with which I have been preoccupied for over forty years, namely the process of Extension. Marshall, talented and brilliant, immediately saw the elegance of this concept. It fit his thinking like a glove fits the hand. Now, one could not say that Marshall "learned" about extensions from my book or from me because he didn't. This concept was a mini-media event and illustrates his thinking, because once one begins to think of media (and all of culture for that matter) as extensions of what was formerly done by the organism itself, you have deleted the artificial compartmentalizing, isolating, effect of much of our thinking and made a step in the direction of giving human beings back to themselves. That is, few people think of the entire medical profession as an extension of the immune system and the body's built-in repair mechanism. It is difficult in a compartmentalized culture to take something as advanced, complex and evolved as the modern automobile, as an extension of the feet and legs. We think of the doctor as one thing and ourselves as something else and our diseases, when we have them, as something else again which brings us together with the physician. Even the physician is likely to separate you from your condition. Yet there are times when it pays to simply let the body do its job, just as there are times when it is well to keep in mind that the automobile multiplies our strength a thousand-fold and if we are angry or upset things happen which would not occur if we were on our feet instead of the throttle.

It should be clear at this juncture the two of us got much from each other. Both of us were what Buckminster Fuller called comprehensive thinkers. And truly comprehensive thinkers are anathematic to those who build systems and think along linear, compartmentalized lines. So it is reassuring to know that there are others whose minds work as our own does. Since this kind of thinking makes connections and does it constantly, it is inevitable that we would be linking ideas and events in different ways. I shall never forget Marshall's description (in *The Gutenberg Galaxy*) of the first use of 3-D description in a printed text. At the time I was writing *The Hidden Dimension* [46] and was looking for boundary lines between different ways of perceiving (and describing space). I knew, for example, that what had happened in art during the Renaissance with the adoption of linear perspective must have also occurred in literature.

Marshall, his friend Ted Carpenter and I all shared an interest in how artists used their senses. Marshall had sent me galley proofs of *The Gutenberg Galaxy*. There it was, in King Lear: as Edgar seeks to persuade the blinded Duke of Gloucester that they stand atop the cliffs of Dover. Reading Shakespear's quote one is there in the spot standing beside the Duke looking down and at the same time carefully examining the reduction in size of objects as they recede in space — a 3-D image of the scene.

Like others I had known, I had found Marshall to have achieved a state of erudition that verged on the unique. Not only was he literate but he could relate things that others had not. It isn't enough just to know history because unless one can do what Marshall did much of the impact of history is lost. Yet one cannot say that one learns to make connections, from someone else. Usually this happens automatically inside the head. But what one can learn again, but from a new angle, is the treasure trove of insights that lie buried, waiting to be mined, in the literature of the past. Marshall broke many of the rules of academe, but in so doing he revealed new ways of viewing the past and relating that past to the present. One would have to look far indeed to discover his equal in this respect. He kept reminding us by his examples that there is the past waiting to divulge its secrets if we are only willing to take the time to look.

While Marshall and I both did our own thing in our own way we were still stimulated by each other, and how does one assign a proper value to "stimulation" in a compartmentalized world? Without stimulation we would perish.

What did Marshall mean to me? What differences did he make in my life? He saw and related some things that I had failed to see. He was company in a lonely world and he provided stimulation, pleasure, ideas and discourse. What more can one ask?

Hall's remark on "learning" recalls the distinction between preliterate rhapsodic-learning with all the senses, and literate book-learning that separates the visual from all the other senses. So also, "to learn" that once meant both to impart and to acquire knowledge, now often means only to acquire knowledge. But our experience of exploring with Marshall was always a two-way process in which we both acquired knowledge from, and imparted knowledge to each other through participating.

In this book, our combination of "parallel actions" or *parataxis*, like the plots and subplots of Shakespeare, is intended to create depth awareness of "participating." We recognize that its visible "plot" may look like a cubist "hodgepodge," but we hope that its invisible "sub-plot" may resound many harmonies of the drama we delight to "participate" inside out.

TONY SCHWARTZ

Media consultant and oral historian, who became a legendary "sound wizard." We began hearing from Marshall about Tony's recordings of New York's oral history during the 1950s, before they had actually met.

When I approached Tony by telephone from Toronto with our two main questions, he called back from New York soon afterwards with his responsive chord.

TONY:

What did I learn from Marshall McLuhan that I hadn't known before? In two words — a lot!

The main thing that Marshall did for me occurred on almost the first day that I examined his book *Understanding Media*. It was given to me as a thank-you present by a teacher whose class I spoke to.

Before reading this book I had great difficulty working with people in the advertising field, because they didn't understand what I was doing with sound. But after reading Marshall's book, I discovered that different media function according to different principles. That freed me instantly from worrying about this difficulty. I recognized that these people and I were playing the same ball-game in different ball-parks: they were playing in a print-oriented ball-park, and I was playing in an acoustically-structured ball-park.

I could now explore the principles that operate in my ball-park instead of worrying whether I was fitting into their ball-park. What I did to get around that problem successfully, was that on every job I did, I arranged in my contract for doing it two ways: the way that the client wanted, and the way I thought it should be done. I agreed to do this for the same price, and I found, about 90% of the time, they bought the approach I had taken.

I used to say to friends that I would give anything to meet Marshall McLuhan and spend an hour with him. One day, "Herb" Brown (a space salesman for *Time* magazine) answered: "He's in my office right now." Herb offered to bring me over to his office, but I said: "No. I would much rather meet him here in my office so that I can show him some of the things I want to share with him."

BARRINGTON:

When was that?

TONY:

May 4, 1966.

BARRINGTON:

Marshall had begun talking about you before that.

TONY:

When I met him he told me that he had already used my records in his classes.

Soon after meeting him, I heard him speak at the YMHA. I recorded his presentation, and found his speech so much more meaningful than just reading him. There were "gems" in his talk.

But I also found every page in Marshall's book could open up a year of "explanation," for his insights were so deep.

For example: "Instant information creates involvement in depth" is a very important statement; it gets behind the reason why we should respond quickly with electronic media to what is actually happening. If people hear a quick response, they get involved much more deeply — like the difference between getting a telephone call that your house is burning, and receiving a letter telling you that your home has burned!

Marshall came to Fordham University in 1968, and asked me to teach with him. He sat in on every one of my classes and it was exciting to have him there!

Regarding his humanity, there is one thing my wife always speaks about: when he came to dinner, the minute it was over, he got up and cleared the table, taking the dishes to the sink.

I call Marshall a shooting star, and we mortals can only follow a little way in his path. The shocking thing about Marshall was that he had such insight. I had worked in my field for twenty years before meeting him; and though he didn't work in this field closely, he had deep and principled insights about it.

Of most people you can say that they do things in "obsoletely" the right way. Marshall didn't. He could respond to new things instantly. I remember one time when he asked me to record a talk of his (I think it was at the Museum of the City of New York) where he was to speak to some 250 museum directors, I refused. In the course of my work, I have recorded more than 200 meetings, and no more than maybe five or ten people had come to pick up a recording.

I figured that nothing is as useless as yesterday's speech! So I said to Marshall, I would much rather record and make cassettes of your speech now, and send them a week or so in advance to all the people coming to this meeting; they could listen to it, and then talk it over with their staffs. When they come to the meeting you can just get up and say "Are there any questions?" He responded immediately, "Yes, let's do it." And we did just that with great success.

Marshall not only opened up areas to explore, but also gave direction as to method. That was the exciting thing: for example, "electronic replay" (one of the greatest advances of the century) reverses the role of cognition and re-cognition.

BARRINGTON:
Do you recall anything comical?

TONY:
One day, Marshall came into the office, as I was editing some tape, and asked, "What are you doing?" I said, "I have a speech here of Mayor Lindsay. I'm taking out all the *ahs* to let him hear what it would sound like without them. Like ladies and *ah* gentlemen." Marshall said: "You shouldn't do that, you should add ha so he would be saying 'Ladies and *ah ha* gentlemen.' It would convey a feeling of discovery."

This anecdote also reverberates Marshall's playful approach to discovery for entering any new territory, as well as Tony's *Responsive Chord*.[47] Marshall's influence on Tony is nowhere more evident than in Tony's later book, *Media: The Second God*[47].

MICHAEL SMART

Michael, who is now Coordinator, Geographic Names, Land and Resources Information Branch of the Ontario Ministry of Natural Resources, was born in Montreal. After post-graduate studies at the Geographisches Institut in Munich and the London School of Economics, he accepted an appointment in Toronto with Ontario Department of Lands and Forests as Provincial Toponymist (responsible, among other things, for the naming of some 250,000 hitherto unnamed lakes and rivers).

Michael had discovered *Understanding Media* during his stay in London, had written McLuhan asking permission to meet him, and received a prompt invitation to do so. Michael's office in Toronto was just around the corner from the Centre, and, on a July morning in 1970, the moment came.

I left my office in the Whitney Block, crossed Wellesley Street and found McLuhan's office tucked away behind a group of stately Victorian houses. I walked up to what used to be a Coach House and knocked; a tall gentleman appeared and inquired whom I might be looking for. (I mentioned the letter from McLuhan's secretary.)

As we mounted the steps to an upper office filled with partly opened boxes of books, papers and assorted journals (recently transferred from another nearby office), he explained that Dr. McLuhan's secretary was not in at the moment and asked: "Could I be of some help? What was the nature of your studies? How do you believe it relates to McLuhan's work?"

We talked for most of what was my lunch hour, soon forgotten, as we launched into an animated discussion revolving around my firm belief that, from my perspective, McLuhan's work was really a marvellously articulate dialectical extension of the evolutionary hypothesis of Pierre Teilhard de Chardin, especially his work on the extensions of man. Finally, as I rose to return to my own office, the tall stranger, who had not yet introduced himself, invited me to join Dr. McLuhan and his associate Barrington Nevitt the next Monday evening at 8 o'clock at Dr. McLuhan's home in Toronto's Wychwood Park. Would I be interested? Indeed I was. He commented on how much he had enjoyed our talk, then introduced himself as Marshall McLuhan. My surprise knew no bounds!

Thus began my association with this great man, and my initial insight into his unique personality and style. On my way back to the Whitney block, I wondered why McLuhan was so intrigued by my reminiscences about life among the Mistassini and Wawanippi Cree (Québec), while in the employ of Hudson Bay Company, but apparently not at all interested in what I believed was the link between his work and that of Père Teilhard.

Later, we asked Michael to repeat a favourite story that he had told on that first visit to Marshall.

On a warm Sunday afternoon in 1955, as I was carrying out, in company of two Cree assistants, a routine geological reconnaissance survey of the trackless wilderness west of *Asinitchi-bastat-Sha-kee-gan* (Five Mile Lake) in the Chibougamau-Opemiska region of central Québec. We lived under canvas, travelled by canoe and float plane, and traversed so-called virgin forests of red pine, cedar, and white and yellow birch over undulating boreal terrain of deep moss, glacial erratics and pre-cambrian rock outcrops. We blazed an east-west line from the lake to provide a grid reference to which we were to plot geological information gleaned from close study of outcroppings of the country rock. Measurements were made by chain (steel tape) and magnetic bearings (compass). Equipped with tracing paper, pencils, protractor, geological hammer, mineral lens, ... we struck west from the lake shore where we left our canoe. My Indian companions were provided with axes, spade and pick to assist in the removal of moss, soil, roots ... covering rock outcrops which might unlock important information on mineralization ... All of this was entered carefully onto the field map I carried, much to the curiosity and mystification of my two companions, who marvelled at the white man's fascinating ability to "read " rocks, yet who was, paradoxically, so uncertain about where he was on the ground that he must consult a little magical box with a swinging needle in it while he intently studied a many-coloured topographic map, or photograph taken of the area from a high flying aircraft, before daring to venture away from his canoe or campsite. And when he sallies forth he is seen to trail a steel tape behind so that he may be quite sure just how many feet separate his survey lines from his outcrops.

While concentrating on getting as much geological information on paper as possible between bouts of swinging the map at clouds of blood-thirsty mosquitoes and moose flies, I realized, with a start, that I didn't know where I was anymore! A deadly serious situation. How could we get to the canoe, or even cut across country to base camp in the remaining light without being securely locked onto a familiar

155

blazed line and grid on that map? Euclid's two-dimensional. world had evaporated before my very eyes. A tree without one of our blazes could be anywhere. The first reaction of my two companions, when I announced that "we" were lost, was disbelief. Then, typical of Indians generally, when faced with someone else's embarrassment or loss of face, they burst out laughing. ... The final blow came when both blurted out, with respect: "We're not lost. We're here, O-chee-mau. Tent lost!" (*O-chee-mau* is the Cree word for leader, etc.). I could see that they had picked up their tools, and I followed them "home" *their way*. ... Since then, I've never been able to see maps in quite the same way. Being friends of long standing my companions never mentioned the incident again.

This anecdote exemplifies the contrast between "modern" and "ancient" awareness — of EYE-people, who are lost without a map, and multisensory-people, who are never lost in their own environment.

Are the "moderns" lost forever in their Global Electric Theatre of the Absurd, where only the unexpected happens? Have they left the nineteenth-century world (dominated by print and visual thinking), and plunged through this century (dominated by electric media and multi-sensory being), without recognizing that the awareness of the "ancients" is now mandatory for human survival?

WAYNE CONSTANTINEAU

As a comprehensivist, Marshall favoured human experience with its actual contradictions, rather than seeking merely logical explanations; and he fostered friendship with fellow explorers, whose human experience was complementary to his own, like our colleague, Wayne.

Two millennia ago, Plato arrived in Athens as the leader of a touring mime troupe. The sensory stress of his world was rapidly changing from EAR to EYE through Greek phonetic literacy. But in the EYE world established by Academe, Plato shunned the traditional magic of mimesis.

Two decades ago, Wayne, who practised international business, took up mime, while the sensory stress of our world was rapidly changing from eye via electric process to multi-sensory media. He encountered McLuhan circuitously in

Paris.

I never met Marshall McLuhan directly, but indirectly by reading one of Edward Hall's books. As a mime teacher in Paris, I was keenly interested in what Hall had observed and, through his bibliography, I sought other related material. I found four books by McLuhan. When I opened the first book, *From Cliché to Archetype*, I read: "The entire world of technology makes sense by miming the human body and faculties."

For the next five years I pored over McLuhan's books, line by line, letting it all sink in. I found practical, mimable examples of what McLuhan was saying. After returning to Toronto, in 1981, specifically to work with McLuhan, I found that he had died on New Year's Eve. Only then, did I find out that he had been famous.

I located his son, Eric, who introduced me to some of McLuhan's colleagues who were trying to revive his famous Monday night Seminars. I then set out to mime Marshall through the imprints he had left on others.

At first, I was overwhelmed. But I had an advantage over his erudite colleagues. Mime let me investigate any medium's effects directly.

I thought with my body, but how did McLuhan think? Eventually, Barrington and the others exposed me to Four Basic Questions for exploring any medium: What does it *enhance*? What does it *push aside*? What does it *revive* that had long been dormant? And, finally, what will it *flip into*? After *Laws of Media* was published I also discovered that analogical ratios played between these effects. The first medium I tried these questions on was the chair. This investigation generated a book — *Our Affair With the Chair* — a medium with effects quite out of general awareness.

The chair enhances the head and it pushes aside the rest of the body. The chair is the only medium I can think of that names the parts of the body as it numbs them: feet, legs, seat, back and arms. The chair also illustrates two other points McLuhan was trying to make about all media: the user is clearly the *content*. And, like all invisible grounds, the chair is out of sight, out of mind — in plain sight, in other words — where it besieges us with its array of rear-guard actions. When we look at it, it becomes a Queen Anne, a Stickle-back or a Bauhaus. A joy to the eyes. We embellish it or collect it. But where we never seem to look, it distends our seat, numbing the largest muscular system in our body, the one pivotal to all postures and posturings.

All power — private and corporate, everywhere and always — organizes itself around the attributes of a posture. Our society shapes power according to chair sitting (Speech from the Throne, Chairman of the board, "Pre-sit-dent," etc.).

The chair — the throne — arrived with writing systems 5000 years ago in Sumeria and Egypt, and it gained corporate power as writing gained influence as a medium fostering a monopoly of knowledge. While writing allowed for action at a distance, the throne stayed at home and created centralism.

One important aspect of chair-sitting, discovered by Elias Canetti,[48] reveals the chair's role as centralizer, shows us the main difference between it and squatting, and prepares us to understand the difference between the chair and the recliner, the medium that obsolesced it. With these three postures we can track a parallel process to McLuhan's understanding of tribal (squatting), literate (chair-sitting) and post-literate (recliner) eras.

Canetti observed that "in relation to the legs of a chair [a sitter] actually is heavy. If he sat on the ground he would make an entirely different impression, for the earth is so much heavier and more solid than any of its creatures that the pressure they can exert is insignificant in comparison." In other words, chair-sitting is the only posture that exerts weight and pressure, and it concentrates this weight on the seat. The role of the corporate body is to carry this *centralized* weight. The centralized authority emanating from the throne corresponds to McLuhan's view of some effects of the phonetic alphabet.

Curiously, both the chair and writing, having arrived together, are obsolesced together with the advent of electric media. Under electric conditions, as all leaders now know, every seat is a hot-seat. So they now stand and we recline.

We began to use recliners (chaises longues) in earnest in the last century, to read the newspaper. Today, as McLuhan had noted, no one can watch TV for very long while sitting up straight or standing. We slouch and sink lower until our heads too are at rest. Only then can television properly do its mimetic work on us: we mime or "body-english" our way through every program. Actually, the TV tube mimes us, plays on our sensibilities while we sit there. The recliner numbs the entire body and the body at rest seems to be a necessary precondition for travelling on electric media. The TV generation certainly was the "laid back" generation.

But how does the recliner — "the La-Z-Boy" — differ from the head-enhancing, seat-centralizing chair? The recliner numbs the head too and spreads the weight more evenly throughout the body politic — private and corporate. Hence, decentralism. The recliner is to electric media what the chair was to writing. The new electric figure reinforms the postural ground.

In brief, the chair enhances the head, numbs the rest of the body, revives the numbed parts as elements in the corporate body and, when all is said and done, the once mighty head flips into the no body, the recliner.

Now, here comes everybody on the "Internet," while their bodies mold in a "meat seat."

MIMETIC VISION

Here is my way of understanding McLuhan.

In order to express myself as a mime I have at my disposal only the four modes of action of the body. I can assume a *posture*, I can *displace* myself in space (steps, walks, runs, etc.), I can *articulate* (bend my joints) and I can contract my muscles (*isometrics*). And these modes of action are also modes of perception, ways of knowing.

In order to imitate another person, a mime concentrates on only one of these modes of action, isometrics: the tensed muscles, the blocked energies. For consider what happens when you isometrically contract your muscles: you *inflate* (*enhance*) the muscles (bulging biceps, e.g.). This *impedes* articulation (try bending the arm at the elbow while upper and lower arm muscles are contracted). Isometrics *revives* posture (of the arm, in this case). It stands out, it "freezes." At some point, the muscles tire and must relax: they *reverse* their effect; they deflate. Or, after a brief effort comes displacement; what you are pushing, a car for example, begins to move.

In other words, every isometric muscular contraction sets up a field of effects parallel to McLuhan's "tetrad" of questions — inflate, impede, revive and reverse. Isometrics, used as the kinesthetic sense, generates these four nodes of awareness. Equally, the ratios or relations that play between the modes of action also play between McLuhan's tetrad of effects. Of course this doesn't mean that I see McLuhan as as fellow mime. But several more parallels and differences are worth noting. [see page 262 for a fuller discussion on tetrads.]

For social reasons, I don't often use the mime's "kinesthetic eye" when looking at other people. This eye strips the body bare to the bone and people prefer to be looked at with an eye that glides over the surface of things. But here is how I use kinesthesia/isometrics as a perceptual tool and how it corresponds to some of McLuhan's work: "putting on" the tensed muscles and blocked energies of another person — inside your own muscles, so to speak — immediately revives posture, lets me know where and how articulation is impeded, and I pick up the rhythmic pattern of the Other's gait long before I hear the sound of the Other's footfalls. I'm "listening" to the silences between them, the ground. And, just as a mime can "hear" the Other's foot-

159

steps before he hears their sound, McLuhan was picking up the "sounds and sights" of his time 30 and 40 years before they were evident to most others.

By putting kinesthesia in charge of my investigation, I use *sight* too, but sight is held in check, in proper proportion, the same way that an isometric contraction holds articulation in check — and in the same way that (according to McLuhan's Laws) a new medium down plays the previous one, another curious parallel.

Every imitated object easily yields these effects. When I mime a hole-digger with a shovel, all I really show my beholders is the shovel's effects on the user, which is what McLuhan was trying to do with all media.

Each of the four modes of action (the mimetic learning-elements), is a way of knowing. Miming someone via kinesthesia, as above, is but one way. I can also mime people by imitating their walk (the displacement door), or even by looking at one of their body parts (articulation's way). For instance, I can give you a detailed profile of people by considering only their feet. Articulation's way of knowing proceeds by breaking the subject into parts, pieces and categories: are their feet open or closed? Do they walk on their balls or on their heels? The list goes on for another ten or twelve "things to look for," and finally I have my profile. Here, I use the eye, in fact the whole sensorium, differently than when kinesthesia leads the learning. The eye/articulation approach detaches the elements before putting them back together again.

Kinesthetics/isometrics and McLuhan's tetrads — as complements to the eye's "slower," more detailed way of learning — grasp the situation, sum it up in one gesture, in a "flash." The mime tries to do it with a muscular contraction; McLuhan, with a tetrad of effects. Of course, McLuhan too had other tools of understanding. And he could do several tetrads on the same subject. But there is an important difference between mime and tetrads. Mime grasps fleetingly and tetrads arrest mimetic action so we can contemplate it properly. With one corresponding set of actions, I get a physical and a mental work out.

Everyone shares with mimes and infants the innate ability to "put on" an object, a situation or another person. In fact, this is how we learn for ourselves and from each other. Aristotle called this process mimesis, but he may not have been trying to express the same thing. As pointed out earlier in the chapter, Aristotle was refering to rhapsodic learning, which goes beyond what a mime limits himself to. Rhapsodic learning included the chanting and the acting out the "epic poems" of the culture, which add even more sensibilities (voice and music, etc.) to the learning process and make it a group activity.

Here, we are examining the mimetic process at the personal, preverbal level, before it becomes tribalized, civilized or electrified.

Edward Hall and the other contributors to this book have learned from McLuhan by miming him. Surely they tried on his ideas, played "let me try on this idea or approach for size." And it is not uncommon for co-workers and close family members to mime one another's physical, emotional and mental characteristics. In this respect, I should question Hall's claim that we learn very little from each other.

I missed meeting McLuhan by a few months and I had to settle for his living spirit, as reflected in those he knew, including many contributors to this book. His thought strengthened my understanding of mimetic processes and of the sensorium's workings. But more than mime and perception, McLuhan gave me words, a set of metaphors for translating mimetic silence into speech — arresting it. And it is through my ability to use these words that I have tried to mime him.

Lest we forget, after *The Mechanical Bride* McLuhan developed his work by replaying the "processes of cognition and creation," like Joyce, Pound and Eliot before him. Mime is another door into the cognitive and creative process, and it reminds us of how little we use our innate abilities to grasp events as they happen.

RAY AFFLECK

Montreal architect extraordinaire, epitomizes comprehensive grasp of auditory and visual space alike in works that now grace Canadian cities. He learned about McLuhan through his writings. He epitomizes McLuhan's "artist" as "the man of integral awareness."[6]

I find the first part of the question "What did you learn from McLuhan" rather difficult to answer. The learning covered so many aspects of my life and came enveloped in such witty insights, metaphors and probes. It might be described as learning through poetry rather than prose.

I well remember my excitement back in 1965, when I first read *Understanding Media*. Every page was a learning experience, every paragraph a challenge to the conventional wisdom.

McLuhan's comment on his own experience (*Playboy* interview, March 1969) says it much better than I can.

My work is designed for the pragmatic purpose of trying to

understand our technological environment and its psychic and social consequences. But my books constitute the process rather than the completed product of discovery; my purpose is to employ facts as tentative probes, as means of insight, of pattern recognition. ... I want to map new terrain rather than chart old landmarks.

This brings me to the second part of the question "that you didn't already know." I found most of McLuhan's work strikingly original, but sometimes I felt I already understood his probes, albeit in a halting, vague unstructured way. What he did was bring it all together in a meaningful way, fitting it into the fabric of the emerging post-modern world. This experience constituted another form of learning, one that had an excitement all its own.

The above deals with learning in a general sense, but there is another aspect of McLuhan's work that was of enormous importance to me, that is, his contribution to my work as an architect. Particularly important were his perceptions about multi-sensual environment: his critique of our tendency to stress the visual sense at the expense of the other senses, particularly the tactile. These and other insights had a profound influence on my design method.

Understanding that the medium of architecture is space itself enabled me to develop the design process around probes of spatial experience, the experience of a subject moving through space using all the senses. This is, of course, in marked contrast to a fixed object "looked at" by a fixed observer — an attitude to architectural design that had come down to us almost unaltered from the Renaissance.

McLuhan's insights also helped me break away from a rigid linear process of design, design development, and decision making. The alternative process involved simultaneity and dialogue among the principal players — replacing a linear process by a cyclical one — that operates through the intersection of imaging, judging, and understanding.

In summary, McLuhan and his collaborators were mainly concerned with manifesting rather than attempting to "prove" the differences between "visual space" (dominating literate Western civilization) and multisensory space" (underlying preliterate and post-literate Western, as well as Eastern, and non-literate cultures).

VISUAL-SPACE STRUCTURE

An artifact of Western civilization created by Greek phonetic literacy.[40] It is the space perceived by the eyes when separated or abstracted from all the other senses. It is continuous, connected, homogeneous, and static. It is like the "mind's eye" or Visual Imagination that dominates the thinking of literate Western people, some of whom demand "ocular proof" even for existence itself.

AUDITORY-SPACE STRUCTURE

The natural space of non-literate people (those who have no experience of phonetic literacy) is like the "mind's ear" or Acoustic Imagination [39] that dominates the thinking of preliterate and post-literate people alike. It is discontinuous and non-homogeneous. Its resonant and interpenetrating processes are simultaneously related with centres everywhere and boundaries nowhere. Like music, it requires neither proof nor explanation, but is "made manifest" through its cultural environment.

Auditory and visual-space structures are both complementary and incommensurable, like History and Myth. This is exhibited not only by the Wave-Particle of sub-atomic matter, but also by Art and Science, by Aphorism and Method, the differing Right and Left cerebral hemisphere activities of the young and the old, non-literate and literate people, as well as the "simultaneities" and "successions" of nature itself.

Only the visual sense in high definition can create the illusion of objectivity by divorcing thought from feeling, as Jacques Lusseyran [43] clearly "saw." We have been trying to make manifest that no language of "rigid connections" (whether mechanical, logical, or visual) can re-present audile-tactile, eco-logical, or "resonant relations." Neither can audile-tactile and visual presentations ever match each other, although they may be complementary. As Marshall constantly emphasized, only the visual sense separates from the other senses, which all relate to each other.

COMPLEMENTARITY OF THINKING AND BEING

Two millennia ago, Chinese sage, Wang Fu, restated already ancient Yin/Yang wisdom that "poverty arises from wealth, weakness from power, order engenders disorder; and security, insecurity."

Two decades ago, Marshall and I replayed these complementaries, and added: "jobs create unemployment" (neither tribal men in their own territory, nor mothers anywhere, were ever unemployed until forced to sell their labour power in "jobs" to earn a living); "knowledge creates ignorance" (there was neither bad grammar, nor bad spelling, until people learned to read and write); and "whites created blacks" out of people to produce the "white man's burden," which has now become the white man.[7, 40]

The style of an artist, in his chosen medium, is his way of understanding multi-sensory existence. Cartoonist Al Capp understood that in depicting the Eye/Ear cultural gap between the "city slicker" and the "country bumpkin," L'i'l Abner: "As any fool can plainly see, Ah can see it!" (not merely by sight, but through manifest insight).

Today, anybody can plainly see that "law creates ordure": both industrial pollution and abstract "legal rights" that subvert manifest justice. Electric speedup fosters retribalization and accelerates not only the withering away of centralized national states, but also the crumbling of all "rational authority" imposed on humanity. Continuing failure to harmonize human means with humane ends is inflaming "us against them," and leading to neo-tribal warfare everywhere. We are now relearning, what the ancients knew: "you can hurt a man's feelings, but not his rage."

In the 1960s, we had already noted that "Frederick Winslow Taylor made himself famous by his time-and-motion studies and scientific management. Like any other avant-gardist, he had one foot firmly planted in the past." Taylorism's "one best way to do everything" by people who learn to serve as mere extensions of any technology, is now being superseded by Humanism with "no best way to do anything" by people who are learning to remake all technologies to serve everybody. Whereas the Old Laws of Implementation converted the new into the dead by using the old means, the New Laws of Implementation will anticipate the effects before creating their causes with multi-sensory perception.[31]

From now on, we shall try to show how everybody may learn to build the new bridges of "perception" that St. Thomas Aquinas recognized long ago as "a proportion among proportions apprehended in our sensory lives." We shall consider such "proportions" (Latin *ratio*) among literate and non-literate, occidental and oriental mentalities, in both modern and olden times, to retrieve ancient human wisdom with fresh meaning for all of us, by using all our wits with humour and comprehensive awareness.

At the turn of our century, Gilbert Chesterton used to admonish "progressives" to consider discarding works of the immediately preceding century, and always to reconsider the previous century's "unfinished business" as a resource.

Meanwhile, as new electric times seem to reduce centuries into decades, Western civilization is being reduced to universal "trivia" by global multi-media.

INTERLUDE

Let us now take time out to unfreeze some of our "frozen categories" (unexamined assumptions) not to destroy them, but rather to reconsider their consequences that may still be more "upside" than "downside." We know that "archetypes" or inventions, whether verbal or nonverbal, are converted into "clichés" by use, and then discarded for reuse in new archetypes through *hendiadys* (one-by-means-of-two) with new meaning in a new situation. Marshall explored such processes with Wilfred Watson in *From Cliché to Archetype* (1970).[52]

As *Homo Ludens,* let us also note with Johan Huizinga that *play preceded culture,* and with Edward T. Hall that *culture is communication and communication is culture.* We may then begin to organize some of our own ignorance by constantly asking ourselves, and everybody else, our twin questions with Marshall's "playful seriousness"; and let us use them, like his 1969 *Distant Early Warning* card deck, to stimulate dialogue by aphorism in Joycean tradition: "The clown is the emperor's PR man," "The victor belongs to the spoils," and "Should old Aquinas be forgot?"

Let us also recognize that the "wireless world" had already obsolesced the "wired city" early in this century (but is now reviving in "global networks" with fresh meaning). Instead of gazing nostalgically into our rear-view mirrors at the fast receding grounds of would-be "problem solvers," let us now learn to look directly at our problems and theirs, not merely in *computerized virtuality*, but in *the actuality* of human existence. Old answers are getting cheaper, faster than ever. New questions have become our main resource. *Today, the action is in resonant relations, not rigid connections.*

Preplayed more than two decades ago by McLuhan's DEW Line Newsletters, his Distant Early Warning approach (not theory) is now being ferociously verified.

The future is not what it used to be (old wit), *and neither is the past* (new wisdom).

CHAPTER 1

WATCHING THE GROUND AS FIGURE

During the Watergate break-ins, two decades ago, "No one knows what goes on behind closed doors" was a popular song. Clark Cunningham, who was then engaged in painting Corinne McLuhan's portrait, asked Marshall if he had heard it, and he replied immediately:

> No, and anyway it's not true! Everyone knows what's going on behind closed doors nowadays in Washington and Ottawa because of investigative reporting and electronic eavesdropping. The real problem is that people can't see what is happening all around them — things that are really destroying our society! — the hidden environment or "ground."

FIGURE/GROUND RELATION

Benedictine Sister Bede Sullivan, a graduate student and close friend of Marshall and his family, celebrated his birthday anniversary in 1981 by "conducting a conversation" on TV Channel 10, Victoria B.C. with Gerry Royer.

GERRY:
Was there any area foreign to Marshall McLuhan — physics, sociology, psychology, economics? The man had such perception, like a laser beam. He saw truth, played with it, using metaphors and language in such a way as sometimes confused people, but once you got behind the scenes, as it were, then you understood McLuhan.

SR. BEDE:
Take his "rear-view-mirror image." Once you caught on, you began to realize the danger of projecting the future from statistics of the past. He would say: "There is nothing inevitable so long as man is willing to think." ...

GERRY:
As you know, we all had to do a final paper for McLuhan, and I did "The Floating City." I was curious to find out how many people were in the air at any given moment. Back in 1963, the general statistic was two million, a population equivalent to that of

Toronto ... so a floating city.

McLuhan operated from a lot of different levels, and saw reality from many different angles and approaches. But he didn't fix on it — never said: This is Truth! That is Reality! He merely drew attention — this is happening, that is happening.

SR. BEDE:

What impressed itself indelibly on my mind was his statement: "Unless you see both Ground and Figure simultaneously, you don't have the whole picture."

GERRY:

Yes, he always said if you look at anything, or hear anything, there is always something else behind it that you don't see. We are unconscious of our environment. Fish don't know water exists until they're beached.

SR. BEDE:

Appropriate to the Figure/Ground discussion is ... what appears on the Three of Diamonds in the "McLuhan Deck" of playing cards: "Should old Aquinas be forgot?" The sayings on these were the subject of the first class we had with him, remember? For depth awareness the American says: "I know it inside out;" the Englishman: "I know it like the back of my hand;" the Spaniard: "I know it as if I had given birth to it," etc.

GERRY:

McLuhan was a tall man, as you know. I will never forget the night he came in from a trip to Texas, wearing a large cowboy hat; he started his lecture on "The Impact of Clothes as Language," which translates: if you take note of the way people dress, you get an insight into what goes on inside their heads. He had a knack and facility of using the given — as it happened — to bring home a truth that should be investigated by an anthropologist.

SR. BEDE:

Wasn't he really more anthropologist than anything? A recent sketch in *Today* magazine shows McLuhan in a telephone booth with a telescope, and the legend reads: "McLuhan puts a telescope to his ear, and says: "What a lovely fragrance we have here!" His critics liked to talk about how he confused the senses. But, in retrospect, we understand better the validity of his statement: "Unless the body can achieve some degree of balance amid the input of the senses, it grows hyper-restless. When we moved into a world heavy on radio and TV ... we got excess in taste and touch as well — a lot of drunkenness and drugs, and of nudity and sex."

Synesthesia

Early Greek and Roman philosophers conceived a *sensus communis* as a "common sense" that could unite all the senses. But art historian E.H. Gombrich has pointed out that *synesthesia* (interplay of all the senses, once considered to be a mental aberration by psychologists) is now recognized as normal by most artists.

> ... the splashing over of impressions from one sense modality to another, is a fact to which all languages testify. They work both ways — from sight to sound and from sound to sight. We speak of loud colors or of bright sounds, and everyone knows what we mean. Nor are the ear and the eye the only senses that are converging in a common center. There is touch in such terms as "velvety voice" and "a cold light," taste with "sweet harmonies" of colors or sounds, and so on through countless permutations.[49]

Gombrich demonstrates that re-presentation is never a replica — no human sensory response can ever match a sensory input. People always make sense or "meaning" in different ways. Their cultural environment (dominated by EAR or EYE, not merely their ideological or theoretical persuasion) creates a "mental set" favouring some kinds of sensory response at the expense of others. That environment also stimulates differing degrees of Left/Right cerebral hemisphere specialization. This mental set engenders both a generational and cultural gap not only between East and West, but also between literate, non-literate, and post-literate mentalities.

Vivid Figures in Shifting Grounds

From an interview by Kevin Doyle recorded at Sr. Bede's home in Victoria, B.C., during 1988.

Sr. Bede:
> Marshall's vernacular was the local slang and expressions of the people he was working with. He didn't speak in footnotes, but in very direct, vivid language, full of good allusions.
>
> At seminars, his normal procedure was to read the front page of a newspaper for the news story of the day about an event anywhere in the world, and to start a dialogue with: "This is the way the newsmen think the world is today." (This is the Figure) "What's behind that? (What is the Ground?) It is not possible to

understand any word or "figure" alone, but only in its context or "ground." The most important thing Marshall taught me was this Figure/Ground relationship.

For example, here is Marshall, Sister Bede, an unidentified participant and I at a seminar in Toronto, January 15, 1973.

MARSHALL:

Take transportation; or, better, urban affairs. Houses are built, but at the wrong location, at the wrong time, for the wrong people. Welfare is provided by a continuing, rather than a liberating philosophy.

Transportation is subsidized, but strangles the city, and drains the resources of the community. But it offers security for the rich and guarantees insecurity for the poor. Of course, these categories are very, very shifting. These are Figure/Ground resources being developed, so that no matter what relationship you look at, that is the Figure. We are talking about psychology.

Toronto's Mayor, David Crombie, is the Figure. What is the Ground in which he operates? Is it public opinion? Or is it his buddies? Or is it the opposition? Or is the Ground, against which his Figure dings back and forth, like the clapper of a bell? Because the Figure does not determine the pattern. The Ground is the pattern, and the Figure is only incidental.

BARRINGTON:

One of the more powerful Grounds surrounding all these Figures is what comes out here in the last column of the newspaper report. It says: "Bureaucrats of similar ecological bias" — it does not matter whether they are from the private sector or not.

MARSHALL:

They all share the bias of ignorance, meaning the subliminal. They have all the subliminal unawareness of the world they live in that anybody has. Let's put it this way: in any community, the ignorance of what is really going on in the world is shared by friend and foe alike. Both are completely ignorant of the Ground they live in.

The only people who have any knowledge of the Ground are artists — in any period, in any country, in any culture. The only people who know what the Ground is in which they are actually operating are artists. The reason is, they do not depend on ideas; they depend on perceptions.

BARRINGTON:
  Of the Ground?

MARSHALL:
  Yes. Of the world they live in. Now, this is where Owen Barfield's *Saving the Appearances* comes in; it is a little Harbinger paperback of about a hundred pages. It studies: what did the world look like to a man in 2000 B.C.? And what would the world we live in right here look like to him, if he used his eyes — his senses — in the same way to look at it? The subtitle of the book is *A Study of Idolatry*. That doesn't help, does it? This is not what we mean by idolatry.

BARRINGTON:
  What he means by idolatry is any concept looked at as an absolute.

MARSHALL:
  In other words, any fixed position. He [Barfield] says: "The same world looked at in the Middle Ages was not the same. The trees, the spaces around them did not look the same in 1200 A.D.; and not the same in 1500 as they did in 1200. In 1800 or 1900 A.D., they looked completely different. That is, the World vision supplied to the senses of the people living in these periods — the world they actually saw — was not the one we see today."

  In other words, the perceptual life of man (the Figure/Ground relationship) is not the same. The Ground changes all the time, and the perceptions thus change with the Ground. The Figure may remain fixed. For example, at the present moment, the motor car has not been drastically changed by the jet plane. What has changed?

SR. BEDE:
  Perception of time and space.

MARSHALL:
  Yes. It has completely altered the whole feeling we have for the world outside us. This hasn't affected the design of the motor car yet. But it has changed the meaning of the highway; and the manufacturing services of the motor car — the whole Ground of services in which it operates. The motor car is a Figure in a huge Ground of services that are changing.

  It is not the Figure of the car, but the Ground that is wiped out by jets. The jet just goes around the highway, and leaves it sitting there. ... The jet plane will destroy the motor car socially, but not immediately, ... It can still be used for getting to airports.

  Like the use of horses for pulling cars out of ditches before high-

173

ways. The horse-driver could see a glowing future; he'd "never had it so good" as when the motor car came in! But this is again a question of Figure/Ground that was not understood.

UNIDENTIFIED:

It's like the airlines having gone into the rent-a-car business. Each airline has its own car rental system.

MARSHALL:

In the meantime, with the movies, the horses came back with a rush, with a vengeance. They have never had so many horses in North America as since the Westerns.

The horses came back as an art form. The motor car will come back as an art form. That's nostalgic. The movies have come back as art forms, not entertainment. TV is the entertainment, and the art gallery is the movies. Always, the old will have a return bout as an art form ... with the Figure/Ground (meaning) completely changed.

Arnold Toynbee was among the first to recognize the new Ground of the Second Industrial Revolution — the "etherealization" of material "hardware" by information "software" — doing "more and more with less and less." United Nations Secretary General U Thant pointed out that it was no longer resource that made decision, but decision that made resource. And Marshall McLuhan (starting with the exemplar of natural language structures) began to explore the power of all human artifacts as communication media to influence what is thinkable or "unthinkable" on differing grounds.

JOURNALISTIC FIGURES ON CURRENT GROUNDS

Sister Bede recalls that on June 4, 1973, McLuhan opened another seminar, based on the rise and fall of buzzwords, that explored "where IT (the hidden ground) was really AT" in journalism. We cite excerpts from the hilarious report of 1973 by Ward Cannel and June Macklin,[50] which launched that discussion with the "Word of the Year" used by people "who tell it like it is."

> *Relevant* (1968) was then the relevant word. During the week of September for that year, to cite a small example: an eminence of public broadcasting called for a more relevant coverage about the bishops; a leader of student activist groups demanded that colleges teach more relevant courses;

a director of a major art museum said many of his colleagues across the country failed to provide relevant exhibitions.

All in all, the word was so popular that it was held over for another year. ...

The power of the word of the year is that it makes some order out of the disarray and disrepair of the human condition. At least it indicates what should be fixed first. ...

One year's word is inevitably replaced by another that is more *profound* (1928), or more *provocative* (1967) with different *priorities* (1959).

Just how a word gets started on the route of having a year of its own is impossible to say — but all at once it is everywhere, ...

Take the 1967 word *charisma*. That word went out by way of the laboratory a year later. According to a Gallup Poll, 1968, Richard Nixon had 13% more *charisma* than Hubert Humphrey, who, in turn, had 4% more *charisma* than George Wallace. Figures of the polls one month later showed a 3% gain in *charisma* for Nixon and a 2% drop for Humphrey. However, over the period of testing, the percentage of *charisma* of Wallace remained constant. But as to which of those percentages was *relevant* — well — it may take decades to find out. But by then it won't matter because by then *relevance* will have lost, and have been replaced by *priority*, or more *viable* or *visceral* (1970).

The whole trouble of "telling it like it is." ... By the time a word gets in, it is on the way out. ... and nothing has been *resolved* (1776).

Slang continually replays old forms, and invents new means to display current "happenings" in our global theatre. As Tom Wolfe has observed, only the Old Journalism still claims to tell us the way IT *really is*; the New Journalism now tries to tell us the way IT *actually feels!*

"At this point in time," (1994) some *specialists* have learned to convert earlier *pollution* into the latest business *product*, "and more." Others have "zeroed in" on *cholesterol*, *Information Technology* that is now called IT by *professionals,* who have "conceptualized" *perception* and packaged *Excellence* on their *Bottom Lines* — ALLFORABIT.[24, 31]

Instead of seeking enrichment through diversity, "lean

and mean" management now frantically strives to produce moreness of sameness faster than ever; touts "today's pain for tomorrow's gain" by compelling the human race to join its global "rat-race" to achieve competitiveness by homogenizing all goods and services on a level playing field; polishes its own image by claiming to negotiate with everything "on the table"; competes for control of "the main chance" on its own terms "under the table," (where there is no love but self-love, and the biggest number is Number One, while "greed makes the world tick"); converts human needs into "packaged oblivion" for today's pain.

During the Age of Reason, moral philosopher Adam Smith, showed how to pave the way to economic heaven with bad intentions by free markets that created the First World. During the First Industrial Revolution, political economist Karl Marx, showed how to pave the way to economic hell with good intentions through administered markets that led to the Second World economies of the post Iron Curtain era. Today, under increasing pressure from both sides, the so-called Third World could find economic salvation via the electric information environment — the Fourth World. The less developed countries could bypass their own collapse, but only by understanding the laws of media of both software and hardware. The last would then be first! WHY NOT?

ABSTRACT FIGURES MINUS ACTUAL GROUNDS

Meanwhile, conventional macro-economic theories continue to measure progress statistically by Gross National Product (GNP) that equates the costs and benefits of Warfare with Welfare: killing with curing. And First-World economic development programs provide subsidies to reduce food production in their own countries, while offering loans to increase it in Third-World countries — to save "the market" locally at the expense of its human users globally.[31] Given sufficient funding, higher "hi-tech" offers to solve such recalcitrant human problems with Artificial Intelligence and Virtual Reality. Both demand stripping natural language of its boundless cultural heritage (beyond definition), and reducing Human Reality to fit the "last word" in Science and Technology: one word with one meaning (by definition). And that would confine rationality to what we now behold via the modern idol of "two-bit wit" — GIGO (Garbage In, Garbage Out), and less!

"It figures," but does it *make sense*? For nothing has any meaning alone, not even "nothing"! The journalistic quest by 5Ws (Who, Which, Where, What, Why, or the like) may probe the Figures, but what questions can expose the Grounds (local, national, global, and beyond) to reveal the dominant laws of our situation not merely for reacting, but for pro-acting. The future of our future is now here, not in some U-TOPIA (no-where).

Today's hidden Ground of electric information, highlighted as a Figure in our quest, has transformed the meaning of every Figure based on former Grounds. All "twains" now meet willy-nilly. That is where I T is really at. How do we get "with I T?" By Instant Replay with suspended judgment,"demonstrated by Ted Turner (CNN) via TV during "Desert Storm" (1991).

FRED AND BARBRO THOMPSON

Canadian Architect Fred Thompson met his wife Barbro, a Swedish Industrial Designer, while working in Sweden. Fred is now a professor at the University of Waterloo, Ontario.

I'll answer the second question first "What anecdote or personal experience demonstrates Marshall's humanity?"

After we had moved over from St. Mike's to the Coach House, it was so crowded you were lucky to get in, even if you were taking the course. During the first term, Marshall said we would have to have a paper ready for delivery after Christmas.

At the end of the first session after New Year, Marshall began: "OK, who's going to deliver the first paper?" There was a deathly silence — not a word. Marshall started to get steamed up about it: "Well, who's going to be first? Can't start without a first one."

Finally, Derrick De Kerkhove said: "Well, if there isn't a first, I'll offer to go second." So I ventured: "If he'll go second, I guess I'll go first." The others looked at me with an expression that implied: "You must be suicidal!"

Marshall asked: "What are you going to talk about?" I said, "Japanese Space."

Winchester [the famous English boarding-school where Barbro

and Fred had sent their two sons] had a motto: "Manners maketh the man." The night I gave that paper on Japanese Space or *MA*, Marshall came up to me afterwards and asked if he could have a copy. It was his right. But that he should *ask* politely for a copy was the only time this motto had ever been demonstrated to me in a university setting!

As for the first question "What did I learn?"

It was after Marshall had given us a list of some 30 books, and said: "Choose any three of these books, and read them (Appendix A). There will be an exam at the end of term." What interested me was how anyone could walk into a room and ask 20 odd students questions on any three books they had selected for a half-hour exam. I wasn't interested in reading the books so much as how he was going to set the exam. On the way to that exam, it suddenly hit me. ...

Marshall walked into the room, took off his hat and coat, pulled up a chair, lit a cigar, and said: "I want you to ask three questions about each of the three books you have read." And he walked out of the room. I had guessed it. That was the most interesting learning experience I gleaned from Marshall. The exam was not to be a regurgitation, but a "probe": *Give me the name of the book and write down three relevant questions.* He knew whether you had absorbed them; it was easy to read; and, possibly, he might learn something he hadn't thought about.

I also learned about the wit and the humour of turning things inside out: one can cheat, but a "spoilsport" is no go. Marshall often cheated for fun: testing whether you knew the difference between cheating and humour.

SPACE AND SPACING

BARRINGTON:

Do you remember anything Marshall said about space?

FRED:

Well, he kept pushing the idea of "acoustic space." I had a hard time separating it from "acoustical," for acoustical space is exemplified by the medieval cathedral; it cannot be understood from a visual point of view, but only as something one moves through. Like the original encyclopedia, it was an oral encyclopedia. It was to encycle, to intone the chant, and to move through those spaces gathering knowledge as you encycled. It's the space that resonates as you encycle. It is of all the senses, not the ear only. The distinction is between an acoustical structure and the actual sensory experience which can be described as "acoustic" — involving all the non-visual senses. Such acoustic space would be audile-tactile with

178

"centres everywhere and boundaries nowhere."

Japanese space of *MA* is a wonderful example of "acoustic" space bias exhibited by an entire culture. Gunter Nietschke has written about it, so have I. Yet the Japanese were so immersed in this environment that they didn't recognize it. I think it was the "fish and water" syndrome. Barbro and I wrote in that paper for Marshall:

> The Japanese space/time concept is embodied in the Chinese symbol, *MA*, which is made up of two parts: the first being the symbol for the two leaves of a door or gate ... and the second being the symbol for sun or moon. Together, the symbols suggest rays of moonlight seeping through the chinks of a doorway.

The element of time implied by the "moonlight seeping through" is of utmost importance to the understanding of the Japanese idea of space. *Space and time are considered as related and relative entities: neither is fixed.* This, in turn, is related to the Buddhist concept of *KU*, or void; that is to say, *space and time are "empty," not having a nature of their own.*

The idea embodied in the Chinese symbol for space is thus quite different from the idea embodied in the Western word "space." To give a quick and over-simplified contrast, let us say, the West speaks of "space;" the East speaks of "spacing."[51]

For example, in flower arrangement, the European arranges the flowers in space, but the Japanese harmonizes the spacing between flowers: their experience of both time and space are essentially different, as Fred had pointed out a decade before and now further illuminates.

FRED:
> The *MA* of painting in Japanese art is that of the relativity of object to object, the spacing being as important as the object. There is no perspective; this would imply an individual point of view denying any sense of obligation to a greater whole that *MA* itself implies. ...The question now open to the Japanese is the connection [relation] of the traditional spirit of *MA* with the contemporary situation, where the spacing has increased to super-involvement and larger obligation.

BARRINGTON:
> Do you think that today's recognition of *MA* in Japan came about as a result of Marshall drawing attention to it?

FRED:

I think it has come about in other ways: Noh drama, for instance, that everybody looks at, but which fewer and fewer seem to understand, although more and more attempt to describe. The best description I know is by an architect, who came from a Noh family but who, because of the war, couldn't make a living in Noh theatre. Now, he can afford to write about it as an architect in terms of *MA* that are easy to understand.

BARRINGTON:

Did Marshall have any influence in sharpening your own awareness of Japanese culture?

FRED:

Marshall's *cliché-archetype retrieval pattern*[52] struck me first in the form of the Japanese Festival — the way they live it. I eventually realized that we live by patterns, not by definitions. For example, the house is not merely a building, it is the household that you belong in. That's the house. It has to do with the *manner of living*. Likewise, the town you live in, as I learned one day when I decided to go off to see a neighbouring village without telling anybody. When I got back, the whole town was in an uproar, because I hadn't kept them in touch with what I was doing. To be out of touch is to be out of *MA* and that's crazy.

When people realized that I wasn't around, they tried to find out where I'd gone; they went from the bus to the railway, to learn where I'd bought a ticket for. When I came back I got a real bawling out; they were very concerned about what might have happened to me. Obviously, I was now a part of them.

Their pattern of life was that everyone knows the things that you can't do on your own. I had been adopted by them, and had to let them know what I was about, just as I should know what they were about. This is a manner of living affecting the rules of courtesy: it includes the manner of living in your house, the manner of entertaining guests, and the manner of treating the gods.

In a Japanese Festival, you are full of the gods, so you can do all kinds of crazy things. But you learn while you're doing these crazy things. That's where you make your mistakes, for they can be legitimized on the grounds that you are celebrating the gods. The only way to take on the gods is to be "non-rational." You are allowed to break ordinary rules, like leaving slippers for the toilet room outside my sleeping room. It turned into a joke at which we all laughed. Otherwise, it would have been construed as Western or ignorant.

But there are customs much more difficult to break: I had a student here at Waterloo, who was born in South Africa of Chinese parentage. She went to Japan, and wrote to tell me how frustrating it was. She had wanted to teach English. But, as soon as she appeared for an interview, there was terrible confusion: as an Oriental, they wouldn't consider her for teaching English. "On the other hand," she wrote, "I was allowed to learn many things that they would tell me, because I wasn't stupid like a Westerner!"

LOGICAL AND UN-LOGICAL RATIONALITY

BARRINGTON:
Did you learn anything about logic from Marshall?

Fred:
What I really learned was about media — trying to figure out what it was about working in Japan that made people able to work together.

As part of the course, I remember going to the Huron Street Public School (Toronto). Accompanied by one of the teachers, I went into the classroom and put a tape recorder on the table. It was Ted Carpenter's little boy who immediately asked: "What are you doing with the tape recorder?" "I'm going to tape what you say," I said. He then retorted: "Don't you know that people don't talk with their voices, but with their eyes!"

The whole business of logical thinking reminded me that the Japanese don't say "illogical" but "un-logical" or "non-logical." If you can make the "gap" or *MA* just right, you can find new things. That's when I started to see what goes on in meetings: all sorts of questioning and positioning, waiting for somebody to make a mistake in logic. And you ask: "Why did everyone twig to the mistake?" It was wrong. But in the wrong there are elements that could be right. It's just because we had never seen anything right in that context before. So let us see what happens when you do wrong things more often.

TV creates the audile-tactile environment that makes some people tumble. They say: "You're teaching everybody wrong." Also: "I didn't say that. Why did you do that?"

"Well, actually, I was thinking you're tribalized all of a sudden," which means: "OK, let's see if it will work and, if it works, let's see if it will work again." That is the logic and un-logic of the Japanese. *The logical is Why? The un-logical is Why Not?* Marshall is both — the whole thing — the "why" merges into the "why not." And this is evidenced in my work with Marshall. It came out of that paper I gave on the Japanese *MA*. In that interval (gap) comes *that* force.

Barbro and Fred had already noted that, before the latter part of the nineteenth century, there was no word for formal "logic" in Japanese (although *Ronri*, a quite different Buddhist logic originating in India, had reached Japan through China and Korea). However, with the introduction of Western thought, the word *Rogiku* (Japanese pronunciation for logic) was adopted. Until this time, their pattern of un-logical thinking called *Haragei* ignored any form of Western logical thinking that equated "rationality" with "ratiocination" or "rationalism." The Japanese preferred to settle problems emotionally.

Ernest Fenollosa contrasts the Western method of abstraction for philosophic discourse with the method of poetry and the Chinese ideograph. If you ask a Chinese what RED is, he puts together the abreviated pictures of ROSE, CHERRY, FLAMINGO, and IRON RUST. The Chinese word or ideogram for RED is made manifest through what everybody knows; and it makes sense, like poetry, by reverberating across the entire language and culture; and like folk wisdom that "love conquers all."

Whereas classical Chinese coordinates, classical Latin subordinates, words and phrases.

FRED:

The other thing that came out of this "gap" or *MA* was that I could teach until I was blue in the face, as a form of entertainment; but as soon as I took that course, the "why not" became "why not go and help Fred in Japan?" There were six in the course and they all bought tickets to Japan. And I promised: "If you will help me with my research, I'll help you find a job." We helped each other.

What is important in any research is to keep your mind on your research and your eyes open for everything else. I remember one of our fellows writing on the blackboard in the village where we were: "If this guy doesn't make up his mind about what we are supposed to be doing soon, we're going to mutiny." It was written for me to see when I came in. But everything we did led to something we didn't expect! We weren't trying to measure something. When I applied for an SSCHRC grant, their officials always wanted to know what the answer was going to be. So I learned to apply for a grant on work already done, while using it to find out something so far unknown.

182

BARRINGTON:

This reminds me of the technique that the Hungarian-American physicist Szilard applied in budgeting his research for the U.S. Atomic Energy Commission. Colleagues celebrating his retirement with him asked: "There is just one thing we want to know — your secret: How did you make budget every year?" "Oh," he replied, "that was easy. Since nobody understood what I was doing, I got the money for the work I did the year before, and then did what had to be done in the following year."

PARTICIPATING

FRED:

What I learned as a teacher was that the students, who shared that experience with me, learned much more than if I had sat down and tried to teach them here. However, our institution would rather have me give a course to spoon-feed students for an examination to prove the work had been covered.

Perhaps, the most informative learning experience was taking those students to Japan. Last year, seven more people helped me to put together an Exhibition there. I paid them, and that led to mutual respect, for everyone was given a place. Four more are helping this year (1988). For me, this approach is exemplified by Marshall. That was the manner of his work. That was his medium, much more than the "content" of what he was teaching.

JOBS AND ROLES

Marshall talked a great deal about specialized "jobs" versus human "roles" because of what was going on in the 1960s. If you are prepared to make sense of any particular action in the constantly changing situation, that's a role. Role-playing is to anticipate and to achieve the desired effect. The effect is uppermost. The job-holder doesn't give a damn!

If we relate that to Japanese Noh and Western medieval drama, the difference is that the *liturgy becomes drama*. In the Japanese liturgy, one plays a role because one puts on the gods by putting on their yoke. If the liturgy turns into a drama, it becomes a job.

SACRALIZING

If you accept Japan on its own terms, there can be no disservice, because of what happened to Japan over time. The Japanese had sacred places where the gods came from and to which they disappeared. These became sacred spaces in the form of temples and shrines. With missionary zeal, they became sacred districts, and eventually resulted in a sacred country. *If the whole country becomes sacred, then nothing can become a disservice; everything has to be a service.* This is the ideal.

When the sister city of Collingwood, Ontario, says they want to have a Shinto priest come over and bless the gates, the Japanese don't know what to do, for it doesn't belong to the sacred land.

Nevertheless, the Japanese do have some shrines in Victoria, B.C. How they can sacralize them I don't know. They aren't sacred just because they are "sacred things," but because they keep giving the Japanese a "sacralizing charge."

When the Americans speak of "recharging their batteries," they are not "sacralizing," but getting a psychological lift. It has nothing to do with their relationship to the eternal, but only to doing one's job better — do what is necessary for a living "come hell or high water!" That is the bulldozer approach. It is entirely different from "sacralizing," which is more like participating in the Mass — to start afresh, not merely seeking new energy, as such, but having the old spiritual pollution swept away — what is left when this pollution is swept away.

The question for Hamlet was "to be or not to be," but for the Zen-man "not to be" is never a question; it's nonsense! Only "to be" can be a question. But, in today's Global Electric Theatre, the West is twirling East, while the East is going West with ever increasing speed: they constantly probe each other with questions in search of solutions that may highlight process patterns, but can never specify answers for current human problems.

This approach to cultural anthropology, was amply demonstrated by McLuhan's earlier collaborator "Ted" Carpenter,[14, 41] and his colleague Edward T. Hall.[45, 46]

GOING OUT VERSUS STAYING HOME TO BE ALONE

During the late 1960s, we began considering the relatively tolerant attitude of North Americans toward TV advertising, compared to the intolerance of Europeans to this invasion of privacy. Some of us still remembered going out to the "movies" when ads were normally displayed before the "feature" started. Many of us had also experienced how Americans (more quickly than Canadians) had offered the warm, and often boisterous, hospitality of their homes to comparative strangers, in contrast to Europeans of similar professional or economic status.

McLuhan often raised this question with visitors to the

Centre; and, one day, a Japanese visitor casually remarked: "Europeans go home to be alone, and go out to be with people." Marshall immediately recognized a big breakthrough — for North Americans, it was vice versa! And that led to many fresh discoveries.

For example, North American automobiles, whether intended or not, were serving as comfortable havens away from home, whereas European models were designed as playthings for display. The North American pattern of behaviour had arrived with the Pilgrim Fathers, who lived and died by "the Book": they went outside to conquer nature including natural man, and stayed inside to be with their families. The electric information environment of the TV-generation has reversed this trend and many another established by their forefathers.

CHAPTER J

PLAYFUL PROBES AND SATIRE

Johan Huizinga pointed out in his classic *Homo Ludens* that play is much older than culture.[75] And there is no greater example of playfulness than the interplays of Penman Shem and Punman Shaun in James Joyce's *Finnegans Wake*.[54] Once McLuhan espoused Joyce's processes of cognition and creation, he assumed the playful stance as well.

Marshall, a close friend of Pierre Elliott Trudeau during the 1970s, often forwarded insights by playful probe to the Prime Minister and his advisors. During the preparation for the 1979 "Speech from the Throne," Marshall suggested that its form be changed from merely "listing" government intentions to creating "the emotion of multitude" by juxtaposing the plots and sub-plots in our current political drama. In other words, McLuhan was trying to tell them to bring the throne speech into the mythic, electric age.

The Prime Minister's colleagues, on the modern stage of politics, recognized the danger of getting too far ahead of their publics, both inside and outside of government, by trying to "put *them* on" with a dramatic substitute for an ordinary throne speech. In effect, although they had acted on several of Marshall's suggestions in the past, their reaction this time was: "Thanks. But no thanks!" But by the 1990s, most people recognize that all such speeches are showbiz — put-ons.

Marshall playfully probed the Canadian political context by retrieving a long-dormant institution. On the medieval stage, the role of the king's jester was to act as a "probe": to display the background of discontents, hidden by "the emperor's new clothes" — what his fearful subjects and sycophantic courtiers dared not mention, but any child could clearly see.

McLuhan's approach, here and in other instances, captures the essence of satire, "probes" and "put-ons" — all comedy — and of myth,

> ... a structure of parallels without connectives. Mythic form
> is necessarily double. Its double-ness is a matter not of

> matching, but of making, not of the mirror and reflection but of the lamp and illumination..[53]

Claude Bissell, (see chapters B & Q), explains the "double-ness of probes" that Marshall was so fond of using:

> Marshall liked to describe his ideas as "probes," not firm convictions, although he always seemed to express them with conviction. They were attempts to force a reconsidera-tion of accepted ideas. These probes were like the "con-ceits" of metaphysical poets, who delighted in yoking two disparate things together, with illuminating results for each part of the conceit and for the conceit as a whole. These probes would often emerge in conversation or in the give and take of an informal group setting.

In our work with Marshall, we eventually recognized how each sense (and each medium) makes (and requires) its own humour. The deaf and the visually-minded prefer "slap-stick." They chortle especially when the visual goes into high-definition and flips into the kinesthetic; the magically violent choreography of the Three Stooges, for example. The blind and the oral cultures, on the other hand, like Marshall, appreciate word play. Marshall was a big fan of the Marx Brothers and of W.C. Field — the foursome and the loner.

In the electric circus, stand-up comics "put-on" the audi-ence to share each others misadventures, misdemeanours, and misfortunes, or misplaced credulity. Stand-up comedy has emerged as the premier mode to handle the unexpected that we expect to find in our global theatre of the absurd. In all communication, the users are the content of the medium. But, in a "put-on comedy" the users are captivated by the pro-cess of being captured as content. They may also playfully protest: "Don't put me on!," which is another put-on.

RICHARD J. SCHOECK

A colleague of Marshall in the English Department, who, was also co-editor of *Patterns of Literary Criticism* and *Voices of Literature.* "Dick" sent us, from the University of Trier, Germany, some nostalgic anecdotes illustrating Marshall's wit and humour.

- At a table in St. Mike's, Professor Etienne Gilson once commented that there were no American businessmen who were intellectuals: "I've never met one." Across the table Marshall was heard to murmur, "All Indians walk in single file. At least, the one I saw did."

- After a lecture, a graduate student rose and said: "Professor McLuhan, I have noted half a dozen instances where you contradicted yourself." McLuhan promptly retorted: "That simply proves that you still have a linear mind."

- After another lecture, someone said to him: "I enjoyed your lecture, but would you mind telling us in a few well-chosen words what you had to say?" "Not at all," replied McLuhan, "You choose the words."

- Marshall had an impatience with the workings of administration and hated committees. He once said to me (at a time when I was participating in a great number of departmental, college and university committees), "You know it's easy to get off and stay off committees. All you've got to do is make a mess of details on one, and they'll keep you off the others."

- Marshall and I used to meet often on Elmsley Place in the middle of the morning — he coming from his building, and I from the English House — to walk up to the mail room for our mail. He began this morning as he often did, "Dick, we've made a breakthrough." And he began to talk about his latest thoughts on cliché and archetype.

  Just before we turned into Elmsley Hall, a student, whom we both had, crossed our path. I simply said good morning to him. But Marshall wanted to include him in the conversation: "Did you know, S..., that if you raise a cliché to its highest potential it becomes an archetype?" The student, dazzled, of course, said, "No," and fled.

- I once asked Marshall whether he wrote poetry, and he said that he used to but didn't any more. I asked, "Why not?" And he replied, "Because if I did, I would want my poems to be better than James Joyce's."

An inventory of current jokes can expose, any time, the environment of unintended disservices created by intended services, whether private or public — the emperor's clothes, old or new. Jokes, whether hurtful or hilarious, cover hidden grounds of grievance. They announce the grievance, put it on stage and make it tolerable.

Jokes, eventually, get stale and "die" as the grievances they expose fade. Some of the jokes that Marshall collected and often circulated are now dated. Today we no longer hear ethnic jokes. TV brings us the grievance and TV, just as quickly, takes it away.

"Things that are current create currency," said Marshall. And jokes must be current. They need the mythic double plot, they need the ground they are borne in — just as a wheel needs an axle. Jokes, put-ons and satire are meant to oil the "sqeaky wheels" of social interplay, loosen what has seized up. Andy Rooney, in his TV presentation on *60 Minutes* makes inventories of complaints that replay the role of jester for consumers, the new emperors of the market.

The jokes circulated by Marshall as "probes," although often attributed to him, were more often collected for him by family and friends. Many are now dated. Listing jokes is guaranteed to make them ineffective groaners. And like taste, there are as many senses of humour as there are palates. We list some here anyway, "modernized" if necessary, and we intersperse them with a few McLuhan one-liners that still display some pith.

- The guy who felt absolutely alone and jumped off the top of his high-rise. As he passed his apartment he heard the phone ringing.

- Cash is the poor man's credit card.

- Some people use statistics as a drunk uses a lamp post — for support rather than illumination.

- It isn't what you know that counts. It's what you think of — in time.

- Only puny secrets need protection. Big discoveries are protected by public incredulity.

- Many a good argument is ruined by some fool who knows what he is talking about.

- The trouble with a cheap specialized education is that you never stop paying for it.

- Mud sometimes gives the illusion of depth.

- The nature of people demands that most of them be engaged in the most frivolous possible activities — like making money.

- Help Wanted: Person to work on nuclear fissionable isotope molecular reactor counters and three phase cyclotronic uranium focal synthesizers. No experience necessary.

- I'd give my right arm to be ambidextrous.
- Food for the mind is like food for the body: the inputs are never the same as the outputs.
- "Well, it's hard to explain without a mirror."
- Living as if each moment was his next.
- A mystery has been committed.
- Summer Course Work for Educators:
    Creative suffering.
    Overcoming peace of mind.
    Career opportunities in ~~El Salvador~~ ~~Bosnia~~ Rwanda.
    Tax shelters for the indigent.
    The joys of hypochondria.
    ~~Tap~~ Lap dance your way to social ridicule.
- A man all wrapped up in himself makes a small package.
- Since the invention of elastic the space occupied by women has been reduced one third.
- Diaper backwards spells repaid. Think about it.
- There are no more great men, only great committees.
- Communication is what people with nothing to say do to people who won't listen.
- All my work is satire.

When a friend once greeted Marshall with a formal "How do you do?" he promptly countered: "Do you really want to hear an inventory of my grievances?" And when a stranger ran up and asked him whether he really believed in life after death, Marshall asked him: "Do you really believe there is any life before death?"

ADRIENNE CLARKSON

Well-known Canadian TV broadcaster and publisher, mediates another one-liner.

I consider Marshall McLuhan to be a genius and feel that everything he wrote was illuminating, but one thing in particular I will never forget is his saying "the miniskirt is the ultimate act of violence."

Taking off your clothes to "put on" an audience is violence in quest of identity; but the nude is "naked" only for civilized, not for tribal people for whom it is custom or "costume." McLuhan also noted that in her dressing room, without an audience to wear, the stripper is just a private person. In his DEW-Line newsletters, Marshall exposed at length the relation of mini-skirts, mini-plans, mini-states, and mini-futures for many "maxi-establishments."

One of Marshall's early colleagues, who wishes to remain anonymous, reveals yet another aspect of Marshall's playful probes and put-ons in this conversation with the explorers. Mr. X also touches on some poignant, telling details of Marshall's rich and varied sensory life.

MR. X:

When Marshall came to our farm, he always came in costume. Each time he came as a different person. In cowboy boots, in a cowboy hat, he was no longer Marshall. He was somebody else. He loved to roam around the place. Of course, he saw us that way too. At the farm we always wore farm clothes, and didn't really think about it. But to Marshall we were in costume.

BARRINGTON:

Marshall would call it, "putting-on a mask," to put-on an audience, and his daughters lost no opportunity to provide new "masks" for him. He enjoyed them all playfully.

MR. X:

Marshall couldn't stand people who had no sense of drama, who were not fun!

BARRINGTON:

When his famous tweed jacket became notoriously inappropriate for some of his business engagements (as his dear wife and close friends had long been telling him), for some reason he turned to me to recommend a good, but not too expensive, tailor. I called Bill Cameron (an old school friend), with the understanding that Corinne would have to approve the final result — a business suit, a sporty plaid, and a seersucker. But Marshall was always inclined to wear the most comfortable rather than the most appropriate.

MR. X:

Marshall hated standing around at cocktail parties, assailed by insipid questions. He would much rather play games, even tossing

192

bean bags or throwing darts.

I don't think I ever put together a meeting that didn't have Marshall in it as a hidden ground. He was a scary figure in the corporate world. So you wouldn't say: "As Marshall said, ..." What I did in practical terms was to use Marshall's direction and ability to see what the real problem was.

I don't feel that I've stolen anything, because an idea you don't give away blocks the next one from forming. Besides, Marshall encouraged the use of his ideas as a means of discovery. Marshall didn't hesitate to appropriate anyone's ideas, if he thought them useful. That was his approach and his role as an artist. He made no apologies for it.

I remember times when Marshall was almost intolerable, if he didn't like somebody, but that varied from day to day and from person to person. If the person was a real idiot, that didn't bother him.

And Marshall couldn't tolerate noise, even before his operation. When driving in my convertible, the top had to be up, and the windows closed. Even then the vibration of the top itself was too much. He had very sensitive hearing, and used to put cotton batting in his ears to protect it.

MAURICE:

Also, when answering the telephone in his office on any call exceeding two minutes, he would say impatiently: "Hang up! Get rid of them!"

And at the time that I was at the Centre, Marshall was receiving something like three invitations a day, from all over the world, either to speak or write.

Marshall was also strongly affected by the full moon, and he firmly believed that it caused many of his personal misfortunes.

BARRINGTON:

Marshall's sensory life, which had always been intense, reached still higher intensity after his operation. Marshall had to use Librium or Valium (to hold down the "adrenalin," as he said, without paying too much attention to what the prescription said). He also suffered in the kitchen, and complained: "It smells like a chemical factory!"

MR. X:

His senses were heightened in other ways too, in a way related to his put-ons. And that reminds me of a meeting held in Canada for top-level IBM management, where a Club of Rome speaker preced-

ed Marshall. After the first speaker finished he received an ova-
tion, doubtless due to his linear thinking — one percentage after
another! Everyone in the room understood him, because that's
IBM's business.

Marshall then got up and said his piece — absolutely the
reverse of the previous speaker — demolishing the Club of Rome's
position with humour, and showing no sign of irritation whatever.
He had fun, so did we.

Marshall loved to pull the petals off the corporate rose, so to
say, because he could foresee unheeded pending disaster. He was
not always right. But he knew that the only thing corporate people
can see is "more" of what they've seen before.

BARRINGTON:

And to think that he told IBM as early as the sixties that they
should move into software. I guess the joke is on them now.

JOHN ROSE

Former Principal of Blackburn College and Visiting
Professor, Lancashire Polytechnic, England; Director-
General of the World Organization for General Systems and
Cybernetics and former Editor of its journal *Kybernetes*.

My impression is that Marshall was a man ahead of his time, with
a fertile brain and plenty of vision and imagination; he also had a gift
for words. Indeed, because of this, I invited him (and his good lady) to
be one of the chief guests of honour at the Lord Mayor's Banquet at
Guild Hall in 1969, in connection with the First International
Congress of Cybernetics and Systems in London. I remember he came
attired in a Scottish kilt, an impressive figure, and made a memorable speech (he sat at the top table).

A few days after, he invited me and my wife to be his guests at the
Royal Gardens Hotel to celebrate their wedding anniversary. We
were the only guests there. It was a splendid meal, ... while a Gypsy
band played on and a violinist serenaded the couple.

JEAN MERCIER

Professor of Political Science, Université Laval, Québec, who
has a lively interest in Marshall's work, sent us an interesting letter and tried his hand at probing à la McLuhan.

Although I was an M.A. student in 1974, Marshall McLuhan kindly answered my letter, addressing me as "Dr. Mercier." I was in Paris doing a thesis on *McLuhan et la Politique*, and had asked to interview him in Toronto that summer. Since he was coming to France for a conference at Le Touquet, he suggested that I could interview him there.

How had I become interested in McLuhan in the first place? I was a law student at Laval, and a friend in sociology said to me one day "You are the type to get interested in McLuhan's theories." Whatever that meant, it proved to be true. I eventually left law for social science. Not only was I fascinated by McLuhan's approach, his way of seeing things, but he also introduced me to a great variety of excellent authors: Jacques Ellul, Alexis de Toqueville, Lewis Mumford, Elias Canetti, and many others. In retrospect, I believe one of McLuhan's great strengths was his capacity to identify, in a sea of social science authors, who had something to say. He evaluated an author in a straightforward fashion that is uncommon in the sometimes hypocritical world of social science.

Physically, Marshall McLuhan was taller than I expected. He was rather slim and, at the time, had a mustache. His back was slightly arched forwards, as one would expect for a person doing a lot of reading and writing.

We walked towards the site of the conference. McLuhan commented on some of the other speakers that had made presentations the day before. I recognized his flair for what was substance and what was not.

McLuhan's humanity, in this case, was to avoid wasting time with the pompous. He was too busy trying to understand the world around us.

On arriving at the conference site, we walked in front of a French, experimental, television set that was turned on. He stopped and told me: "That is high definition TV, very different from the television I have been talking about. This is more like cinema."

While sitting beside McLuhan, as we listened to a journalist, I wrote a note and passed on to him: "Typical newspaperman, oral man who values print." McLuhan smiled and wrote back: "The newspaperman always dreams of writing a novel. Does he not see he is deep in fiction already? Journalism is *roman collectif*." I still treasure that piece of paper, and while listening to the evening news, I often recall his comment. I inquired about the possibility of a more formal interview, and he told me to wait until we were on the train to Paris. Seated with McLuhan were his wife, Corinne; Jean Cazeneuve, a French media scholar; and Derrick De Kerkhove. For the interview,

McLuhan invited me to sit facing him, and asked not to be tape-recorded.

In answering my questions, McLuhan was patient, but rarely repeated the same elements, preferring to approach a subject by allusion, by metaphor, almost in a poetic style. He showed his humanity by his patience in letting us into his world. McLuhan's work was very much a work of understanding unconscious social processes.

Two years later, I went to the Centre for Culture and Technology in Toronto to give McLuhan a copy of my M.A. thesis. He invited me to participate in a seminar that evening. It was the last time I saw him in person.

I sometimes wonder what McLuhan would have said about phenomena he did not live to see: break dancing, AIDS, star wars, perestroika, or neo-conservatism. I try to imagine his comments:

On break dancing: "When we move from the mechanic to the organic, the mechanic appears as a form of art." On AIDS: "Sexually transmitted diseases generally transform sex into a hot subject again." On star wars: "Star wars become almost totally software." On *perestroika*: "Communism has been dead in communist countries for decades. *Perestroika* is the only way of acknowledging the failure." On neo-conservatism: "I have said for years that the ultimate effect of new media is to make us all conservatives."

HARRY BOYLE

A pioneer Canadian radio broadcaster and journalist adds some pertinent details about Marshall's use of put-ons.

I didn't know Marshall too well on a personal basis. I wrote several articles about him. We also had a brief collaboration as so-called "consultants" with an outfit that aborted. The people organizing it simply didn't understand what it was all about, and thought they could capitalize on the two of us. ... Incidentally, for anyone who believes Marshall was inept about business matters, I can only say that he had enough sense not to get involved in the scheme once we determined that we would be exploited.

On a few occasions, I also arranged for Marshall to meet people who were mainly curious about his ideas and who, I felt, he would have a healthy curiosity about. I remember one unforgettable dinner at the Windsor Arms with a mad childrens' book author, a young popular designer, and a hot-shot adviser on culture to (our federal-government minister) Judy LaMarsh. They came expecting to find a REV-

OLUTIONARY and he played the role of CONSERVATIVE. It was hilarious for a bystander. Marshall knew they were play acting, so he put on a role (to "put them on").

My impression was that of a rather humble man, with a mind like an exploding cosmos. He lit one idea off the end of another. If you were lucky enough, and caught one of his sparks that fitted your experience, you could often end up with some amazing insights.

I think we're still too close to really assess him. For instance, in that meeting with the "revolutionaries," it was apparent that they wanted hard-sell theories from him. For, like all revolutionaries who say they want to be liberated from dogma, it is really dogma that they are searching for. And he wasn't about to give it to them.

The more I learned about Marshall McLuhan, the more I was convinced that he wanted people to explore for themselves. He was a gadfly. Some of his points were well taken. For example, TRIBALISM: if you watch music-videos and current TV commercials, you will find a lot of something that looks like tribalism. And if you look at what people are wearing, from colours to materials, they seem to be Tribalizing. [Tatoos, pierced rings for ears, noses, lips and practically every other part of the body. Is art now something to wear? the ultimate put-on?]

We not only adopt "Jeans," but the latest fad a la Ralph Lauren — to dress up in faded and worn clothes that will make you look as if you're catching the 7.23 from Ealing Station, with a jacket that had a shine to it, even if you'd just bought it from a Lauren store. Have you seen what is inside those stores? Faded carpets, horse-brasses, and all kinds of gew-gaws from what would appear to be English country homes.

Can anyone deny that TV kept Reagan in power, front and foremost in the voters' eyes? There doesn't seem to be any memory concerned. The scandals raged on and he seemed to be unscathed. For the voters are not watching a politician; they are really looking at him like John Wayne and a host of others. Gary Cooper could do no wrong in High Noon. Sheriff Reagan could do no wrong in Irangate.

Perhaps TV has fictionalized everything and Americans have no memory of what has gone before. A commentator calls Iran a barbarous country, a savage country — ignoring Persian history, and refusing even to think of interference in the affairs of that country in the reinstatement of the Shah. Likewise TV portrayed Nicaragua without mentioning Somoza, the Dominican Republic without mentioning Trujillo. There is no memory on TV, except in the form of a documentary. And popular fancy says you can watch that without being affected, for it is only history.

TV has perpetrated some things McLuhan foresaw: the public debates by leaders, TV dominated events, TV dictated events with no liberty or free flow of ideas. They are straightjackets, formalized by formalized questions with no real value for enlightening the public, with about as much freedom for the participants as ballroom dancing in a submarine! And yet they are taken seriously, with newspaper commentators and pollsters solemnly making something out of them.

McLuhan, it would seem, prophesied "Ronnie" Reagan as early as 1966. "Within fifteen years an actor will be elected president." And before the end of the 1960s, by extending the process patterns of the current ground, we had already pre-dicted the accelerating retribalization of our planet.[23]

In the 1970s, we could also foresee what Harry Boyle con-firms: "The Future of Economics is Politics, and of Politics, Showbiz," for that had already happened.[31] Unable to mea-sure the value of anything, economists calculate prices for everything, while our rulers provide *panem et circenses* (bread and circuses) to the ruly and unruly alike — junk food and electronic games for the masses and *pastimes* for the elites.

Gerald Mason Feigen

A proctologist and amateur ventriloquist (who used the lat-ter talent in working with autistic children), Gerald ("Gerry") was a close associate of the late Howard Gossage of advertis-ing fame (whose 50,000 stickers WATCHA DOIN MAR-SHALL McLUHAN? were plastered on almost as many cars in North America). Both also did much to introduce Marshall to the world by organizing a McLuhan Festival in San Francisco during 1965.

Gerry (now deceased) outlined "what I learned from McLuhan that I hadn't already known." He presented these insights as hypotheses to be "disproved" in proper Popper style, or as postulates of empirical thought" in Kantian terms, or as "manifests" that accord with Marshall's approach.

- The medium is the message.

- Each new medium produces a new cultural environment that

becomes invisible, while that of the previous culture becomes visible.

- All new media are extensions of man.
- Relative use of eye and ear changes with differing media.
- Media are both "hot" and "cool."

In reply to our letter, Gerry wrote:

I corresponded with Marshall for about six years preceding his death. At our first meeting, we began discovering how many jokes and puns each of us knew. I had cross-indexed about 2000, and he was anxious to hear as many as he could. He suggested that we write a book about humour, but we settled for including a pun or a joke in each letter we wrote.

One of his favourites was: "Message to deep-sea diver, 'Surface at once. Ship sinking.'" He wrote this when he was visiting Professor at Fordham, and during that period he would blithely plunge into the absurd at any opportunity. This was more enjoyable to me than any other humorous side of the correspondence — an ongoing joy in sharing words with a kindred punster, his probes — his unforgettable contribution to understanding the technological revolution.

WAYNE AND SHUSTER

Wayne and Shuster exploited current grievances to create humour in comedies that replay "gripes" as TV art forms that McLuhan greatly appreciated. Wayne and Shuster (W/S) recently discussed their approach with us in a conversation (cited from memory) that we also greatly enjoyed.

W/S:
Is there a "village idiot" in the Global Village?

WE:
Yes, in the rear-view mirror!
How do you account for the long life that your show seems likely to continue enjoying?

W/S:
By resisting the normal drive to produce more shows more often, and carefully controlling the spacing between them for more than two decades, we have avoided overkill. We always start by considering how the audience enjoy themselves, and create our own

material orally. We write only to guide production. But we edit the production ourselves after long consideration, and set our own pace if possible.

WE:

How would you describe your mode of satire?

W/S:

We show the weaknesses of the things that irritate. We do not try to be vicious. We try to do it in such a way that everyone laughs at the incongruity of the thing. It isn't intended to upset the sensibilities of people, but to expose the ridiculous which is taken for granted. We want to be humorists that laugh at the nonsensical things that surround us. McLuhan starts with the humourous thing to get to the serious; we start with the serious thing to get to the funny thing.

WE:

What examples best illustrate your approach?

W/S:

We lampooned all critics in "The Restaurant Critic." And in the dialogue of "The Baseball Game" we tried to reveal the spirit of Shakespeare's language (mainly in his sub-plots that replayed the speech of the common man of his day) in parallel situations for today's school children: "So fair a foul I have not seen. Get thee to an optometrist!"

WE:

Marshall shied away from the "deadly earnest" and was inclined to be most playful when most serious. Playfulness was his way of converting breakdowns into breakthroughs. He didn't treat himself seriously either. He wanted to know the searching questions, not the simple answers.

W/S:

Some time ago, we were sitting in a restaurant discussing whether to try this approach on an Ed Sullivan show. There was a dishwasher standing nearby who came over and asked: "Are you the guys that did the Shakespeare Baseball Game? Are you going to do it on The Sullivan Show?" We said, "Yeah." And he asked: "Do you think they'll get it?"

What is the point of exposing the humour, if people don't comprehend? You can't hold up a painting to a blind man and ask: "What do you think?" You must know your audience. But many teachers and school children alike have given warm approval of our Shakespeare.

And, after our replay of the "play within a play" of Hamlet, Marshall McLuhan sent us a most encouraging and much treasured note (dated October 1, 1979, just after his massive stroke on September 26th).

> The Western Hamlet was great!
>
> The parallel between the two art forms was most effective in throwing light on Hamlet too.

So we are continuing to broaden our repertoire in this spirit.

WE.

What you have been doing inadvertently on TV, Marshall was doing deliberately in writing — "Satire," directed against the human situation in general rather than any human being in particular.

Marshall's type of satire, (dubbed "Menippean" after Menippus, a Greek Cynic philosopher), permits the use of any and all techniques; verse and prose; uni-lingual and multi-lingual; digressions and dialogues — as required to do the job, the job of retuning the reader's sensibilities. As for techniques, didn't Diogenes wear a barrel, and hold a lamp high at noon, looking for an "honest man?"

Eric McLuhan tells us, after his far reaching study of this kind of satire,[54] that each medium embodies its own unique form of this satire. We find Cynic/Menippean satire in writings by Rabelais, Erasmus, Swift, Sterne, Flaubert, and, of course, James Joyce. The great Cynic/Menippean satires get produced at a time of great technological change: Diogenes and Menippus with the advent of the phonetic alphabet; Rabelais and Erasmus with the printing press; Flaubert with the newspaper; James Joyce with the press, radio, film and TV. McLuhan, with the advent of satellites, got us thinking and talking about our new global village. With the computer intensifying the effects of electric process, we rephrased the term to global electric theatre of the absurd, where only the unexpected happens.

Eric also tells us that this type of satire, while open to a multiplicity of styles, imposes at least two strict rules: you use *only* what is necessary to create the desired effect, and it can only be directed against the reader and not against a figure in particular. The idea is to encourage a retuning of the reader's sensibilities in the process of reading. This last point, more than anything else, distinguishes Cynic satire from all the other forms of satire which may stew in sarcasm, drown in laughter, or even moralize.

Marshall became a "Menippean" writer when he stopped adopting the moral stance as an investigative technique, as he had in the *Mechanical Bride,* and began to play with "the processes of cognition and creation," like Joyce and the other Cynic satirists before them. He sought to retune his readers sensibilities through new approaches to language that would resonate with electric times.

By the end of the 1960s, we extended the language of "doubleness" to figure/ground relations in all our work.

CHAPTER K

METAPHOR AND MEDIA MAGIC

In what he called Structural Analysis, Marshall McLuhan constantly stressed the changing ratios of Sensory Response (that he abbreviated SR, or SC for Sensory Closure or "fill-in") induced by various media in differing social contexts; and most particularly that the sensory response or "space" created by television is much more audile-tactile than visual in character. Whereas VISUAL SPACE (what the EYE perceives) has centres with margins or boundaries (abbreviated C/M), ACOUSTIC SPACE (what the EAR perceives) has centres with no margins or boundaries (i.e., C-M). Understanding how the metaphors of EYE and EAR influence our thinking is now essential not only for recognizing, but also for anticipating, the message of every human artifact — the new Nature that constantly remakes old nature (see Chapter H).

At every stage of human history, the dominant technologies reverberate in current metaphors which translate unfamiliar aspects of existence into familiar forms (Greek *metapherein* and Latin *transferre*: to carry across). In biblical times, the allusions were to agriculture and household arts, to fishing and seafaring, and to tribal warfare. Its millenial metaphor was the Garden.

After Gutenberg and the Renaissance, there were perspectives and points of view, telescopes and microscopes, water-power and clockwork, navigation, and gunpowder that ushered in the Age of Reason with its mechanical "forces." The First Industrial Revolution introduced steam-engines, lineal rails, production lines, "evolution" (paradoxically, unrolling the ancient Book of Nature) and "missing links" that led to step-by-step "progress." Its centennial metaphor was the Machine.

Today, in the midst of the Second Industrial Revolution, we speak of "fields," "feedback," "resonant chemical bonds," "quantum leaps," and information traveling at the speed of light via electric media. But the age-old metaphor of The Great Chain of Being still exerts its power along with the now obsolescent (not obsolete, but increasingly familiar) Bottom Line.

Metaphors and models both help and hinder thinking; like language, they shape perception and (for the unaware) can determine not only what is thinkable, but even what is unthinkable! Metaphors also tend to favour either visual or audile-tactile perceptual modes. Users of any metaphor or medium make sense of its program by filling in what is lacking, either consciously or unconsciously. What users bring to this process of comprehension is profoundly influenced (not absolutely determined) by their previous experience — their "mental set" — shaped by the current social context. Simplification often complicates understanding.

The prevailing media environment biases perception either toward the literate EYE or the tribal EAR, and becomes the dominant metaphor, whose effects are normally ignored. In studies of "media magic" (sponsored in more academic terms by the American National Association of Educational Broadcasters in 1960),[55] McLuhan and his collaborators normally started their investigations by considering the sensory effects of a particular medium, in both High Definition (HD) and Low Definition (LD). First of all, they explored how each conventional medium transforms one kind of Sensory Impact (SI) into another kind of Sensory Response (SR) through Sensory Closure (SC), in a given cultural environment. Sensory Input/Sensory Closure (SI/SC) charts[55] of their observations reveal many hitherto unexpected relations that Marshall outlined in his *Understanding Media.*

For example, when a sensory input is in High Definition (HD) the response of the perceiver will also be in HD, but not necessarily of the same sense. HD auditory input produces HD sensory responses of both visual and tactile nature. Senses lacking in the Sensory Input (SI) tend to be filled in by Sensory Closure (SC). McLuhan explored under what circumstances and to what degree this depends on individual sensory bias toward Ear or Eye (E/E) in relation to the sensory environment of the dominant culture.

The origin and prevalence of popular myths and legends, the continual changes in already existing forms of art and current advertising, the reversals of centralizing and decentralizing tendencies in human organizations also exhibit the sensory effects of new media.

From both "lab and life," both Science and Art, we learned that conventional media not only filter, distort, and add "noise" to the "information" input quantitatively, but that they also transform this information qualitatively during the actual process of human communicating. We observed, for example, that SLEEP is induced by dimming down one or more of the sensory inputs. We learned too, that elevating the sensory impact of a single sensory image, or of a tribal drum-beat, can produce HYPNOSIS by reducing both sensory closure and interplay.

Repeated, intense sensory inputs can also induce uncritical conviction — BRAINWASHING, which requires some sensory interplay, but no "fill-in" or sensory closure. At the opposite extreme, by removing all sensory inputs, we can maximize sensory closure and thereby produce HALLUCINATIONS. Moreover, when all sensory resources are stretched to a high degree for a prolonged period, the result is NUMBNESS. Eternal vigilance thus creates its own opposite — INDIFFERENCE.

Between these extremes lies normal consciousness, which results from the constantly varying interplay of all our senses. Super- or Extra-sensory Perception (ESP) is whatever remains undefined, or beyond definition: "what must be left to silence," as every Zen-man knows (see Chapter L).

FRED RAINSBERRY

Former CBC Supervisor of Children's Programming of Radio and Television, recalls how Marshall's approach to "metaphor" deeply influenced his academic work and subsequent career.

I first met Marshall in his garden on St. Mary Street in Toronto in the company of Hugh Kenner in the summer of 1952. I was working on my doctoral dissertation at the Library of the University of Toronto, putting together a chapter on Kenneth Burke. Once or twice a week, I would drop in on Marshall to talk about my ideas. I never left his company without new insights about my work. While his insights were always refreshing, he inspired one's confidence in one's own ideas. When my thesis on *The Irony of Objectivity in the New Criticism* was finished, it was a privilege to acknowledge my debt to him for the stimulation and understanding he gave me, helping me, in many ways to produce a critical work which has ever since influenced my work and my career.

A central contribution which Marshall made for many of us who knew him in those days, before he became interested in the mass media, was his unique perception about metaphor. It was in conversations with Marshall that I came to understand that a metaphor was essentially pictorial and not simply a "decorated idea." Of course, this perception lay at the root of the work of James Joyce and Ezra Pound about whose works he was a most imaginative and perceptive critic. The notion of metaphor as pictorial, able to stand as an independent poetic object, goes back to Aristotle's *Poetics*, where one finds the first recorded relationship between analogy and the pictorial. A valid metaphor has four terms arranged in analogical form: viz. A:B :: C:D :: E:F and so on. Each relationship in the analogy creates a pictorial image or figure. As the analogy develops parallels, there must be a common ground to enable the reader or viewer (whichever the case may be), to perceive the element of identity common to all the parallel images. Only by this means can one experience the richness of metaphor.

Marshall defended poetic objectivity against any attempt to reduce poetry to rational self-consistency. He often criticized Yvor Winters for this approach to poetic criticism. In his *The Anatomy of Nonsense*, Winters gave an interpretation of the following lines from Shakespear's Sonnet 104

> Ah! yet doth beauty, like a dial hand,
> Steal from his figure, and no pace perceived:
> So your sweet hue, which methinks still doth stand
> Hath motion, and mine eye may be deceived.

as follows: "Subject is change by which we measure Time, but especially as that change occurs in the human face: conceptually there is no irrelevance here: the comparison is used to make a fearful judgment absolutely certain and inescapable." [56]

Concerning Winters' interpretation, McLuhan says that the metaphor is allowed to amplify only the concept. He excludes any notion of T.S. Eliot's meaning for metaphor in his idea of the "objective correlative" as a precise counterpart of a moment in consciousness and yet every metaphor is just that. As indicated above, there are four terms to a metaphor as a "figure of thought." If we deny the metaphysical reality on which the metaphor is based, truth itself becomes mere self-consistency or tautology.

We may thus interpret the first line of the sonnet analogically: Just as your beauty is to your face, so is the dial hand to the face of the dial. The second line introduces the word "steal." As the hand of the dial is to the thieving of Time, so is your beauty to your face. One readily observes the pun on the word "steal" implying "robs," "sneaks away." Instead of Winters' insistence on relevance, we have from Shakespeare an intellectual surprise in the manner in which Donne was later to surprise his reader. The word *"figure"* becomes loaded with ambivalence about the declining wealth (Time) of day; its lengthening shadows and changing hue. The phrase "Steal from his figure" involves not only the face (French "figure") which is losing shape, but the physical figure which is getting pursy. It is not, then, beauty which is being stolen but beauty which is the cause of the theft.

There is still beauty in the face but "no pace perceived." Since "peace" was pronounced "pace," the rationale of beauty as thief becomes more apparent: there is still beauty but no peace in your face. It is now obvious that the literal interpretation which Winters gives is clearly inadequate because it seeks to settle once and for all the poet's meaning on an univocal level of meaning. Metaphor becomes a mere representation of an idea without any objective quality at all.

Marshall watched little television. In fact, he had a deep suspicion of the motives of the promoters and producers of programs and commercial messages to be seen on the screen. And yet, what he did see, he saw with a most creative eye. There has been little comment about the relationship between his ideas about metaphor and what he frequently called "the grammar of television." Having worked with Television for many years, I owe a great debt to him for insights which enabled me to see, use and program television in a creative way.

Good television is essentially analogical, presenting images in montage so as to create meaning without words, a technique with which McLuhan was thoroughly familiar from the study of James Joyce's novels where prose is written in a non-syntactical way. Verbal images are juxtaposed with one another so as to create a montage of images. With careful pre-planning, the producer can create a visual organization which is both aesthetically pleasing as well as informative. Marshall used to set the analogical in apposition to the univocal as a way of explaining the misuse of television when producers could be more verbal than visual. How often have we seen commercial messages in which the announcer speaks in a loud voice, expounding the virtues of the product while the visual is not only overwhelmed by the sound but the pictures themselves are inconsequential? For years, educational television was misused because the educators preferred a "talking face" to a visual sequence which would have diversified the classroom presentation with input from another medium. The analogical organization of imagery enables the images to speak for themselves while the univocal is strictly verbal. Thus it was that I was able to see the unexplored opportunities of the visual media derived from the most creative elements of metaphor in poetry. In short, there are bad poets and bad producers in the visual media. A good poet and producer have much in common when they seek ways to present human experience in whatever field so that the reader or viewer can participate in an aesthetic experience where he is both learner and creator.

WILSON BRYAN KEY

President of Mediaprobe Inc., Steamboat, Nevada, and former Professor of Communication Studies, "Bill" Key introduced us to *Subliminal Seduction*[56] practiced by "embedders." Bill confessed that he enjoyed revealing how "airbrush" artists can hide or embed subliminal sex or Freudian "death-wishes" as programmed magic to increase their clients' sales. He also pointed out that US Patent 3,278,676, granted to Hal C. Becker on October 11, 1966, describes more sophisticated ways of "imparting useful information to an observer by subconscious stimulation" for advertising as well as other purposes.

What did I learn from Marshall McLuhan, either directly or indirectly, that I did not already know?

I was in relatively frequent contact with Marshall over a six year period — 1969-75. I had an educational background in statistical, empirical and cognitive studies in language and behavior, some 300 research productions for governments and private corporations: Marshall's influence literally dynamited me out of the simplistic perspectives and conventional wisdoms of North American social science. After Marshall, my world was never again the orderly, sequential, Chi-squarable, logical array of assumptions which were programmed into me as a graduate student and later as a corporate problem solver. My view of media realities had been micro, the tiny bits and pieces that can be fitted together into a sound, verbalizable, and convincing basis for corporate investments. Marshall drove almost everyone around him to distraction with constant admonishments, "Question your assumptions, all of them, constantly!" This is difficult to do, agonizing if you keep doing it too long. But, intellectual growth has never been a painless process. For most, growth congeals at the moment fame and fortune are derived from a new wisdom that, in its turn, becomes the momentary eternal truth.

Marshall's most important contribution to my life and career was the sly manipulation he could manage where his audience, often against their own better judgment — at first anyway — would end up doing an end run around their own biases and discover that biases could lead into new, more flexible biases ad infinitum. After a few years of Marshall, I could laugh uproariously at the superficial verbalism of the likes of B.F. Skinner and Wilbur Schramm whose major thrust was to conceal rather than expose the inner-workings of media. Marshall reveled in a freedom of inquiry hardly ever experienced by graduate students or tenure perusing faculty members.

Best of all, Marshall was good fun. After three or four hours of his Monday-night seminars, I usually found myself in turmoil, turned on with new insights, concepts, and objectives for several weeks. I was never quite certain he fully approved of the directions I traveled after our long, exciting, and provocative meetings. I perceive him as really quite conventional in his unconventionality. My work resulted in the painful sacrifice of numerous sacred idols in the North American cultures, not the least of which was an exposé of the fraudulent, perceptually manipulated integrity of the mass-communication industry. I want to believe, nevertheless, he would have said privately, "Good show! Now, go out and find another mountain to conquer."

What anecdotes or personal experience demonstrated Marshall's humanity?

I never knew Marshall to turn away a human in need of help, support, conversation, a friend, a curious or troubled student, individuals at war with their environments. He appeared able to fit everyone into his crowded schedule, though it was certain this meant many late nights of labor to make up for time lost. So many of them, in my perception, ruthlessly wasted his time with lost causes, hopeless ventures, and endless unresolvable troubles. He was a kind, dear, and good friend to virtually all who needed one. I believe Marshall would have wished to be remembered as a man who cared very much about everyone and everything.

Do we need to ask why the practice of "subliminal seduction" is still vigorously denied by admen whose livelihood depends upon it?

Likewise academics, seduced by Western culture, refuse to recognize: "The medium is the message" as a symbolist hyperbole that highlights the greater power of the medium to create (desired or undesired) effects by ignoring the lesser role of the user as co-maker of the experience. Marshall once told us what he remembered of its origin.

> "The medium is the message" is a phrase that came to my mind during a conference of radio broadcasters in Vancouver in 1959. TV was threatening the radio world at that time and I wished merely to draw attention to the fact that each medium created its own public and set up a unique equilibrium in its users.
>
> The idea that there can be an equilibrium or *homeostasis* among the components of any living system, individual or corporate, stems from the work of Claude Bernard (*Le Milieu Intérieur*) in the middle of the nineteenth century. Taken in a psychological or social context, any new component disturbs the balance of the entire system by requiring some kind of partial compensation for the new factor.
>
> *Gestalt* or figure/ground considerations are natural accompaniments of any equilibrium theory, and in the phrase "the medium is the message" there is an interplay of figure and ground in that the "medium" can be figure and the "message" can be ground, or vice versa. To illustrate, the motor car is ground for the figure of the driver, but the same car is figure against the highway and the basic services of industry and fuel which sustain the car as a social fact.

DAVID OGILVIE

Marshall greatly enjoyed and highly recommended Ogilvie's book *Confessions of an Advertising Man* (Longman's, 1963). In contrast to the "subliminal seducers," Ogilvie confesses his own good fortune: "I spend my life speaking well of products in advertisements; I hope that you get as much pleasure out of buying them as I get out of advertising them." Marshall was inclined to emphasize that: "The role of advertising is not merely to sell good products, but rather to confirm your own good judgment in buying them."

After returning from Fordham with urgent need for a literary agent in Toronto to handle his increasingly complex international affairs, Marshall turned to me for suggestions, and David Ogilvie immediately came to mind. His unqualified recommendation was Matie Molinaro, who became a valiant defender of Marshall's literary patrimony.

However, Ogilvie's note from France (on July 19, 1988,) some two decades later, speaks for itself:

My answers to your questions:

I learned nothing from McLuhan.

Never heard any anecdotes.

The whole McLuhan thing mystified me when he was alive. After he died, I never thought of him until I got your letter of June 12th.

CHAPTER L

Meaning and Content, Medium and Message

In his "anonymous history"[57] Siegfried Giedion reveals how new ideas that died in America went to Europe to be reborn. For example, the insights of Edgar Allan Poe, father of the detective story and symbolist poetry, became exemplars for Charles Baudelaire,[58] who invited his *"Hypocrite lecteur, mon semblable, mon frère"* ("Hypocrite" reader, my likeness, my brother) to put on his poetry like a Greek actor's mask and become its content.[58]

Whereas T.S. Eliot from America and James Joyce from Ireland came to France to "participate" their symbolist poets, Marshall McLuhan came from Canada to "participate" them all "over there." Are old American ideas still going to Europe to die? like Servan-Schreiber's *Le Défi Américain* (The American Challenge) in the 1960s?

After returning over here, McLuhan learned from his colleague, economic historian Harold Innis, how staples — fish, fur, paper, timber, and wheat — act as communication media by creating their own messages: unique material, mental, and social environments. He went on to discover that every technological extension of humans — every human artifact, whether hardware or software — is a communication medium; and the message of any communicating process is the totality of its effects, regardless of any intent or program. Unlike Dr. John Henry Watson, who had a theory for every fact to fit, McLuhan proceeded like Sherlock Holmes, who never had a theory until every fact fitted.

Herbert E. Krugman

General Electric Company researcher, proceeding in Karl Popper's scientific style, went to the laboratory to disprove the "McLuhan Hypothesis." Krugman reported his unexpected finding.

> The basic response of the brain wave is clearly to the media and not to the content differences within TV commercials,

> or to what, in our pre-McLuhan days, we would ordinarily
> have called the "commercial message". ... The old theory
> was concerned with the fact that the message was transport-
> ed. The new theory must be concerned with the fact that the
> viewer is transported, taken on a trip, an instant trip — even
> to the moon and beyond.[59]

Marshall was delighted. Although we all recognized the limitations of scientific proof and disproof, Krugman's "lab" experiment confirmed rather than contradicted our experience of life.

In contrast to the prevailing TRANSPORTATION theory of communication that equates a program of signals with the message — treating information software like material hardware for delivery from sender to receiver — McLuhan and his closest collaborators developed a TRANSFORMATION approach to communication[20] that is humanistic rather than scientific: it is concerned with digesting, rather than regurgitating, information.

This approach begins with a human experience or INTENT that is "outered" or uttered or ex-pressed by a PROGRAM in some MEDIUM (such as the text of this page). The users (both reader and author) put it on like a mask or costume and become its CONTENT, but they make sense or MEANING of the program/medium (text/context) interplay individually, in relation to their own "mental set" (visual or audile-tactile sensory bias) rather than any ideological persuasion. *The medium is never neutral*, for it transforms their sensory inputs into differing sensory responses. Their mental representations are never mere reflections of some outer reality, but arise from, and constantly interact with, the whole of human existence, past and present. The program may either enhance or reduce, but never nullify, the effects of the medium. People communicate with each other through change that is shared.

The MESSAGE is made manifest in the material and mental and social consequences of the entire process in "aetivity" (forever after), whether intended or not.

Communicating anything new requires anticipating the effects not only of the program, but also of the medium on its actual users. It is both magic and miracle, not impossible but very difficult. It is normally hindered by what Marshall dubbed the "motivated somnambulism" of the dominant many. For the persistent few, it is like finding *le mot juste* (the exact word) in poetry, which according to Richard Aldington, "does not mean the word which exactly describes the object in itself, it means the exact word which brings the effect of that object before the reader as it presented itself to the poet's mind at the time of writing the poem."[60]

Marshall was not immune to this difficulty in revising his approach to human communication outlined in *Understanding Media*; for that had treated old media as the "content" of new media: speech as content of writing, writing of print, print of books (also telegraph), books (also plays) of movies, and movies of television.

Communicating the new is Art, not Science. There is no possible scientific formula for communicating anything really new — to share the reality of unrepeatable percepts — precisely because neither repeatable words nor concepts can ever re-present the uniqueness of direct human experience. Whereas "the Means are the Ends" for mythic Midas and modern "Bottom Liners" alike, the "Medium is the Message" is a rhetorical exaggeration designed to highlight the effects of the MEDIUM by ignoring the user as the CONTENT and co-maker of the MESSAGE — the total result of the actual communicating process. The PROGAM is the "bait" designed to catch the user. And every medium is a metaphor that transforms one kind of being into another at its interface with any user. Why are these processes of human communicating so difficult for so many?

ROBERT FLEMING

President of Robert Fleming International Research Inc., and General Editor of *Canadian Legislatures*, is a former Administrator of the Ontario Legislatures, as well as Executive Secretary to the Royal Commission on Book Publishing (to mention only a few of his many roles).

I first met Marshall McLuhan at a conference held at the West End Resort near Freeport in the Bahamas. I had flown over from Los Angeles where I was founder and editor-in-chief of *PACE* Magazine, a world publication aimed at the 16-34 year-old generation (the 60's generation), the purpose of which was to search out the most interesting and enlightened men and women in the world, and to report on international trends. The theme of the Bahamas meeting, which was held in January, 1970, related to the future development of business corporations, and included "luminaries" from many fields. This was an ambitious undertaking.

I will not forget watching Marshall McLuhan with his old friend — of Geodetic Dome fame — Buckminster Fuller (both of whom had been featured in the pages of *PACE* Magazine) talking to the long-range planner from Coca-Cola in Atlanta, Georgia who was trying to develop a new approach to bottles, and the office-landscape planner from a Chicago design firm. *LIFE* Magazine was trying to report these extraordinary discussions and photographer Harry Benson was clicking away. I was also photographing the scene (as a young man I had trained as a photo-journalist). I won't forget it especially as a former *Time-Life* editor turned inn-keeper on the banks of the Hudson River at Tarrystown, New York stepped in to suggest that I should throw my cameras away and ponder a career outside publishing.

As a result of the Bahamas meeting I saw Marshall on a number of occasions during the next years. There is no question he had a considerable impact on my thinking, although I didn't understand him at the time, or rather what he was saying. It had something to do with the fact that he was throwing out questions but he didn't really want answers. A right or a wrong answer was beside the point. This type of communicating was definitely unsettling to the person used to certain labels, frames, designations, etc.

I think I learned from Marshall that what was really important in life was not what was directly in front of me in terms of day-to-day tasks and commitments, but the broader perspective of being open to new patterns of thinking; that to contribute anything of major value in the world you have to live in the realm of ideas, concepts, visions and inter-relationships.

Marshall McLuhan was rooted firmly in the past — the "Elizabethan era" — and yet he was totally geared to the future. He showed that man has to have certain roots and traditions and then on top of that he has to be an explorer. Marshall was an explorer on mankind's road; always searching out the new, never stopping to set up camp. This style has increasingly become my style in recent years.

The "terribly important" things in life are probably not the nuts and bolts issues or achievements in politics, business, the media, academia or whatever but another set of values entirely which have something to do with whether or not we as human beings are working to inch mankind ahead in an unfolding universe. Are we merely rushing about, gaining satisfaction from some type of action, or are we really trying to accomplish that which is important? What I learned from Marshall helped re-orient my life to these priorities.

There seem to be two groups of people in Canada (and the world): those who are searching for and encouraging change and those who are passionately determined to maintain the walls around their lives. Marshall seemed to be saying, "You must not try to pin anything down. It will change."

During recent years I have been involved very directly with government and politicians in Canada and now produce Canadian Legislatures an annual publication which in addition to providing information about legislative institutions attempts to act as a "signpost" to help provide some direction to those who are traveling on the legislative road. In my Foreword to the 1987-1988 Edition I quote Marshall McLuhan: "Politics offers yesterday's answer's to today's questions." Marshall made this observation in 1967. If our political leaders would take the time to ponder that statement it could radically affect the state of government worldwide and transform our societies. I probably wouldn't have understood this statement in 1967. I must have come a fair distance on Marshall's road.

What Anecdotes best illustrate Marshall's humanity?

West End, Bahamas was plunged into a sudden "deep-freeze" in January, 1970 with the temperature plummeting to about 30 degrees Fahrenheit. Marshall and his friend, "Bucky" Fuller made the best of it. They frolicked barefoot on the beach and in the shallow water. Marshall wore a 10-gallon hat. Their trousers were rolled up. At the time it struck me as pretty remarkable that two such "brainy" people could have so much fun. Marshall at times had a naive, almost childlike quality about him. "Bucky" had difficulty with his hearing and I can recall him trying to listen to Marshall through two very large circular hearing aids.

At one point I called on Marshall in his coach-house office at the University of Toronto. It was about 4 o'clock in the afternoon. I walked in the door and called out for him (the building seemed deserted). "Come on up" he responded. There he was, seated at a tiny table, I think with a typewriter. I had an impression of books piled everywhere. In the middle of it all was a kettle and a tea pot. The kettle was boiling. "Let's have tea," said Marshall. It seemed incongruous that one of the farthest out thinkers of the day should be so surrounded by tradition — books, tea pot, leaded windows, etc. Yet that was Marshall.

In 1972, General Richard Rohmer who had developed the Mid-Canada Corridor concept came up with the idea of a University of Canada North to be possibly based in Inuvik, NWT. A planning conference took place at Inuvik, I think in February, to which native leaders, government officials, academics, businessmen and northern development experts were invited. I had the idea that we might video-tape Marshall speaking about what would be required of a new university in Northern Canada. We met at Ryerson College and I soon realized that I would have to conduct the interview as the interviewer did not turn up. "How would you begin a new university in the North?" I asked. "Well," he responded with a twinkle in his eye, "It should not be like the University of Toronto...we should throw out all previous concepts of a university...it's a different environment, a different setting, a different set of circumstances...its entirely different to anything we've ever done before in Canada...start from there."

I think it was in the Fall of 1972 that I received a telephone call from Marshall's agent, Matie Molinaro. Would I be ready to go over to his home in Wychwood Park, Toronto next Sunday morning to take some portrait photographs of Marshall. Some were needed and she had a feeling I could do a good job. I agreed. I found Marshall bright and eager. After looking at various rooms in the house I decided to photograph Marshall outside. At one point I had seen a small television set in the form of a walkie-talkie. It seemed sensible to relate him to television. He flipped the switch and on came Senator McGovern from Washington, D.C., close-up. I took close-ups of Marshall with the TV-set cradled in his arms. From time to time he would spin it around like a pointer or a gun. He was relaxing and having fun. The photographs were used at various times and one was published by Teleglobe Canada a few years ago on the introduction of the McLuhan award.

Marshall struck me as being intensely interested in the views of other people. It was as if he was operating by radar, and drawing from those conversations his remarkable unfolding philosophy. Who people were, or what they did, didn't really seem to matter to Marshall. He could learn something from all which would then become part of his kaleidoscopic view of the world. There was humility mixed with humanity and all who were with him must have felt that quality.

Jacques Giard

Director of the School of Industrial Design, Carleton University, Ottawa, learned about Marshall indirectly through seminars conducted at Carleton by Georges Singer (Professor of Communication, Université de Québec à Montréal) and from me.

[McLuhan's] analysis of communication media, their pervasive nature in our lives, but, more importantly, their power to influence at a subconscious level, formed the basis of my own explorations in the semantics and rhetorics of product form.

It was not until later, during my doctoral studies, that the seeds planted in those formative years began to manifest themselves in my own work. My research took me into an area one could call visual linguistics and the language of products. It culminated in a more specific study: comparing visual language of the same object in various cultural contexts. The premise of my research was the belief that everyday objects were more than simple tools of a strictly utilitarian nature, but could also reveal a great deal about the nature of the context that originated them.

Marshall McLuhan gave me the keys that opened the doors to this exploration, and the courage in later years to forge my own way.

In 1987, Jacques presented his Ph. D. thesis (comparing high-speed train designs in Britain, Canada, France, Germany, and Japan) at Concordia University, Montreal. Since then, his overseas colleagues have continued inviting him back to discuss his unique discoveries.

A.E. Safarian

Dean of the School of Graduate Studies at the University of Toronto, during part of McLuhan's tenure, is not only a top-ranking academic, but also a close friend of Marshall and his family.

Much has been said about Marshall McLuhan's prose. It has been described as discontinuous, enigmatic, scattered, and lacking any logical structure, to use some of the less critical comments. He has been described as a rhetorician, which can mean one who uses language effectively or one who uses language for effect only. McLuhan often lent credibility to these views, for example, by stating that he dealt with perceptions rather than ideas, and by insisting that his writing was largely satire.

There is no lack of examples of all of this in his work, especially his later writings. It could hardly be otherwise since one of his main contributions was a form of literary and intellectual iconoclasm, of breaking up the old forms of expression and of ways of thinking, with a view to reshaping them again. But McLuhan also had formidable intuitive powers. It was my experience that he always had a point and that he usually provoked one to think about it. He disdained the lock-step processes of simple deduction and often used language in a confusing way, particularly for "merely visual man." But there was a message in the medium for those who were not simply put off or mis-led by the style. That message usually related back to some larger idea, linked to his view of the impact of communications in society, which he had worked out very fully.

Let me cite just two examples from the period of the early 1970s when I saw a great deal of him in the Graduate School at the University of Toronto. On one occasion the School needed forecasts of graduate enrollment over a five-year period for all its units. McLuhan's response was to ask what the future role of the University should be, given all the changes both society and the University were undergoing. Having settled that to his satisfaction — it was a much smaller institution, with its training function displaced to other organizations — he proceeded to make an enrollment forecast. On another occasion he wrote me about something I had written on federalism in which I took a centralist view on certain economic powers. By contrast, he believed Canada was blessed by a more decentralized federation than was the United States, one more suited to the decentralizing forces of information technology.

In these and other instances I was tantalized by his use of language but not sure whether I agreed with his conclusion. I was never long in doubt, however, of where he was going, and how it fitted into his larger set of ideas, or rather, perceptions. And, ultimately, I believe his was an optimistic (even, his protests to the contrary, a dialectical) view. A précis of *Take Today*, a book he wrote with Barrington Nevitt, concluded

> Today we can maintain visual values only if we choose to moderate the intensity of the acoustic resonance, even as we might choose to turn down the sounds of a Rock concert in order to engage in dialogue. Knowing, as we do, the con-

stituents of both civilized and tribal cultures, of both the private, rational individual and the corporate, mystical, tribal man, it becomes our privilege and responsibility alike to mix and harmonize these factors even as the Greeks chose to alter the Dionysian fury with Apollonian detachment.

DENIS DINIACOPOULOS

Professor of Communication Studies at Concordia University, Montreal, recalls the exhilaration of studying *The Gutenberg Galaxy* and *Understanding Media* with his colleague John Buell and other academic staff, as well as their students.

That same academic year, The Student Association invited Marshall McLuhan to give a presentation...he had nothing in common with any university professor I knew. He appeared natural, spoke naturally in an informal manner, presented simple jokes perfectly to the point, in a slow pace, and used simple words; it was clear that he cared a lot for his audience. He made himself understandable. He was simple and natural. And he always appeared naturally human in all the subsequent contacts I had with him in Montreal and Toronto. ...

I remember one day, in Toronto, McLuhan was more lively than usual, and this means a lot, because, like all involved men, he was already rather enthusiastic. His eyes were sparkling, a constant smile was dancing on his face, he was exuberant and talking more than usual. He was immersed in joy — somebody whose intelligence was satisfied at last. Through the flow of words I heard: "All media are utterances," and the flow continued. ... After a long period of "directed thinking," I realized that Marshall McLuhan had discovered the first level of the psychological origins of the media.

ERIC WESSELOW

An ecumenical scholar and innovative artist, is not only our close collaborator at Concordia, but also a fellow explorer and good friend of Marshall. Eric's innovations in the design of stained-glass windows exhibit his deep understanding of the differing sensory effects of "light through" (his windows) and "light on" (his paintings) that Jonathan Miller disputed in his *McLuhan* (see Chapter B).

- Once, in a discussion, Marshall asked me: "What is art?" I began by expounding that, etymologically, "art" could simply mean "make something." "Actually, art is what you can get away with," was Marshall's suggestive statement.

- "What is a portrait?" he asked me another time. Of course, I felt that I had a lot to say on that subject, but Marshall quickly answered his own question: "A portrait is the picture of a person where there is always something wrong with the mouth," he explained. Yet he was a most attentive listener when I mentioned the difficulty of pictorially "freezing" in a portrait a sitter's most expressive features, particularly the eyes and the mouth. I explained that this was also why I would engage a sitter in talk and motion of features in order to render a sum of expressions in time.

- At my Toronto Dominion Centre show Marshall arrived with a group of friends. One of my exhibited pieces was the black-and-white glass relief of an angel. The panel was backlit, and the light was in motion. Everyone studied the work for a while, but nobody seemed to find out what produced the ever changing light pattern. Marshall looked at it and immediately remarked: "Ah, you have a black-and-white television screen working behind it!"

- Marshall had a never-failing sense of humor, the very source of which must have related to his unique modes of perception. Hence his deep understanding of the processes of art. On the occasion of this exhibition, I had a good many of my own sayings written on small pieces of cardboard and displayed all over the show. Among those which he seemed to enjoy most:

- It seems easier to answer ultimate questions than to solve immediate problems.

- People who are bored, are boring.

- Complexity is simplicity gone overboard.

- Talent is that part of one's body one must not sit on.

- Every coin has three sides

One day, when I dropped in at the Centre, Marshall wanted to know about progress with my stained-glass window-project, "A Glance into the Heavens." Eric McLuhan, his son, was also present. I told them that on the previous day I had addressed the board of the congregation and that in my talk I had referred to the etymological difference between "Heaven" and "Sky." "What would those be?" Marshall asked curiously. I explained that "Heaven," deriving from

Old English, and further back, actually means "to lift, raise," and "Sky" deriving from Latin means "shield." Thus "Heaven" could be thought of as an open hemisphere or dome, "Sky" as a covered one.

On the third anniversary of Marshall's death, I dreamt I was having a discussion with him on a famous saying of his which, years ago, he had written in our guest-book: "The rear-view mirror shows the foreseeable future." In our dream-conversation, I pointed out that in German "rearview-less" is *"rücksichtslos,"* which actually means "ruthless, rude, inconsiderate." In my dream, McLuhan was quite surprised by this discovery, ... So was I, when I woke up.

What I Learned from Marshall McLuhan:

• The dynamics of probings, instead of rigid theories and illusory certainties.

• The importance of Figure/Ground relationship.

• Better understanding of the function of art media and their communicative force. For instance: the "content" of contemporary art bearing on the collective sensitivity of a society and its culture.

• The importance of humor in discovery.

• One can be both conservative and revolutionary.

• Finding confirmed, in the case of Marshall McLuhan, that great humans are simple, humble, and good.

DENNIS MURPHY

Associate Professor and acting Chairman of Communication Studies (1987-88) at Concordia University, Montreal, learned about McLuhan through his writings and from seminars that I conducted. Dennis is now engaged in extending the Transformation Approach to Communication into Cybernetics and Systems Research and other academic disciplines not only in Canada, but also in England, France, and Germany. In a recent paper[61] Dennis reviews how he has tried to cope with difficulties encountered in explaining our approach to his colleagues.

Concepts are essential to any organized decision making. But their very service to human beings, that is, as generalizations and hence immediate re-cognition of any particular situation, obscures immediate experience. How can we transcend this limitation while maintaining our distance from events with its own inherent advantage — "seeing the whole picture?"

Some hints lie in the comparison of the notion of "overview" with that of "details." Notice that the former is singular; the latter, plural. In this regard we can profit from the technical terms used in film and television production when speaking of an "establishing shot." Film, with its wide screen, tends to favour the "long shot," taking everything in. Television, with its smaller screen and weaker definition, favours the "close-up shot" for establishing what is important. These two approaches are not hard and fast rules for shooting, but they do allow us to grasp how concepts include as much as possible from a distance in a single shot; whereas percepts work much more with details, the choice of which depends upon the situation as well as the vision of the maker. Percepts suggest a plurality of views; concepts suggest a particular and intentional filtering of these details. Both serve, however, to make sense. In Nevitt's words

> Understanding is neither a point of view nor a value judgement. To understand something is to grasp its multiple facets simultaneously in their constantly changing relationships to each other, and to environments, both visible and invisible. Understanding is not merely conceptual; it requires perception involving all the wits and senses.[62]

In terms of the integration of the human and the technological, we can now address the making of an inventory of effects for any medium, in order to make manifest both its "meaning" (for each of us) and its "message" (for all of us).

Taking media on their own terms assumes that an ideology is present but does not stop there. Taking media on their own terms also assumes that beyond ideology and politics we come face to face with how we know; that is, what-we-make-use-of to understand whatever it is we encounter. ... WE are the "content" of any medium (as users and co-makers of the human experience), not the program as we usually think of it. Our detached (academic) approach to understanding the integration of the human and the technological assumes that the content is the same as the message or program. This is valid for purely mechanistic forms of message transfer.

For example, the Shannon-Weaver mathematical model of communication (sender to receiver via channel and noise) is appropriate for assessing the technological transfer of data on telephone lines. But content in this case begins and ends with the telephone, to take our example. Content in this sense does not ignore the human being at the sending and receiving ends; content in this sense simply does not need human beings at all. All the variables concerned can be measured and assessed without human receptivity.

But once we enter the area of us-as-content, what becomes important is how each of us makes sense, how we make meaning out of all the data we encounter. McLuhan and Nevitt addressed this point directly: "The meaning of meaning, does not ignore the human being at the sending and receiving ends; content in this sense simply does not need human beings at all. All the variables concerned can be measured and assessed without human receptivity is a relationship: a figure-ground process of perpetual change. The input of data must enter a ground or field or surround of relations that are transformed by the intruder, even as the input is also transformed." [63]

Please note that we are now speaking of "transformation," instead of our previous notion of "transfer." We are shifting from a transportation notion of communication to a transformation notion of communication. In the former, the "message" is brought along as so much baggage. In the latter, the person as creator and sustainer is central to whatever takes place in making sense.

The most difficult notion in this quote is that of the input being transformed. ... This is because we do not accept that WE are the content of any medium. We stay with the notion of program or message as content, or with the notion of ownership of media as determiner of content. ...

In order to get past this we have to ask different questions — questions which are not steeped in the ideology of program-as-content. The questions that need asking stem from our previous mention of "inventory of effects" as well as "manifest." What do these two terms imply?

There is a story, among the Dene people in northern Canada, of a young Cree boy who was called to be a witness at a trial held by whites. He was asked by the judge to swear "to tell the truth, the whole truth, and nothing but the truth."

"Oh, no!" he replied: I can't do that. I can only tell you what I know."

This illustrates the essence of what is meant by "inventory of effects" and "manifest." What the boy referred to was his ability to speak clearly about what he knew — and only that. His witness was a manifestation of his understanding.

Each of us, as this boy knew, can only tell what he or she knows or feels — and that is all.

But it is in the comprehensiveness of the manifests, the fullness of all our testimonies, that we come to an inventory of effects. We can come to know the relationship of the human, and the relationship of human beings and information media, by listening to people reflect on their experiences. This process discloses the terms particular to media by disclosing their consequences.

In short, we distinguished between a theory based on abstract hypothetical causes that can be disproved, and an approach where observed effects are made manifest, requiring no further proof. We shared the exhilarating experience of constantly reconsidering every human artifact (including our own approach) as a communication medium. Several of us worked toward discovering the "laws of media," work that was brilliantly completed in 1988 as *Laws of Media*.

CHAPTER M

CO-AUTHORING AND DIALOGUING

GEORGE LEONARD

Former editor of *Look* magazine, generously gave us permission to republish part of "Jamming with McLuhan, 1967" which describes his own experience of co-authoring with Marshall.[64]

The first time I met Marshall McLuhan, we talked for thirteen hours straight. We started at his house in Toronto at ten AM on Saturday, October 8, 1966, and didn't stop until eleven that night. We went out to lunch and dinner together, visited the men's room together, never once breaking the flow of our conversation. ...

"The Future of Education" was the title of our proposed collaboration. I was already fully prepared to write about the future of education without McLuhan's help. ...

McLuhan lived almost entirely on the mental plane. Though he reacted with excitement to ideas and to the information about schools that I brought to the dialogue, he rarely, if ever, asked about my personal life. He told me his mind never stopped. Sometimes, he confessed, he could hear his friends' ideas in his head through a kind of telepathy. "It's a great bother, really," he said.

However abstract, McLuhan's mind was a marvel to behold. Among the mental tactics for which he was known were his "probes" — sudden, unexpected leaps of thought. During our nonstop conversation, we kept coming back to the subject of competition. Why did schools use so much competition in the educational process when research showed that it generally failed to improve performance and often produced negative side effects? Late in the afternoon, while we were talking about something else, McLuhan suddenly raised his finger.

"I've got it," he said. "Competition creates resemblance."

For a moment this went right past me. Then I got it. In order to compete with someone, you must agree to run on the same track, to do the same thing, only faster or better. This "probe" was to figure in a section near the beginning of the article devoted to a critique of present-day schooling:

Specialization and standardization produced close resemblance

227

and, therefore, hot competition between individuals. Normally, the only way a person could differentiate himself from the fellow specialists next to him was by doing the same thing better and faster. Competition, as a matter of fact, became the chief motive force in mass education, as in society, with grades and tests of all sorts gathering about them a power and glory out of proportion to their quite limited function as learning aids.

Then, too, just as the old mechanical production line pressed physical materials into preset and unvarying molds, so mass education tended to treat students as objects to be shaped, manipulated. "Instruction" generally meant pressing information onto passive students. Lectures, the most common mode of instruction in mass education, called for little student involvement. This mode, one of the least effective ever devised by man, served well enough in the age that demanded only a specified fragment of each human being's whole abilities. There was, however, no warranty on the human products of mass education.

That age has passed. ...

The ideas bounced back and forth between us, gaining velocity and momentum with each bounce. I flew back to San Francisco with the notes of our conversation and wrote "The Future of Education" with relatively little effort. It was a thoroughgoing criticism of conventional education and a brief for the use of modern technology, especially computers, to create self-paced, individualized learning, to break down the rigid walls between school and the world. "The Future of Education," the lead story in February 21, 1967, *Look*, had plenty of McLuhan in it, but was essentially, as one critic later pointed out, a précis of my book-in-progress. ...

McLuhan loved "The Future of Education." He began phoning, often late at night, with ideas for other articles. We had dinner in San Francisco in late November; then, in early January, I dropped in on my way to New York to lay plans. We brainstormed future topics. I suggested "The Future of Sex." He liked "The Future of War." ("War," he said, "is speeded up education.") I came back with "The Future of Power." What we were planning seemed far more than a series of *Look* articles — another book, another whole career. What was I letting myself in for?

At the end of March we talked again in Toronto about "The Future of Sex," and again we had a wonderful time, a jam session in ideas. We agreed that sex as we now think of it might soon be dead. I described sexual customs in primitive cultures, ... McLuhan pointed out that the Romans had coined the word sexus, probably deriving it from the Latin verb *secare*, "to cut or sever," and we agreed that that was exactly what civilization had done to man and woman, especially in the industrial age. I brought up the idea of the narrow-gauged, specialized male, a creature who is essentially hard, domineering, and unfeeling. McLuhan speculated that the narrow-gauged male of the industrial age produced — in ideal, at least — the specialized woman, the one who is passive yet armed with feminine wiles. We foresaw the end of this specialization, the cooling of hot sex, the creation of a world in which all of life is erotic.

In mid-April McLuhan and several members of his family visited San Francisco. With them was Father John Culkin, a communication expert from Fordham University, which had awarded McLuhan the $100,000-a-year Albert Schweizer Chair in the Humanities, beginning the next September. We all went to a peace march at the panhandle of Golden Gate Park at noon on Saturday. The marchers were mostly members of the Haight-Ashbury hippie community. Price Cobbs joined us. We stood next to McLuhan at an intersection and watched them go past, their faces painted, their bodies adorned with beads and feathers and a wild variety of improvised psychedelic clothes.

McLuhan was fascinated and bemused. He kept shaking his head. "There is no question," he finally said in his most professorial voice, "that this is a result of the new tribalism of the Electric Age. Whether I can deal with it is another question." ...

I felt warmer toward McLuhan that night than ever before. I had enjoyed working with him. I liked the two articles we had done together. I knew he was eager to get started on "The Future of War." Yet it was precisely then that I started pulling back. There was the matter of my work overload, which was truly overwhelming. But there was something else, perhaps even more decisive: McLuhan's name was listed first in our joint by-line, and I could tell from the letters in response to "The Future of Education" that almost all our readers assumed that the ideas were his, that I was simply the writer that put them down. Quotes in the newspaper from our article were attributed to McLuhan alone. Not that such an assumption was not understandable; he was famous for his ideas, whereas I was not. But in truth we shared in the production of the ideas in these particular articles, in addition to which I did all the writing. The time had come, I thought, to make my own statement and put my own name on it.

In retrospect, I can see that my brief but intense relationship with Marshall McLuhan was more valuable than I then realized. His ideas — on the importance of the media of communications, on the Electric Age, on the global village — might have been expressed in neon rather than sober scholarly tones, but he was essentially right. Only in the late 1980s can we clearly understand just how right he was.

The hazard of being hidden behind McLuhan's famous name created obstacles to long-term collaboration for many of his co-authors. Only those who could submerge their egos, without too much regard for authorship credit, could continue to enjoy the excitement of dialoguing and co-authoring with him as fellow explorers.

BRUCE POWERS

Professor of English and Communication Studies at Niagara University, Lewiston, N.Y., co-authored *The Global Village* [65] that replays work of many other co-authors with Marshall.

Bruce has kindly allowed us to replay a slightly revised version of his conversation with Marshall during 1978, outlined in the preface to their book.

"When we went to the moon," Marshall said, "we expected photographs of craters. Instead, we got a picture of ourselves. Ego trip. Self-love."

"The mirror," I countered, "is another way of saying water, which stands for a change in man and nature. Narcissus fell in love with his image in water."

"No," said Marshall, "that's the popular conception. Narcissus, as Ovid paints him, is a primal youth; has never seen a mirror or his image. He fell in love with someone else. That's the mythical and satirical point. For him the watery image was death."

MARGARITA D'AMICO

Professor of Communication at the University of Caracas, and occasional contributor to the widely circulated Venezuelan newspaper *El Nacional*, has also given us kind permission to cite excerpts of material, co-authored with Marshall during her visits to Toronto before and after his visit to Caracas.[66] Just before his arrival, *El Nacional* devoted an entire page (25 April 1976) to a "collage" (in Spanish) of Margarita's previous conversations with Marshall and me. Our translations of the following samples indicate Margarita's skill in "McLuhan's approach" throughout

Venezuela, and beyond.[66]

"I Neither Interpret Nor Explain, I Explore and Investigate" says the vibrant director of the Centre for Culture and Technology of the University of Toronto. "I do not make value judgements. I am not interested in proving the validity of my investigations. I simply have a lively interest in understanding what is happening."

In trying to understand him, it is not enough to know, to accept or reject the maxims, aphorisms, paradoxes, proverbs and metaphors that have made him famous. It is not sufficient to perceive the imagination, the skill, the wit and the humour of this great master; his immense culture, his humanism and learning, his profound knowledge of history, esthetics, rhetoric, literature, art, the evolution of contemporary thought through science and philosophy; his epochal spirit and sense of tradition.

It is essential to get rid of prejudices and inflexible opinions in order to understand what is happening in our world. But to understand is never a point of view, because it requires the simultaneous apprehension of all facets of a situation. "To understand," say McLuhan and his collaborator Barrington Nevitt, "is to find the structures of current processes, the effects with their causes, not sequentially, but simultaneously and on every side."

MOSAIC AND COLLAGE

"Our world," say McLuhan and Nevitt, "is an invisible *Rim Spin* — all the communication that surrounds us. It is like a cyclone, a vortex that has transformed the old world of visual connections into a new world of audile-tactile resonances: a global theatre of instant awareness."

We live in an acoustic space...like discarnate minds floating in the magnetic cities of radio, television and satellites. ...

Our world is a great multimedia poem. To understand this world we must study its processes, investigate their effects to recognize their causes: to program our future. We must express our ignorance, to seek solutions in the problems themselves. We must comprehend what is happening with our "hardware" and our "software," with the "figure" and its "ground," with the media and their messages. We must explore by probing things at the same time.

It is clear that our approach to contemporary processes can be neither unilateral, nor determinist, nor dogmatic. We can have no univocal meaning for each and every thing. Perhaps our one possible approach may be of mosaic type or collage, rather than a lineal one of logical demonstration. ...

Mosaic emphasizes that all elements together create the total effect. As for collage, the association, arrangement and juxtaposition of objects, phrases, different concepts, both heterogeneous and absurd, that comment upon and influence each other, all of this has very close affinities with concepts of chance, accident or "serendipity" (making accidental discoveries of valuable, but unsought, knowledge), important concepts in present science and culture. Although McLuhan is engaged in both mosaic and collage operations, he did not invent, nor claim to have invented, either mosaic or collage. Nor the concept of medium as an extension of man.

There are some Venezuelan communication investigators who should avoid the obsession of trying to see who influenced whom, for McLuhan himself doesn't hesitate to say who his inspirers are. His works, his books, are full of references to numerous thinkers of the most varied disciplines. But one must read the books, and above all, not stop at *Understanding Media*. Much has happened in the world since 1964 and McLuhan has written much since then. ...And his thinking is also changing.

But, if McLuhan was not the first to have used collage, it is he who has best captured the totally new character of the new mass means of communication and the social impact of new technologies.

ONE REVOLUTIONARY AND THREE REVOLUTIONS

Once upon a time, primitive men lived in an oral universe, tactile and participatory.

The First Revolution was due to the invention of the phonetic alphabet that destroyed their world and converted it into a linear, abstract form.

The Second Revolution was ushered in by the printing press that, through mechanization, intensified the effects of the phonetic alphabet, and fragmented their sensory life, by orienting it toward the linear, the visual.

The discovery of electricity brought about the Third Revolution that began with the telegraph and has reached television and the computer.

It would be fatal. This revolution reversed the effects of the second, and restored to man his audile-tactile senses, reintegrating his experience. The phonetic alphabet and the printing press had led to individualism; the new inventions return man to neo-primitivism and tribal participation.

McLuhan explores and centres his investigations around a series of contrasts: written and oral; linear and mosaic; individualism and participation; tribal existence and civilization; fragmentation and organic unity. ... Print and electronic media; high definition, low definition; "hot" media and "cool" media; meanings and messages. ... And the global village, the theatre, the invisible maelstrom, nature and ecology.

And always intriguing, in the midst of all, that famous discordance: "The medium is the message," launched in *Understanding Media*. Nobody understood it in 1964. McLuhan ... clarified it in *Take Today* which, so much the better, his detractors have not read.

WHAT IS HAPPENING?

Twenty-five hundred years of rational culture are in process of dissolution. Age-old habits of conceptualization will not serve to train observation on the effects of the new man-made forms of energy. Since Plato, philosophers and scientists have ... refused to recognize any patterns of energy arising from man-made technologies. Having invented 'Nature' as a world of rigorous order and repetition, they studied and observed only 'Natural' forms as having power to shape and influence psyche and society. The world of man's artifacts was considered neutral until the electric age. (TT. p.7)

The Greeks identified technologies with their gods mythically, and hid all their disservices in Pandora's Box.

For twenty-five hundred years we have continued studying our technical evolution as if it were a matter of abstract figures, but we have ignored the effects of the resonances caused by our technologies as they were transforming us ecologically.

REINVENTING NATURE

When the first satellite was launched (Sputnik on October 4, 1957), the Earth was immediately transformed into a Global Theatre. Its inhabitants became not only the observed, but the observers. This sudden change made them participants, actors playing a role on a global scale.

Man has to reinvent nature, recreate it as an art form perfectly adapted to the totality of human needs and aspirations.

ANTICIPATE EFFECTS TO PROGRAM FATE

MARSHALL MCLUHAN:

I study the effects to arrive at the causes. I study everything in 'play-back.' I learned it from publicity. The symbolists discovered it. They said that to write a poem they had to start by knowing the effect it would create and that would determine what they put in the poem.

BARRINGTON NEVITT:

At the speed of light we cannot give ourselves the luxury of waiting to see what is happening. Instead, we must know in advance the physical, psychic and social effects of our decisions. Today, we can choose the effects before creating their causes, because thought travels much faster than light. We can anticipate the effects so as to avoid hitherto inevitable Fate.

"Feedback" based on past experience is now too slow. "Feedforward based on recognition of present process patterns is essential for reprogramming fate.

SUPERANGELS OF ECOLAND

Yesterday's reality was to match the old in visual space. Today's reality is to make the new in acoustic space with all our senses. In this acoustic space, it is impossible to keep fixed points of view. Only change is stable. ...

In the era of electronic simultaneity, man has acquired a new dimension. He is everywhere as a discarnate spirit. With electronic media THEY are here and WE are there simultaneously. "Communication transports us everywhere, as discarnate minds by metamorphosis, in super-angelic forms."

THE CONTENT IS NOT THE PROGRAM

"The medium is the message" does not mean that the program is the content. ...Man (reader, spectator, listener), the "user" is always the content of the medium. It is he who forms it, and it moulds and transforms him unconsciously. He wears it like clothing.

All technologies, whether "hardware" or "software" are extensions of man, who, as user, is always their content. The meaning is the sense that each individual participant makes of the communication process, and the message is the totality of its physical and psychic and social effects, today and ever after, regardless of any intent. That is the message of any technology.

SHARING IGNORANCE

The only way to hold a dialogue is to express your ignorance — not to be like a specialist who has answers to sell or exhibit. ... The explorer says: "Give me the question." It is necessary to share ignorance, because the knowledge that lies hidden behind ignorance is boundless. Our knowledge is finite. Ignorance is infinite.

Therefore, start by finding the solution in the problem itself. The solutions are not outside, but inside, the problems themselves. For that reason we say that questions, not answers, are today's main resource, not only in science, but in education and everything else.

More than a year later, Margarita also recalled in *El Nacional* (October 30, 1977) what she learned in her last dialogue and interview with McLuhan, subsequently reprinted in *McLuhan en Venezuela.*[66]

On a sunny Sunday morning, McLuhan invited us to breakfast at his century-old house in Wychwood Park. But it had to be after Church. So, after Mass, we settled down to wait for him in the garden. It was the third time that professor McLuhan had granted us the honour and privilege of interviewing him. The first was in Toronto in 1973; the second in Caracas at the International Seminar on Radio broadcasting; and now, as his latest book, *Laws of Media* was about to come out.

And thus, between cakes, fruit juice, and scrambled eggs prepared by his wife Corinne, with music by Juan Vicente Torrealba — a record, given to him in Venezuela. ... As we left around noon, after this delightful repast and stimulating conversation, the professor said: "Fine, come to the Centre tomorrow and let us work a while."

Two o'clock Monday afternoon at the Centre for Culture and Technology, University of Toronto. Present at the conversation: Barrington Nevitt, author with McLuhan of *Take Today*, and author, individually, of *The Communication Ecology*, a book that had not yet come out. (I had already received a typescript copy from Barrington.)

McLuhan begins by speaking of the guide that he had made for secondary school students, to broaden learning resources — the ambience in which they live. They study the streets, the newspapers, the radio programs, and the traffic — the total environment (Marshall was referring to *The City as Classroom* co-authored with Kathy Hutchon and Eric McLuhan).

TRAINING PERCEPTION

McLUHAN:
    The idea is to train perception. We do not train them in theories but in percepts.

D'AMICO:
    Why do you say that you do not make theories, but that you are only concerned with percepts?

McLUHAN:
    I train in percepts, not in concepts. Percepts are different from concepts.

D'AMICO:
    What is the difference?

McLUHAN:
    Concept is a replayed percept. When you see something on TV,

that is percept. When you reproduce it, go through it again, it is concept. *To cognize is percept. To re-cognize is concept* [our italics].

McLUHAN:

I also re-cognize, but I cognize first.

D'AMICO:

What are the main things that you recognize in our culture?

McLUHAN:

Patterns.

D'AMICO:

"Patterns," models of what?

McLUHAN:

Of everything that is happening all around us. For example, the quest for identity, roots, origins: many negroes in America want to see where they came from. That is re-cognize. The problem of seeking roots arises for someone who has no body. In the age of electricity one has no body. When you talk by telephone, or appear on television, you have no body. All who have no body seek their origins, their identity. When one moves and lives at the speed of light, one feels discarnate, helpless. The new reality is discarnate man.

D'AMICO:

What would the solution be?

McLUHAN:

When you lose your natural body, you must have a supernatural solution. Religion is the only solution when you lose your body, when you are nobody.

D'AMICO:

Any kind of religion?

McLUHAN:

In practice yes, but ideally no. Many people will use drugs. ... It isn't easy. In other words, if Christianity insists on a human body that is incarnate, it is the right religion for discarnate man who has lost his body. Let's move on to another question.

D'AMICO:

Your new book *Laws of Media* (LOM). Part of this book was published in the journal *ETC*.

McLUHAN:

It explores "Four Basic Questions" (what we call "Tetrads") that concern all human artifacts, — all media, from a pin to a pun or a tractor: What does the medium intensify or amplify? What does it obsolesce? What does it retrieve? What does it transform into?

D'AMICO:

How did you arrive at these laws?

MCLUHAN:

By a structural focus. The structuralists, beginning with Ferdinand de Saussure, and now Levi-Strauss, divide their focus into two categories: *diachronic* and *synchronic*. Diachronic refers simply to development, to the chronological study of any cultural theme; synchronic assumes that all aspects of a process pattern are simultaneously present in each of its parts. Although I have concentrated upon the simultaneous focus in these *Laws of Media*, each of them can also be studied in a diachronic perspective.

Information speedup leads to a simultaneous structuring of experience that represents all directions at once; and it is "acoustic" and "synchronic." Diachronic perspective, on the other hand, represents one step at a time, and is visual in its analytical pattern. Few people seem to be aware that visual space and order are continuous, connected, homogeneous and static. In that regard, visual space is very different from other spaces, such as tactile, kinetic, acoustic, or olfactory space. Only visual space can be divided.

D'AMICO:

Could you explain Laws of the Media with some concrete example? *Electric media*, perhaps?

MCLUHAN:

Electric Media: Amplify the radius of simultaneity and the information environment; obsolesce the visual, the connected and the logical; retrieve subliminal, audile-tactile dialogue; flip into "etherealization": the sender is sent (as a discarnate mind). By telephone, for example, "they are here and we are there," simultaneously. When something reaches its limit, it flips into its opposite form.

Another example, *The Satellite*: Amplifies the planet; obsolesces nature; retrieves ecology; converts nature into an art form. The world is transformed into a global theatre where there are no spectators, because we are all actors. Take another subject.

THE TWO HEMISPHERES

D'AMICO:

Another theme concerns the Third World. You say that the Third

World is becoming First World and vice versa. Would you comment a little on that?

MCLUHAN:

First of all, we should remember the two hemispheres of the brain: the right and the left. The first controls the left side of the body, and the second the right. (McLuhan points to a chart indicating the characteristics of each.)

LEFT HEMISPHERE: "Hot" (non-involving), EYE-world, verbal discourse, logical, mathematical, detailed, sequential, controlled, intellectual, domineering, worldly, active, analytic, reading, writing, naming, sequential ordering, perception of significant order, complex motor sequences, quantitative.

RIGHT HEMISPHERE: "Cool" (involving), EAR-world, spacing, musical, acoustic, holistic, artistic, symbolic, simultaneous, emotional, intuitive, creative, tranquil, spiritual, receptive, synthetic, "gestalt," facial recognition, simultaneous comprehension, perception of abstract patterns, recognition of complex figures, qualitative.

The right hemisphere has very special qualities. It is Third World. The First World is the world of quantity, of technology, machinery, lineality, the consumer society: more, more, and more; it is left hemisphere. At the speed of light we are going more toward the Third World, the primitive. [Cerebral hemisphere specialization is itself an artifact of Western civilization.]

Do you see that picture by Picasso over there? It is primitive, simultaneous, acoustic: the inside and outside are seen at the same time in a bi-dimensional plane. It is Third World. The Third World is trying to convert itself rapidly into First World (left hemisphere). Caracas is both Third World and First World, and China will be the same, as well as India and Africa. The Second World is socialist, but in Russian socialism there are still acoustic people who have been pushed toward the First World very violently.

D'AMICO:

How so, professor, that's more than fifty years!

MCLUHAN:

Yes, but they still resist it, and therefore have five-year plans to push it. They have no motivation, except war, to become First World. Look at Quebec, it is Third World, but doesn't want to live like people of the First World. It wants to return to its roots, its ancient tradition.

D'AMICO:

Do you have any other books in progress?

McLUHAN:

Certainly. For many years, I have been preparing my doctoral dissertation for publication. It is called *From Cicero to Joyce* and is a study of Thomas Nashe and his times. It is a history of the Trivium.

D'AMICO:

Do you go to the cinema, professor? Did you see Woody Allen's film "Annie Hall" in which you appear?

McLUHAN:

I haven't had time to see it yet, but sooner or later I will. Instead I see a good deal of television.

The other night I saw a program: "The billion dollar movies" that sampled fragments of fourteen films among the "hits" of the last two years, from "The Exorcist" to "Earthquake," "Jaws," etc. I no longer enjoy movies as entertainment; besides films are no longer amusing; they have no story line and are all "right hemisphere." I am a "left hemisphere" person, I was trained in that form.

D'AMICO:

But you live in a right-hemisphere world, with your mind, in your work.

McLUHAN:

Yes, I have been taking note of that.

D'AMICO:

Do you listen to radio?

McLUHAN:

I would, if I had time, but I don't.

D'AMICO:

You work a lot, then.

McLUHAN:

One always works a lot. Part of my extra work is what I'm doing now. I should be doing other things.

D'AMICO:

But, professor! Don't you take into account that, if you talk about these things with a journalist, you inform many more people? It's not like talking in the classroom where only your students learn.

McLUHAN:

>That is why I do it. Many thanks for having come to visit us. It has been a pleasure.

ERIC MCLUHAN

Besides serving as editor for Marshall's *Dew Line* (Distant-Early-Warning) newsletter (published in New York during the late 1960s by the Human Development Corporation), Eric was a boundless resource for all of us: sharing his deep and detailed knowledge of *Finnegans Wake* — the subplot of most of our work with Marshall. He also taught a few of us the art of "speed reading." During the last years of Marshall's life, Eric became his father's main collaborator as well as co-author of *Laws of Media*.

I'm having the darndest time answering your two questions: What did I learn?, and How has his work influenced mine? The answers, of course are obvious, since he was my father: "nearly everything" and "completely." Had I not grown up in time to discover the exhilaration of his work and of working with him, I'd probably now be an engineer or scientist somewhere, or a pilot in a commuter airline, for much of my early fascination was with things mechanical and electrical. As, in fact was my father's. He built and sailed boats, made radios, studied engineering ... until literature found him.

However, "everything" and "completely" are less than satisfactory, although those are the first things that occur to me as his son. Here, though, are a few of the things I learned in the role of collaborator — a role I played off and on for about twenty years.

One of the chief things was **tenacity**: keep gnawing away at something and sooner or later it will give. But keep at it. If the problem can't stay at the forefront of your attention, because workaday matters intrude, "put it on the back burner" and keep it simmering. That is, keep coming back to it again and again until it yields. When he decided, for example, to look for media laws, three quick answers (laws) "came" to us in one afternoon at the Centre. Anyone else might have stopped there: he kept at it. Three weeks later a fourth came. For the next seven or eight years he looked for a fifth and sixth (and kept trying to find an exception to the first four). It amazed me to learn from a draft of Bill Kuhn's biography of my father that he'd planned as a young man to search out exactly the kind of basic laws of communication that he spent his last years discovering and refining. Tenacity.

A companion quality, **patience**, undoubtedly helped make him the great teacher (and discoverer) that he was. He often observed: "no short cuts: the short cut is the long way round." And "when you're sure you've found the answer, keep looking: there's more." Also "there's no right way to find the answer" to a problem, no correct approach: attack it in as many ways as you can find, continuously, until it yields, and then some more. For that reason he always involved as many others as he could in whatever was the current problem — colleagues, students, visitors — by bringing their faculties to bear as his resources. This was for him a means of shifting perspective rather than picking someone's brains — though to the unimaginative they're the same thing. Equally, in teaching, his effort was not to get from students "right answers" but to limber up their thinking, to develop in them a flexibility of responsiveness to literature. "Every style," he would say, "is a new way of knowing."

Consequently, hard work (there was no other kind) meant **serious play** — "low seriousness," to parody Arnold. You just cannot approach something from a dozen different directions at once — have your mind in a dozen different shapes at once — unless you're mighty playful. So work was always riotous fun at its most serious: any serious artist (in Pound's sense) will say the same. My father simply learned this from The Tradition and brought it to bear on media and culture as much as literature. Every poem is a comment or gloss on all that preceded it and vice versa. So it has to be approached by bringing the entire tradition to bear at once.

"The Tradition," by the way, means pretty much what Eliot meant in his essay ("Tradition and the Individual Talent"), the old *translatio studii*" of texts and commentary and interpretation, sacred and secular, on which my father wrote his doctoral thesis. For him, as for a practising artist, it was not something static, finished, to be learned, but alive and there for application, for **immediate use**.

Use of the tradition does not mean plunder, but enrichment: every use added to knowledge. (As "Bucky" Fuller would often observe, every time you use your knowledge it increases.) "Use" meant involving — bringing to bear on the present text or present problem all those minds and faculties, all those 2000 years of ways of thinking and of seeing ... simultaneously. Playfully; seriously; just as one "used" colleagues, visitors, students. Small wonder he found the narrow specialist outlook of the "communication experts" too confining! Small wonder, too, they find his insight baffling, enigmatic. (Also, this may shed a little light on his frequent insistence that he didn't have "an opinion" or use a "point of view" — he had hundreds, at once. Your own private ones just got in the way.)

To use the tradition properly calls for **humility** — you are engaging all the best sensibilities of your culture, to learn by and from them — and unremitting **honesty**. And **honour**. You are an insignificant part of the tradition: it is there for you to use, if you can. Using it demands the utmost in honourable comportment. If you are untrustworthy, so will it (and others) be.

Of course, this all leaves you wide open to theft, and quite a few (no names, please) have claimed and will undoubtedly claim to have been the "true" author of this or that insight — to which one can only respond, look at their other work: is it of a piece? "By their works ye shall know them." Another of his maxims, instilled by using the tradition: "give more credit than you take." This makes little or no sense to the specialist, complete sense to a real artist. It also plays havoc with those who need to connect and footnote everything, like the folk who are now trying to concoct a "Toronto School" of communication. Pure fantasy.

For example, my father never hesitated to praise any colleague's work that helped him in the slightest. It's a natural impulse in a teacher: you do it when your students get near or on the right track, to encourage them. By a hyperbole, he once noted that his work was "a footnote to" that of Harold Innis. Now, a score of earnest and unimaginative communicationeers have seized upon this literally to claim that "McLuhan's work derives" in part or wholly from Innis's. (The loathing which so many at the same university privately evince for the one or the other, or both, makes it all the more comic.) Innis's communications studies were an extension of his work in economics: most see them as a departure from that work. My father's communication studies, on the other hand, were an extension of his work in literature and a profound application (you might say, updating) of grammar and rhetoric. His work will not be fully comprehended except in that light.

There was one technique he used constantly and, as often, recommended. He got it from Coleridge's *Biographia Litteraria* (nor, of course, was it new with Coleridge): if you really want to know what someone knows, find out his ignorance. That is, go first for his ignorance, find its pattern, and the knowledge will quickly fill itself in. Going the other way, it can take you as long (or nearly) to learn a man's knowledge as it took him. Life is too short!

I once asked him about the lack of dedications in his books, or acknowledgements. How do you acknowledge a debt to thousands — to the tradition as a whole? He said he'd never dedicated a book to my mother because he never thought any of them worthy.

When you read my father's books and articles, you find his texts replete with bits of the tradition — a phrase here, a line there, a quoted verse. Not the usual fashion of literary men to ornament and elevate one's statement with sweet sentiment and polite word-dropping. He too had the book of verses underneath his brow, but he used them as working tools, never as ornament. And his most frequent recourses were to Wyndham Lewis, Ezra Pound, T.S. Eliot, and James Joyce. Especially Joyce. For Joyce, more even than Eliot and Pound, could mobilize the resources of our language and tradition, and bring them all to bear in an instant; he was, and is, *the* graduate curriculum in poetics ... and that means in media and culture too. He showed me how to read Joyce and together, over the years, we worked our way back and forth through *Dubliners*, *Ulysses*, the *Wake*. (One year we even read together all of Eliot and Pound, and more Joyce! The while, we collected material for a project to revise his thesis on the trivium, and wrote and discussed bits for what became *Laws of Media)*.

Joyce was a fountain of play, insight, "**low seriousness**," and inspiration. For some years, every time he or we made some breakthrough we'd open *Finnegans Wake* and find, within a couple of pages, that Joyce had been there before us: there was no envy in this, rather independent confirmation. Using the tradition. *The Wake* is a seismographic record of the perturbations of our senses, language, culture by our media. (It is to my father's work what that, in turn, is to the rest of media study in our time). Joyce's "ten thunders" stand at the climax of poetic achievement: they both encode and perform the major media transformations of culture and sensibility. Some of this we indicated in that essential little essay, *War and Peace in the Global Village* [Bantam, R3845, 1968]. My father constantly, in our years together, exhorted students, colleagues, collaborators to read Joyce, to use Joyce. A few lucky ones did.

My own experience of co-authoring with Marshall starts from a different point. First of all, I am three years older than Marshall. On the rare occasions when he was briefly tempted to take a professorial stance with me, I reminded him of my advantage, and we would both smile. But if we couldn't agree, Marshall would say: "you're a numbers man and I'm a letters man" as we both struggled to become comprehensivists. Our chapter headings are in fond memory of Marshall's vast preference for "letters" rather than "numbers" in organizing the "main verbs" of all his work.

Our fifteen years (1965-80) of dialoguing and co-authoring

included one book, more than thirty articles, and some hundreds of seminars, which required not only mutual respect and trust, but, above all, firm friendship and complementary interests. The only major obstacles we encountered were due to Marshall's contractual obligations with publishers who would not permit him to share authorship either with me or anyone else.

Marshall had his own rule-of-thumb for "fair use" of copyrighted material by any author including himself: 20 words of poetry, 500 words of prose. He also urged students to study and to use advertisements that are not only free of charge in the "public domain," but are also the "greatest art form of our age" — devouring more artistic talents and resources in one year than all the "fine arts" of previous ages put together.

Although not so often in books, we did try to continue our long and close collaboration in articles. But Marshall, already grossly overloaded, was suffering from his irreparable loss of Marg Stewart, and that, I believe, finally led to our irreplaceable loss of Marshall himself.

On the morning of September 26, 1979, when Marshall was struck down by aphasia, Hans Preiner (a program director of the Austrian Broadcasting Company), Peter Noever (a professor of architecture and also Director of the Austrian Museum for Applied Arts), and I had already had breakfast in the centre of Vienna at Peter's home, just behind Stephan Dom. We were founding the "Club of Vienna," with Marshall as our President, to bypass the old Club of Rome; for, by ignoring potentials of the "present," its "futures" still projected "past-times" to ineluctable Ruin. We planned to launch the new club from our Institute for Media Studies in Vienna (whose President was also Marshall) through its widely circulated journal *UMRISS*.

Peter promptly sent a colour snapshot of this "happening" to Marshall, who kept it beside the kitchen telephone at Wychwood Park, which had been a centre for so much of his work. There, it continued to represent the reality of our electric age with "centres everywhere and boundaries nowhere" as long as Marshall lived.

CHAPTER N

FROM ART TO SCIENCE AND VICE VERSA

A famous Canadian scientist, who has known McLuhan for many years, but wishes to remain anonymous, said in reply to our questions: "I never regarded McLuhan's opinions very highly, for he seemed to ignore the facts. But somehow he often came up with the right patterns."

He then asked: "Was it evidence for my tentative theory that genius may be due to brain damage or malfunction? I have never found anyone who could support that either." Nor could we. Our interest was to explore with Marshall the *somehow* that led to the right patterns. As Frank Lloyd Wright once noted: "The truth is more important than the facts."

Literate Greeks invented *phusis* — Nature in visual space — by abstracting it from *chaos* — the "buzzing confusion" of multi-sensory existence. Upon this abstraction their successors have built Western civilization that separates Thought from Feeling to create the illusion of "objectivity." This culture also substituted Aristotelean YES OR NO *logic of statements* for Heraclitean YES AND NO *dialectic of existence* itself.

More than two thousand years later, we now recognize that a comprehensive study of the origins, structures, and "laws" of existing "logics" is still unfinished business. Rosalie Colie makes that manifest in *Paradoxia Epidemica: The Renaissance Tradition of Paradox,*[67] which struck a "responsive chord" in Marshall's "medieval" spirit that resonates with our times. Th. Stcherbatsky's two-volume *Buddhist Logic*[67] is a study of great Indian and Tibetan Buddhist logicians, done with awareness of the history of Western logic and philosophy until the end of the 1920s. Since then, we have witnessed the spread of Zen Buddhism from Japan to the West, and of Buddhist economics through E.F. Schumacher's "small is beautiful," everywhere.

In contrast, Hegel and Marx retrieved Heraclitus in concepts minus percepts to convert breakdowns into breakthroughs in theory, while achieving the opposite in practice!

Electric information speedup has created a new all-embracing environment — a *Global Theatre of the Absurd, where only the unexpected happens* — that is now recreating us. This Second Industrial Revolution, has obsolesced the old ground rules, based on Aristotelian YES OR NO logic, by ushering in new process patterns that are retrieving Heraclitean YES AND NO dialectic with new meaning.

Since the dawn of Western civilization, *art has preceded science,* precisely because the perceived effects always precede the conceived causes! Technology (derived from Greek *techne*: art or skill of the artisan) preceded science until the Age of Reason, which, pushed to extreme, became "mother of modern revolutions" — a new chaos.

In the First Industrial Revolution of material "hardware" production, "value-in-exchange" via markets prevailed over "value-in-use" for humans, and restructured their thinking and being. During this Age of Humpty Dumpty, technology became "applied science," as all arts and sciences, thinking and doing, were further fragmented and separated. Physics stressed measurement of quantifiable aspects of material bodies, Alchemy (concerned with transmutation of metals from "base" to "noble") became Chemistry that stressed qualitative transformations of all materials (now, through "resonant bonds, "rather than "mechanical connections").

In the Second Industrial Revolution of information "software" production, the old logic of the Excluded Middle still prevails as the hidden ground of thinking in revolutions and counter-revolutions alike. By treating software like hardware, this logic becomes "two-bit" wit that fails to achieve the human potentials of exchanging information, when neither participant loses and both may gain, by making something entirely new.

Rather than more specialist knowledge, this new *New Science* demands comprehensive awareness of its own assumptions. We can find clues for a new "unity of science," embracing all human knowledge, by studying the effects of our own artifacts, in the processes of human communication: the Tradition exemplified by Cicero's *Doctus Orator*, Bacon's *Novum Organum*, Giambattista Vico's *Scienza Nuova*, Joyce's *Finnegans Wake*, and the McLuhans' *Laws of Media*. Hitherto, Western Science has organized knowledge for retrieval, while its Art organized ignorance for discovery.

In contrast to the Next Industrial Revolution, now "foreseen" as visible FIGURES by "hi-techies" in their latest rearview mirrors, is the invisible GROUND of the Next Next Industrial Revolution,[31] now here via electric media. And that revolution will embrace both market and non-market economies, as consumer and producers merge like audience and actors. It will also usher in the next Next Cultural Revolution, which demands that we look behind all visible FIGURES to find their GROUNDS: to make sense of our human situation not only after, but *before* creating its causes. We can thus learn to cope with the new chaos that becomes a boundless resource in our Global Theatre via Instant Replay, by recognizing its complementary process patterns in our actual times and spaces.

Having already learned to ask "WHY?" logically like Western EYE-men, we must now learn to ask "WHY NOT? unlogically like Eastern EAR-men. Both are essential to restructure our present situation. In the real ground of constant change, in pristine and modern chaos alike, only stable figures really need explaining. The NEW *New Science* will embrace Art, Science, and Religion — all human knowledge — both perceptually and conceptually.[68]

The impact of scientists on Marshall was through the metaphors underlying their theories in particular, but whatever impact McLuhan had upon scientists was through his process-pattern metaphors in general.

GORDON THOMPSON

First Fellow Emeritus of Bell-Northern Laboratories, Ottawa, in 1967, "Gordie" persuaded his company to publish a series of monographs entitled *THE* (the last word in *Finnegans Wake)* to explore problems of communicating with people via media. In reply to our questions, Gordon noted that a complete record of Marshall's influence upon him would be "quite voluminous," but he pointed out:

Amongst other things, Marshall McLuhan taught me about the importance of effects. My training in physics left me with the notion that the electron, for example, was the reality. Nor did my engineering training lead me to question this position. McLuhan changed all that when he led me to realize that it was in the electron's effects that reality was to be found: one never sees an electron, only its impact or effects. This change of vantage point became the basis of my research on past communication revolutions.

Gordon and I used to conduct seminars for Computerniks: Gordie, in the morning, on what a computer can do; and me, in the afternoon, on what a computer can't do. We also explored problems of sharing multi-sensory spaces in teleconferencing systems.

We had long recognized that current Science starts with hypothetical causes and discovers effects that fit. (If they don't, it starts again with another plausible hypothesis in this unending process.) In contrast, Art begins with desired effects and discovers causes to recreate them.

ABRAHAM KIRSHNER

Professor and practitioner of Optometry in Montreal, has devoted much of his life to discovering not only current causes, but also actual cures of Dyslexia (learning disabilities in the broadest sense), with vestibular stimulation. Doctor Kirshner has discovered and applied processes of sensory retraining that involve the interplay not only of the "seventeen scientifically identified senses," but also of the unidentified ones, in his Perceptual Motor Program established during 1969 for the Reading Research Institute in Boston.

Marshall McLuhan has had a profound effect on my work. I work with children of normal intelligence who have learning disorders. After many years of clinical experience, I learned these children differed from their peers in being unable to synthesize sensory and motor data. Marshall McLuhan pointed out that the alphabet technology had the effect of stripping the visual process from its acoustic and tactual environment. He suggested it would be good practice to integrate these processes in a treatment program.

As an eye specialist, I was deeply interested in the reading process. I served as an instructor for Rapid and Effective Reading at the university. Part of my course was devoted to the analysis of propaganda. Marshall smiled when he heard of my efforts and he added his famous phrase to my vocabulary. This is how it all happened.

My colleague, Dr. Arthur Hurst, introduced me to Marshall. I was overwhelmed to meet this great man. I began to posture and spout reams of research on perception. Marshall waited patiently for me to pause and then said kindly, "Kirshner, when a man tries to make an impression, it is usually the only impression he makes."

"Wow!" I exploded, we laughed and then he asked what I did with children who had learning difficulties.

I told him that I follow the Gesell Model of child development. Training to improve eye movements, body balance, hand/eye coordination, auditory-visual integration. When these skills are in place the child makes spontaneous gains in academic and social development.

Marshall asked me how I train students to analyze propaganda. I begin by giving them an experience in visual perception. This is what I do: Look at this form at a reading distance. Make sure it is well illuminated. Stare at the form on the next page for 120 seconds without moving your eyes. This will make a retinal imprint. Now look at a blank page and you will see the image of the form projected on the page. Stretch your arm and you will notice that the image becomes enlarged, now quickly hold the white paper at 12 inches or less, notice that the image reduces in size.

Hold the picture at reading distance. View under bright light. Do not move the eyes or the image for 120 seconds. Look at the afterimage from a far and then a near distance.

The image on the retina is the message, but the interpretation of this message depends upon the plane upon which it is projected. Celebrities are seen as larger than life. Information is judged not by the content but by the reputation of the author. To bring home this lesson I stage two scenarios. I ask the janitor to come into my class wearing his street clothes, to slowly look around the room and ask whether or not I would require the projector for my class. The second experiment is to have a passage from the *Encyclopedia Brittanica* copied both as a typed message and handwritten.

For the first experiment, I tell the students that we will have a distinguished visitor address the class on the subject of creativity. My wife who is the president of the Hospital Womens' Auxiliary has arranged for Dr. Jonas Salk, the inventor of Salk Vaccine to pay a short visit to my class. At the arranged hour, the janitor walks in dressed in his business suit and the students look with awe at the great health researcher. Later during the discussion, some members of the class said that they actually saw the man shrink before their very eyes.

For the next experiment, I circulate a handwritten and a typed

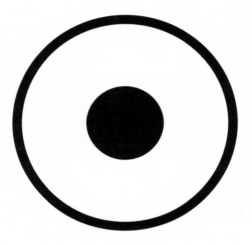

This diagram is for the "retinal impression" experiments described on the previous page.

message and have the students compare these to the original passage that they read in the encyclopedia. Once again they could recognize the plane on which they projected the image. One of my students was a bookseller and he confessed that now he realized that he always treated a hard cover book with more respect than a paperback.

Marshall smiled when he heard my story and said I can give you this lesson in five words: THE MEDIUM IS THE MESSAGE (see Chapter L).

Marshall McLuhan provided me with the theoretical framework for my work with learning-disabled children. Marshall postulated that the Gutenberg print technology (1) would isolate the visual sense to create the "literate eye"; this is in contrast with the "tribal eye" which preceded it. The "tribal eye" was a harmonious integration of all the senses in movement. In order to understand the effect of print on the visual sense, it is first necessary to relate the role of vision to survival. Sir W. Stewart Duke-Elder, the eminent British ophthalmologist said that sight was designed to direct and guide movement. When this capacity is lost, the organism faces extinction.(2)

Many children who enter the school system show a visual disability which manifests itself in poor eye-hand coordination and poor auditory-visual integration. Arnold Gesell (3) systematically catalogued the development of the child's sensorium. Objects in space had no meaning until the child reached out and touched, tasted and manipulated the objects around him. The child begins to bind the visual data to the touch, texture, smell, taste and resistance of the objects that he discovers. Later, if the lesson is well learned, he will see the "apple" and immediately bring to mind the taste, the smoothness, the roundness, the color and the total experience of the apple. It is this capacity to see and know that helps him master his world.

When the child is confronted with print for the first time, he experiences neither color, nor familiar form, not surface, nor smell, nor thing. The print configuration of the word "apple" does not have any apple in it. There is only a procession of strange shapes on a smooth ground. For the first time in the short life of the child the visual sense must grapple with forms that have no taste, texture, resistance, gravity or "thingness." The child's behaviour would have to undergo a transformation so these strange shapes on a smooth ground would conjure up the apple. At this point he transforms his tribal eye to the "literate eye."

I remember a conversation with Marshall in the early sixties. He said, "Kirshner, let's pack our bags and go to Greece and make a study of Greek children before they introduce television." It was too late to do this in America because television had been a part of the community for more than a decade at this time. Although this trip was never made I nevertheless had a strong impression of the behaviour of children in the "head-start" program at the time. I was working in early childhood education and attended conferences on the effect of head-start programs on the learning behaviour of the children. There was report after report from head-start children who were heavy TV viewers: 35 or more hours per week during their pre-school years. What amazed the head-start teachers was the fact that when these children came together as a group they were silent. Television precludes (visible) response on the part of the viewer, either verbal or motor. Whereas Gutenberg technology isolates sight from the sensorium, television isolates sight, sound and motion from tactility, gravity and kinesthesia. There is ample evidence to show that distortions in sensory motor development impose an often insurmountable barrier to successful learning and adaptation to the norms of society. Studies show that juvenile delinquency and learning disorders are highly correlated. This may lead to early learning disorders, "wilding in Central Park" and rapid job turnover and unemployment. Integration-training, to make up for the deficit induced by television and reading, may help our young people adapt successfully to our complex society.

These are my personal views based on the insights of Marshall McLuhan. We are all fortunate that this man lived among us and created a better understanding of our society. We can stand on his shoulders to reach ahead without having to re-invent the wheel.[69]

In studies of children at a training school for delinquents, Allan Berman and Andrew Siegal, two colleagues of Dr. Kirshner, observed two decades ago that 70% had measurable learning disabilities; and they also noted increasing symptoms of hyperkinetic impulse disorders among children throughout the USA:

> ...recidivism rates among delinquents have climbed to a point hovering around 85%. ... the average age for the first incarceration for delinquents is now below 13 years for the first time and is decreasing yearly ... we must think about the possibility that we are using the wrong approach to the problem.[69]

Meanwhile, Dr. Kirshner has continued reversing the undesired effects of TV not only on children, but of sensory excess or deprivation on everybody. Since 1990, he has begun demonstrating how to reorganize the "mental maelstrom" of Parkinson patients.[69]

ARTHUR HURST

Doctor Hurst, another colleague of Dr. Kirshner, tirelessly pursued his own researches with McLuhan into the "causes" and "cures" of dyslexia as a direct result of TV watching. Arthur and Marshall sought in vain for funding to extend their studies of the effects of TV on "vision and reading achievement," summarized by Arthur in 1979.

> Excessive television viewing may still pose the greatest threat to literacy in the Western World. Therefore, it is imperative that TV in the first five years (of life) be eliminated or its viewing severely restricted. [69]

ROSS HALL

Ross is Marshall's cousin. After being invited by McMaster University, Hamilton, to set up their Department of Biochemistry in 1967, he became a regular participant in the Monday-night seminars. Ross gave us a delightful oral history, from which we have chosen excerpts that recall Marshall's influence upon his growth as a scientist.

I'm fifteen years younger than Marshall. My first recollection of him was when I was about four years old sailing in a boat on the Red River in Winnipeg. At that time, my father Reginald Hall, (brother of Marshall's mother Elsie), took his family to Aggasiz just outside Vancouver. He kept up a lively correspondence with Elsie and was always talking about her as well as Marshall and Maurice. She came out to Aggasiz in 1937. My sister and I will never forget a fascinating performance she gave for us.

Marshall also showed up for a brief visit. He was 26 by this time. You can imagine how impressed I was as a small-town boy confronting this tall, good looking graduate of Cambridge. I didn't see him again until 1948, after graduating from the University of British Columbia in my early twenties, when I went to the University of Toronto as a graduate student.

I had kept up a correspondence of sorts with Marshall and he very kindly found me a lodging not far from St. Joseph Street, where he and Corinne were living with their three small children (Eric aged six, and the twins [Mary and Teri] about four years younger) in a small house rented from the University. As a grad student and unattached, I used to go over and baby sit quite often and got to know the family very intimately.

The house was always full of guests. I recall the Bissells when Claude was an English professor, and the Basilian Fathers who seemed to enjoy the atmosphere, and frequent visits of Father Kelly (President of St. Michael's) and Father Phelan, famous for his medieval studies. It was a lively household.

In the evening, Marshall would spend an hour reading Robert Louis Stevenson's *Kidnapped* to Eric, who was six years old at that time and seemed very interested. What impressed me most was that Marshall, who didn't do any of the cooking, always did the dishes religiously. He also did the laundry. And, when Corinne wasn't well, he would pitch in and do other household chores as well.

From 1948 to 1950, I was really very much a part of the family. What impressed me even more at that time as a budding scientist (a post-grad student in Chemistry at the U of T) was that Marshall (a post-grad in English) could pose and discuss some very penetrating and interesting questions in Chemistry. I didn't understand what he was doing then. But later on, it suddenly struck me, that he was not looking at the details — chemical formulas and reaction mechanisms — he was looking at the process.

You don't have to understand the intimate details or the language to understand the process or the patterns. He would structure his questions around the processes that were very relevant to what I was doing. Although I was flabbergasted at the time, I now understand that what he was doing has helped me immeasurably in later life. I now think in terms of process rather than detail.

Marshall never talked about trivia, for example, the weather. He would read from a book that he happened to be reading when you came in. He just carried on, commenting on the politics of the day, or from a play. ... He was always interested in my Chemistry. He was interested in how the scientific world was functioning. In religious matters, he never discussed his position, nor imposed it upon me.

After I had been at Toronto University for a couple of years, I realized it was not the place I wanted to take my Ph.D. I still held the recollection of Cambridge which Marshall had ingrained on my youthful imagination when he had visited Aggasiz so many years before. So with Marshall's encouragement I applied for a scholarship that was awarded in 1950. Marshall had gone to Trinity Hall, I entered Christ's. There I was associated with one of the top Chemistry professors of the Western World who later received a Nobel prize. I found it fascinating and graduated from Cambridge in 1953.

Biology entered my post-Ph.D. work at Buffalo University, where I spent many years as a research scientist, and began to move into other areas of research. Marshall certainly gave me reason to believe there were other careers to pursue, but I saw very little of him until I returned to Hamilton in 1967 to head the Department of Biochemistry at McMaster. By this time Marshall had become a world-famous cult figure. Although already in my forties, I was somewhat apprehensive about re-establishing contact.

But I started to go to the Monday-night seminars and often went up afterwards to Corinne and Marshall's home (then on Wells Hill Avenue). But, over the years, as the children all left home, what struck me most was that they came back at every opportunity.

Marshall had a profound influence on me. I was now much more mature and therefore better able to understand and grasp his concepts. Most scientific work is analytical, in other words, reductionist. You reduce something down to a point where you can analyze it, and then make some kind of judgment based on the analysis.

What Marshall taught me was synthesis: bringing large and diverse things together to form a common idea. What synthesis asked of science really intrigued me, for "global" science is holistic. But an extremely small portion of science is holistic. I was especially interested in this aspect of science, for I had developed an interest in environmental issues. And I began to apply these holistic, synthetic concepts to environmental problems in conversations with Marshall that were most helpful. I'm still applying "synthesis versus analysis" in my work. But in textbook writing I ran afoul of publishers who remain unconvinced.

I therefore set off on another tack and came up with the idea of presenting science newspaper fashion. As Marshall used to say, reading a newspaper is like stepping into a bath: becoming immersed in the stories. There is no one particular place that you begin. Start reading it where you want: read one article then switch to another and back again. It's a non-linear, holistic approach. That's the way I read a newspaper until I've read each article I want. But publishers are still hooked on a linear approach: start at the beginning and keep reading until you reach the end, or just drop out.

I would certainly give Marshall credit for moving me away from the straight and narrow, highly reductionist, approach of science. In contrast with the holistic approach, the reductionist approach means that you ignore anything you can't explain. You must also have a directly linked cause and effect. Today, we have learned that everything causes everything else. Scientists would not entertain such an idea because it is too complex, although it is beginning to be taken seriously in the political field of environmental concerns. Science in general also avoids the playful side of things, for it is too messy for scientists, who prefer to deal with abstractions.

During 1967-1980, I was able to relate to Marshall in a mature way. He still talked about his own interests, but the way he approached things made it possible to interact with anything and everything. You couldn't call him a Generalist because his patterns were comprehensive.

A medieval scholar, for example, could know all the facts about all the subjects there were to know. That's the kind of person Marshall was. He had a vast knowledge where everything fitted together. So it wasn't a question of knowing something about Chemistry, or conditions in New York City, as separate departments of knowledge. He could relate them. To call him merely an encyclopedic man is to do him an injustice, precisely because he had this capacity to relate anything to anything. I practice this "secret" in my professional work today.

In contrast to the Generalist — a multi-specialist or polymath of Western culture — the Comprehensivist can grasp the patterns of all cultures, both analytically and synthetically, as first noted in *Take Today*. Such was Marshall. He never claimed to be a Specialist either in Art or Science, but he quickly learned from fellow explorers whatever details he needed to discover with them many hidden process patterns of both art and science. In science, Marshall learned much from cultural anthropologists "Ted" Carpenter and "Ned" Hall, and other scientists too numerous to mention; and in art, from muralist York Wilson (close friend and neighbour), painter Harley Parker (co-author of *Through the Vanishing Point)*, and sculptor Sorel Etrog (for whom he wrote the text of Images from the Film SPIRAL). Marshall had long ago become a Comprehensivist, both an ancient and a modern in thinking; and he also observed that these terms reversed their meaning with the ebb and flow of EYE and EAR sensory stress through prevailing communication media (as each gained or lost dominance, exhibited by the relative importance of Logic and Rhetoric in Western school curricula from Cicero to Joyce). But he still considered himself a medieval man in feeling.

Ross Hall, a modern scientist, also reveals himself as a Comprehensivist in his book *Food for Nought*[70] which proves, among other things, that breakfast food containers are sometimes more nutritious for rats than the breakfast food they contain.

CAROLYN AND ROBERT DEAN

As regular participants in the Monday-night seminars, Dr. Carolyn Dean and her husband, Bob, (archivist and broadcaster) were strongly influenced by both Marshall McLuhan and Ross Hall. They were also aware of the psychological and social consequences of conventional communication media.[71] Carolyn notes:

Tom Wolfe fretted that McLuhan might be right when he warned us that the electric environment was going to have devastating effects. Well, I know that McLuhan was right. The electric environment is changing our very cell structure. Those of us who have been waiting for the body count before recognizing that he was right have only to pick up the latest medical journals which are documenting the electrified casualties. The most extreme effects are exemplified as a higher incidence of cancer in radar and shortwave radio operators. In his book *The Body Electric,* Dr. Robert O. Becker has heavily documented the research into effects of the electric environment. He lists the dangers:

1. Extra-low frequency (ELF) electromagnetic fields vibrating at about 30-100 hertz, even if they're weaker than the earth's field, interfere with the cues that keep our biological cycles properly timed; chronic stress and impaired disease-resistance result.

2. The available evidence strongly suggests that regulation of cellular growth processes is impaired by electropollution, increasing cancer rates and producing serious reproductive problems.

3. Electromagnetic weapons constitute a class of hazards culminating in climatic manipulation from a sorcerer's-apprentice-level of ignorance.

For years, the notion that our poor state of health, the rising rates of arthritis, cancer, infertility, impaired immunity and chronic disease was due to inadequate and faulty nutrition seemed obvious to me. However, it is only within the last few years that the medical establishment has made statements about the correlation of poor diet and disease. The battle of recognition has taken over 30 years and is still barely won. What about the struggle to make people understand both the service and disservice aspects of the electric environment?

In my practice as a doctor, I can now share Marshall's idea of himself as a new Pasteur who recognizes new causes of disease that were invisible and protected by public incredulity.

We expect that unexpected new medical discoveries will be in the nerve "gaps" rather than in network "connections": through low energy resonant figure/ground relations of the brain with its invisible material, mental, and social environments rather than through visible high energy impacts. Miracles of healing are the "message" of recognizing that both doctor and patient are the "content" not merely of limited medical media, but of our unlimited multi-verse.

In discussing our questions, Bob added:

I learned from Marshall McLuhan an approach and a means to bypass any brilliant and persuasive ideologies and philosophies.

In today's world we have, through the very perfection and instantaneity of our means of communication, made it impossible to resolve the conflicting claims of the numerous societies and cultures which are now in close association. Neither can we hope to impose any one culture on all the others and reduce them to a single form, or model.

Never before, in this state of perfected communication, has there been so much confusion and breakdown of communication.

During the early 1960s, Marshall had recognized this identity crisis created by electric speeds, as new unfamiliar process patterns superseded the old familiar ground rules. Since the end of that decade, Marshall and his co-workers have constantly pointed out that information scientists, educators, and politicians alike still equate improving communication with merely increasing the accessibility, scope, and speed of their media, while raising the quality of its programming, whether cultural or technical. By ignoring the effects of media, as such, they have thus failed to recognize the *Paradox of Communication Speedup,* which is a main theme of *Take Today* (Chapter 8).

Electric speedup annihilates the very image of one's self. The young are deprived of both identity and goals. They react in a kind of narcolepsy or apathetic somnambulism. The Unperson is the inevitable result of improved communication. When all barriers of private consciousness are overcome, the resulting collective form of awareness is a tribal

258

> dream that leads to violence as a quest for identity in prelit-
> erate and post-literate societies alike. [Now made manifest
> as global Re-Tribulation by local Re-Balkanization.]

Ever since Pythagoras replayed his "music of the spheres" in mathematical language, scientists have ignored audile-tactile space metaphors in favour of visual-space models that Democritus had reduced to irreducible atoms and total void. The power of such metaphors to shape scientific thinking and logic alike is discussed in *ABC of Prophecy* and in "Coping with Chaos."[68,72]

All axioms are culturally determined. Today's science manifests its visual sensory bias in its language. We categorize our artifacts, hardware and software alike, in a "Book of Nature" for matching the old. Highly logical philosopher of science Karl Popper has now reduced all science to what can be "falsified" in categorical statements; and such science can never "prove" what is true logically, only what is untrue. But to get a dialogue going with scientists willing to organize mutual ignorance for discovery, Marshall used Popper's statement as a "probe" like detective Holmes rather than Doctor Watson.

> The empirical sciences are systems of theories. Scientific
> theories are universal statements. ...statements can be logi-
> cally justified only by statements. ... In so far as a scientific
> statement speaks about reality, it must be falsifiable: and in
> so far as it is not falsifiable, it does not speak about reality.[73]

Nevertheless, Niels Bohr had already observed that "the opposite of a correct statement is a false statement. But the opposite of a profound truth may well be another profound truth."[74] Nature itself negates logical "disproof" by manifesting its effects directly through percepts, not concepts. But that demands a *perestroika* (restructuring) of normal science — starting again with actual manifests of many kinds of effects rather than a few plausible, hypothetical causes.

In much of this, James Joyce had preceded most of us, before his early death in 1941.

CHAPTER O

PHILOSOPHIZING AND COMPREHENDING

In Greece at the dawn of Western civilization, the Ground shifted from bardic-oral to phonetic-literate culture. In brief, the barter economy of the extended family, gave way to the market economy based on slavery. Ancient tribal democracy, inseparable from aristocracy, recognized the ideal of *kalos kagathos* (the good as beautiful, and the beautiful as good) embodied in its timocracy based on manifest human values. But, in the Ground of market economies, timocracy became rule by market values, through oligarchy that led to tyranny, while the "purse of gold" replaced the "palm of victory" as the ultimate prize for achievement. Greek city-state history exemplifies the ebb and flow of tyranny and democracy due to the constantly changing influence of such Figure/Ground relations.

Today, in the now obsolesced First and Second World alike, anyone can plainly see that the TV generation "wants it all and wants it now" with no inkling of how to get it. And, in search of new identities, the less-developed Third World intensifies the ferocity of its internecine strife with no end in sight. Meanwhile, the world of Academe is self-destructing with "correctness mania" as a substitute for old courtesy and uses language to separate people instead of bringing together all worlds, to convert breakdowns into breakthroughs.

The Dialectics of Nature[77] (Engels) of the Second World that called itself "national in form and socialist in content," equated freedom and democracy with administered markets. And it considered the First World as "national in form and capitalist in content," whose Book of Nature identifies freedom and democracy with free markets. Both ignore that no ideology, no philosophy, no abstraction can be the content of any institution we create, but only "WE the people." And WE *must now learn to anticipate the* EFFECTS *of means upon our ends* BEFORE *creating their* CAUSES. (See Chapter L.)

Meanwhile, the Third World is merging and emerging

with their former "superiors" in a Fourth World — a new Maelstrom of information flowing at electric speed — that has no fixed boundaries of any kind, anywhere. Only by recognizing the new laws of this new situation in its own terms can we now survive by foreseeing and bypassing their undesired effects; and these laws decree combining new technical knowledge with old human wisdom in new ways.

By the early 1940s, James Joyce had anticipated everybody in the second cycle of his *Wake*. By then, giant "Finn" could deliberately choose either to fall asleep once more and revert to tribal mud and blood, or to stay awake and remake his previous Fate, as "Finn, again" with the hard-won "keys to. Given!" (Like St. Peter's keys, both mechanical and musical, not only to Data, but Heaven too!).

LAWS OF MEDIA

McLuhan persistently denied that he had any theories, or that he advocated any kind of "McLuhanism." But he did discover an approach to understanding the effects of all man-made Nature, past or present or proposed, whether of information software (especially his own approach) or of its embodiment in material hardware, by asking four basic questions, his *Laws of Media*.[78]

In *Take Today*,[8] (1972) we considered many consequences of trying to reduce the musical harmonies of actual existence to the logical connections of artifical Nature. In "Causality in the Electric World"[80] (1973), we were trying to create an "epistemology" of human experience based on Instant Replay and its "suspended judgment" of percepts (not concepts), as an attempt to cope with constant change. Although somewhat resembling Structural Phenomenology, it is not definable in merely philosophic terms, but only in poetic terms, or in Aphorism, as Francis Bacon understood long ago. Tetrads are forms of aphorism, imploded messages.

During the 1970s, much of our work with Marshall was devoted to *discovering the realities of existence "beyond objectivity" directly in their own terms.* We began by re-cognizing all human artifacts as human communication media whose contents are their human users, and whose messages are the totality of their effects, regardless of any scientific theories or human intentions.

Since 1973, we have been asking FOUR BASIC QUESTIONS (a TETRAD[78, 81], after the Pythagorean *tetractys)* about any artifact as a communication medium, in order to discover its process patterns. Marshall had invited everyone to engage in exploring these Grammars of the Media, and to consider them either as "laws" or "hypotheses" to be disproved scientifically. We use tetrads essentially as multi-sensory resonant probes (means of perception) which act both sequentially and simultaneously.

These elements represent a classic four-part metaphor as the prime example of the action of technological effects. They are rearranged appositionally by the McLuhans in the *Laws of Media*[78] to highlight their dynamic process relations. We symbolize them below as analogical ratios: E:R = T:O, and E:T = R:O not only to organize knowledge for comprehension, but also to organize ignorance for discovery.

LAWS OF MEDIA

(Enhancing Pattern)   *(Transforming Pattern)*

What does it amplify
or enhance?

What does it flip
into when pushed
to extremes?

E   T

R   O

What does it revive or
retrieve of similar
nature previously
obsolesced?

What does it erode,
replace, or obsolesce?

(Reviving Pattern)   *(Obsolescing Pattern)*

Depending on the context, we often use other words to highlight the transformative action of these patterns. For example, (E) *enhancing* as inflating, amplifying, or playing up; (O) *obsolescing* as down playing, impeding, numbing, or pushing aside; (R) *retrieving* as replaying, reviving, or bringing back; and (T) *transforming* as chiasmus, reversing or flipping into.

GREEK PHONETIC ALPHABET

Enhances
private authorship
and individual ego.

Transforms into
history as the
corporate record
of private life.

E   T

R   O

Retrieves or
revives secret
inner life.

Reduces aural-oral
memory.

THE AUTOMOBILE

Enhances privacy
(*see page 185*).

Transforms country
into city.

E   T

R   O

Retrieves or
revives countryside
in a new way.

Pushes aside
horse and buggy.

One tetrad cannot reveal all of the effects of a process pattern. This tetrad provides the broad ground, the main verb. And, depending on the specific ground we are examining, we will get different answers to the four questions. We re-ask the questions so as to reveal the physical, phychic and social effects of the medium. The automobile does more than obsolesce the horse and buggy, for example. Among other things, it pushes aside the jobs and skills that go with them. And this, in turn, emotionally, physically and socially strains all concerned.

Once one set of ratios has been worked out, as above, it becomes a resonant pathway to uncovering other related patterns. Each flip prepares the next reversal.

MONEY

Enhances transactions.

Transforms into pure information (credit).

E   T

R   O

Retrieves or revives personal power.

Pushes aside bartering.

And what does pure information or credit, transform into once it becomes ground? Debt?

GLOBAL ELECTRIC MEDIA

Instantaneous speed.

The simultaneous information environment.

Sender gets sent: you are there, they are here instantly as discarnate minds.

E   T

R   O

Revives audile-tactile dialogue, tribal involvement, and occult.

Erodes visual and logically connected order, the sequent.

Television has inadvertently created a new form of cognition halfway between percept and concept that is now replacing the old game for many sports fans.

INSTANT REPLAY

	Transforms experience
Amplifies	into process
percept.	pattern recognition.

E T

R O

Retrieves structure	Obsolesces cinematic
of a past event.	reality and attention
(concept)	to visual images.

Instead of projecting old "figures" into the fantasies invented by Futurists, we can learn to sharpen our awareness of present "grounds," like Comprehensivists, to change the actual shape of things to come.

INSTANT PREPLAY

	Transforms into
Enhances ground	ecological
awareness.	design.

E T

R O

Retrieves synthesis	Obsolesces logical
of causes and effects.	analysis and the
	emphasis on causes.

Several versions of a tetrad are possible, (interactively, on the "internet," for example). We invite our readers to submit additional tetrads.

The main effects, indicated by such laws of the Nature that we make, can be expanded to include unlimited material, mental, and social side effects through "glosses." Tetrads can also present desired effects as preceding their yet-to-be designed causes, including their Laws of Implementation.[31, 89] But divorced from their relationship to the hidden ground — the totality of nature — tetrads can become idols like any other pure abstraction. Yet tetrads illustrate the approach used by Marshall and his co-workers to understand the effects of man-made Nature, ancient and modern and proposed.

Tetrads can probe the nature of statements or theories about existence, but they cannot package the nature of nature (which, like pristine chaos, has neither grammar nor syntax, but speaks for itself). Tetrads can also expose limitations of thinking and being, as well as reveal visions of the unseeable.

The diagonal **E** to **O** highlights quantitative variations of clichés, whereas diagonal **T** to **R** spotlights qualitative transformations of archetypes as natural processes. The question of the Transformations of Quantity into Quality has always been a central one in classical dialectics.

TRUTH AND REALITY

I recognized long ago with Marshall, that the pure Objectivist believes he can stand naked in this world, whereas the pure Subjectivist believes the world to be his own clothing. In contrast, the pure Empiricist is like the criminal being led off to execution, who says, "This will teach me a good lesson!" Truth is not something to match. It is not a label. It is something we make in a process of remaking our world as that world remakes us — transforms the nature of our "human being."

In our Global Electric Theatre, both man-made Nature and nature-made man now reveal themselves perceptually by making the new through Instant Replay; for that has resurrected the *panta rhei* (everything flowing, like fire and water) in "multi-sensory space" patterns, recognized twenty-five centuries ago by Heraclitus (before phonetic literacy had finally imposed its "visual-space" thinking upon Greek bardic culture). In preliterate times, reality and its re-presentation were united. In post-literate times, the multi-sensory image has again become reality. (I once overheard a child say to his dad who was changing a flat tire: "Why don't you switch the program, daddy?")

Failure to take into account multi-sensory awareness is the blind spot of modern science; for constantly changing process patterns now interrelate everything and everybody in what is actually happening; and that has obsolesced the dichotomies of Aristotle's Law of the Excluded Middle. This *tertium non datur* (there is no third choice: "either A is B, or A is not B") is the underlying assumption not only of every computer, but of all Artificial Intelligence and rational civilized thinking alike; for Aristotle — "The Authority" — had concluded: "It is impossible for anyone to suppose that the same thing is and is not, as some people think Heraclitus said."[81] Since then, guardians of Western culture have continued to substitute logical statements about abstract Nature for actual existence in which there are no separate or static things, but only interacting processes (with nothing excluded).

In the middle of the 1990s, we can prophesy the obsolescence (not extinction, but proliferation and futility) of old dictatorships, Left and Right; for that process is still accelerating. We are manifestly retrieving classless society with Heraclitean percepts of everything flowing, and no definable economic, political, or philosophical concepts to count on. Today's Liberty and Democracy, pushed to extreme, can still re-produce their opposites by pure-market measures. But the Whole is always here as the ultimate background, as silence is to sound.

JOHN CAGE

Was one of the great experimental musicians of the 1960s and 70s. He is noted as having defined silence as "all of the sounds of the universe at once."

Marshall McLuhan suggested that I write a piece of music that would use the ten thunder-claps of *Finnegans Wake*. I learned from him that I could do it. Atlas Borealis and The Ten Thunderclaps. He told me The Ten are a history of technology. Rain falling on the earth, then on other materials, history, finally remaining in the air (the winds, the Present). Orchestra and chorus. The strings filling up the envelopes of actual raindrops, the voices the envelopes of actual thunder-claps. It would be not like going to a concert but like going to a storm. I have not yet done it but I think of it as something I will do. I think of him when I think of it.

I remember being with him at lunch, not what we ate. He asked me questions (he wanted to know what patterns in society I heeded). I couldn't respond; my mind doesn't work that way. For me his books, his questions, his statements were all mysterious and therefore useful. They still are. They keep understanding at a safe distance. He continues to protect us from what we see is happening.

The mystery of what cannot be said remains in the mystery of the boundless Multi-verse — in the silence of its infinitude of unheard sounds as Cage understands.

Cosmological Probing

"Big Bang" cosmology assumes that the observed "red shift" of light from galaxies, which increases with distance, is evidence for a Cosmos that is expanding in empty space. Why not consider how light energy decreases with time by vibrating an invisible medium to its limit, instead of vainly trying to reduce the Eternity of an actually boundless Multi-verse to a History of Time in some imaginary Uni-verse limited by visual-space thinking?

In May 1992, cosmologists were celebrating recent confirmation of the Big Bang "Spontaneous Inflation" Theory of cosmic creation. This reminded me of a conversation Marshall and I had in the 1970s about Anaximander's boundless *apeiron*, a metaphor rejected by ancient and modern "atomists" alike. Marshall easily remembered for he had published my essay, "Space in Physics and Cosmology,"[72] in *Explorations* during the 1960s. He had an on-going interest in the nature of gravity, and was intrigued by my suggestion that (like Mach's "explanation" of the shape of any watery surface in a rotating bucket) it was possibly due to the hidden ground of *apeiron* acting in all directions simultaneously. This is a typical figure/ground relation in multi-sensory space; but, whatever we may wish to call it, the ground remains beyond sight.

We can thus start with the effects and then try to discover what causes might create these effects and no others. But metaphors are culturally determined, and they often hinder our thinking. In this case, any mechanical "ether" is bound to fail as a metaphor to explain the electro-magnetic propagation of light. The Michelson-Morley experiment actually demonstrated this: it was interpreted, however, as "proving" the absence of such an "ether," and of any ground or medium of propagation whatever in "visual-space" terms. And that, in process pattern terms, is a perennial replay of Democritean "atoms and the void" (previously obsolesced, but not obsolete) which still dominate the hidden ground of visually biased modern science.

As well, Hubble's "red-shift" of light from distant galaxies does not consider loss of energy as evidence of "tired light," but as due to "expansion of the Universe." This red-shift, like Eddington's "wavicles," appears as a *figure* minus any visible or invisible *ground*, as a propagation medium. The ground of this conception is mathematically conceived as a universal "container" having no centre anywhere, but having a postulated beginning "somewhere — a utopian no-where." The Big Bang was postulated as the mother of all centres, in virtual vacua, rather than actual plena, expanding endlessly.

Any process pushed to extreme reverses or transforms its previous effects: *prominence is the precursor of obsolescence.* Where can we now go for any rational (not merely logical or mathematical) ending except via a structural shift from visual to other sensory spaces? Or will cosmologists continue to strive unendingly in the spirit of *sozein ta phenomena* ("to save the appearances" of visual space) by merely reverberating the ancient cosmological conflict of Appearance and Reality (whether the heavens revolve around the earth or the earth revolves in the heavens) in new form, without perceiving its new meaning? Are we needlessly devoting our limited research funds to limitless maxi-mega-colliders for discovering a micro-mini-particle with no grounds whatever?

Why not consider a boundless Multi-verse of *apeiron (an irreducible material process, not particle)* with centres everywhere and boundaries nowhere as a multi- and super-sensory world that makes its own space-time with neither absolute beginning nor ending, but only dynamic inter-penetrating processes in eternal ebb and flow? After light-years of travel and travail, why wouldn't individual light energies die down to the temperature of background radiation (or below), and also constantly rise again through many processes in "empty space" (that may well be a *plenum* almost inconceivably full rather than a *vacuum* no longer conceivably empty)? The meaning of all such abstractions and speculations is determined by their contexts, not our definitions.

Meanwhile, we can both initiate and investigate light's quantum "splashdowns," (as figures without grounds,) whenever and wherever we look. But their meanings are in their unique figure/ground relationships, where the ground (like *apeiron*) remains forever invisible, while their total effects or messages are always immeasurable, like the *logos*.

Will cosmologists ever recognize that nobody can ever explain Eternity in terms of History? Like audile-tactile and visual-space structures, they are complementary, but not commensurable. Cartoonist Sidney Harris gives us a clue to this hang-up: two scientists, with wings and halos attached, are discussing their new situation. "I'm beginning to understand eternity," one of them admits, "but infinity is still beyond me."

CHAPTER P

FAITH AND THEOLOGY

As boys, Marshall and Maurice attended the local Baptist Church, their mother's preference for them. Although their father was a Presbyterian, he recognized the importance of compromise and attended the Baptist Church with them. Maurice continues:

Mother rarely came. Its evangelical emphasis did not appeal to her pragmatic nature. She had no evidence that by seeking first the Kingdom of God, all things would be added unto us. If by "things" was meant material prosperity, the very reverse proved true for our family. Mars was twelve, and I ten, when we were baptized by immersion into membership of the Baptist Church.

During his undergraduate years, Mars preferred attendance at any other church where the preaching seemed more interesting. However, he made a habit of reading his Bible daily, not only for spiritual sustenance, but also for its literary value.

In 1934, a team from the Oxford Group, led by Frank Buckman, came to Winnipeg exuding an infectious gaiety of spirit that challenged both of us to personal surrender to the will of God, revealed in Christ. At the height of the depression, many young people were attracted to this approach.

Mars attended one of their large public meetings but remained aloof from the Group itself. Later, he told me that he was looking for a spiritual "city" which had foundations; and this he was to find in the Roman Catholic Church. He believed that this Church exemplified historical continuity dating back to St. Peter, the first Bishop of Rome. Having already accepted the Incarnation, he found spiritual nourishment through its Sacraments.

Among undergraduates, during the depression years, the cure-all for economic ills was to be found in ideologies, such as socialism or communism or their opposites. Mars took exception particularly to political "communism," only to be told that his arguments reflected the theology of the Roman Catholic Church. This quickened his interest in what the Church espoused. In the course of his investigation, he encountered G.K. Chesterton, Hilaire Belloc, Father Martindale, Gilson and Maritain, and other articulate Roman Catholic spokesmen. These men proved major influences affecting Marshall's eventual decision to seek membership in that Church.

It was during his attendance at Cambridge that Mars became a convert. This radical change from his Baptist origins, would, he knew greatly disturb mother and dad; mother more particularly, because she could foresee that his professorial career would be drastically compromised. Gone would be any possibility of becoming president of Harvard, or even of recognition as a professor.

On receiving a letter from Mars outlining his reasons for becoming a Catholic (in which he confessed to having spent two years in prayer that this decision would not affect his parents adversely) dad took the letter to the leading United Church minister in Winnipeg — Dr. James Clark of Knox. After reading the letter, he said to Dad: "Mr. McLuhan, if I had a son who had spent two years in prayer concerning his conversion to the Roman Catholic faith, and hoping to avoid the alienation of his parents, I would give him my blessing." Dad was satisfied.

Mother, on the other hand, having received a similar letter, while spending a couple of weeks with me on a mission field, reacted in her own way. She wept copiously. It was the end of all her aspirations for her talented son. Unfortunately, mother was not spared to see her son achieve his true vocation.

KATHY HUTCHON: (see Chapter D)
I remember that we had a sing-song at my home. Marshall, Corinne, Sister Bede, and Maurice were present with my family. Maurice was playing some of the old Baptist Church hymns, and Marshall was singing lustily. Later, Marshall observed that there just wasn't enough singing of hymns in the Roman Catholic Church. He did speak to the Fathers of his own parish (Holy Rosary) suggesting the need for someone to lead in the singing of familiar hymns. He even proposed inviting the organist and choir leader of nearby Timothy Eaton Memorial United Church to teach the hymns to the congregation (we don't know what came of it).

"GERRY" FEIGEN: (see Chapter J)
Occasionally, Marshall and I would discuss things other than communications and media. I recall one day driving down towards Santa Cruz College, when he said, "Democracy belongs very profoundly with Christianity, and is something I take very seriously indeed. The Christian concept of the Mystical Body: all are members of the Body of Christ. This becomes technologically a fact under electronic conditions.

I asked him several times about how he had determined the existence of God, and he said that he had asked for evidence and received it. It was strong enough to lead to his conversion. He suggested that if I had asked God to reveal Himself to me, I too would find Him. This was almost put to the test for me. I once made a fire walk in the South Pacific, walking over thirty feet of hot coals, and came off it relatively unscathed. He never asked me vocally if I had discovered God at that point; but his one eyebrow was up, and there was a look as if "...well, are you going to tell me anything?" I didn't.

Mrs. Kamala Bhatia interviewed by Maurice and me.

BARRINGTON:

Many people accorded to Mahatma Gandhi almost the same stature as Jesus. But Gandhi claimed that Jesus was being covered up by his interpreters. At the same time, Gandhi was dealing with the situation in India in ways that one couldn't ask Christians to do better.

KAMALA:

I was there when Gandhi was assassinated. We used to go to his prayer meetings on Friday evenings. (It was on a Friday in a garden that a man came forward and shot him.) In his meetings he discussed The Lord's Prayer, and passages from the Muslim scriptures that speak about love and kindness and hospitality to strangers, of a man's doing his duty without regard to rewards. And from the Jains, who forbid the destruction of our ecology, to worship nature — not to be unkind to the life around you (the animals), for that is the life that supports you. So those were the prayers he offered when he spoke of life and humanity. Love your enemies. Do good to them that despitefully use you and persecute you. The kingdom of God belongs to all of us.

BARRINGTON:

He tried to hold the Moslem and Hindu together as brothers. A Hindu shot him.

KAMALA:

Another interesting thing. When the body was laid out and we all went to pass by, there was a Mohammedan priest, a Christian priest, a Parsee priest, a Hindu priest, a Sikh priest, all claiming that he belonged to them. They were reciting all the prayers together.

Marshall McLuhan didn't stress his own value system at all. He tried to conceal it. That was the difference between Mahatma Gandhi and him. Gandhi came out and stated his value system, because he wanted to emphasize certain values, but McLuhan never did.

BARRINGTON:

He would come out with his opinion when driven hard. But people would have to make him very impatient before doing that, and he would be sorry for it afterwards.

MAURICE:

Were you aware of Marshall's intense religious conviction?

KAMALA:

Well, I went to church with him several times. I was always happy to go with him. I was honoured.

BARRINGTON:

After the service, I would always put something into the Poor box, and he would say, "Barry, you don't have to do that!"

KAMALA:

At heart, I think he was a transcendentalist and that Roman Catholicism was only on the top.

MAURICE:

He was mainly interested in the sacraments, rather than the theology.

BARRINGTON:

He used to say to me, "Barry, you seem to understand the fundamentals, why aren't you a Catholic?" He would often send dropout priests to me and say, "I'm too short on the fuse. I get annoyed with them (hung up 'half-way between sanctity and depravity'), but you don't seem to, and may do them some good." "I enjoy meeting them," I admitted. "They probably entered the Church too soon, before they knew what they were doing. They may be lost as priests, but not necessarily as Christians."

He reassured me, "Don't worry about that, Barry. The only things that really count are the seven sacraments. All the rest is secondary."

Marshall conducted two summer schools for priests, which I had the privilege of "participating," to study the liturgy and ritual of the Church and what the media were doing to it. Marshall recognized that, in this regard, the Catholic hierarchy had the same problems as any other human organization — problems of human communicating.

Subsequently, in 1974, the United Theological Seminary of the Twin Cities, New Brighton, Minnesota, invited me to discuss our findings.[82] For example, with the advent of the microphone in religious service, the High Altar had reverted to a Communion Table.

The priest cannot turn his back on the congregation when he is using a microphone; nor can he continue murmuring in Latin, or in any other language, to sustain an aura of mystery.

KAMALA:

Well, I was brought up in two religious traditions. My mother was a Christian. I loved reading the Bible, and the hymns appealed to me; but the Hindu culture and traditions attracted me. My husband was a Hindu. I formed my own ideas about religion, based on the *Vedas*, and *Upanishads*, the Bible, and the great religions of the world.

BARRINGTON:

Marshall was very partial to processions.

KAMALA:

Good Friday is considered a holiday along with Corpus Christi in India, but not in Canada.

BARRINGTON:

One morning in 1970, as we were working on *Take Today* at the Centre, Marshall heard the sound of band-music outside. He jumped up immediately, "Let's go, Barry, it's a parade." Out we went and saw the Orangemen in full swing. It was their day. During the 1920s, it was celebrated with immense pride and pageantry by the Protestant community in Toronto. But on that morning, the most visible and vibrant band displayed the banner of a local Catholic High School! As "Jim" Joyce reminds us, "Pastimes are past times."

Sr. Bede Sullivan continues with Kevin Doyle.

KEVIN:

What impression did you form of his (Marshall's) religious faith?

SR. BEDE:

Very strong. He was one of the readers at his parish, The Holy Rosary.

He consistently went to the noon Mass (at the Basilian church on campus). He would leave guests in the Coach House while he went. He always sat in about the same place. I sat on the other side about four seats behind. He wasn't leafing through anything, but was in total rapt meditation with God all through the Mass. You could see it all over his face.

When we were invited into the Vatican Council, he and my other professor ("Ed." Fisher of Notre Dame) were asked to write some kind of statement to Rome about communications in the

Church. That's when I heard him express himself most succinctly.

"Do you think the Church has any idea of what microphones do in the practice of religion?" That's the kind of question he'd ask. He said preaching had been changed by hearing things in English.

"Do you think the priests are ever going to read any of this stuff? They're still living thirty years behind. Some of them have never updated their theology. They can't even accept John XXIII."

Sr. St. Michael Guinan (see Chapter D) also added.

Marshall is one man who found his way into the Roman Catholic Church through deep reasoning to find the gift of faith. I think he was a very holy man. I think he was a saint. I know that he inspired me. The inspiration consisted in the awareness that here was a man of tremendous intelligence, who could offer that intelligence to God.

SANDRA CONTI

Who graduated in 1983 from Concordia University with distinction in Communication studies, is an author, editor, and *Auxiliatrice des Petites Soeurs de Notre Dame du Sourire.*

Through Marshall I saw the Father's Life in all things ... that there was a spiritual and mystical side to all things, and especially so in communications and other technologies.

In discovering his work in late adolescence, I felt warmed and delighted to know as a young spiritual and mystic — and aspiring communicator and communication student — I would not be alone in this work and view of life.

Though I had always felt that the Father was with me, even in early childhood, it took more than 17 years for me to know that I was also with Him, and others I would come to know and love as brethren and His and my children.

Marshall McLuhan's approach and my other similar studies in the field of communications confirmed this for me. I often said that each of us are members of the one Christ body, each a priest or minister of Christ, either leading his children to Him, or away from Him and his Mother. Marshall helped especially to lead me to Him.

Pierre Babin presents us with a comprehensive "mix" of Marshall McLuhan's and his own views on religion in *Autre homme autre chrétien à l'âge électronique.*[83] From this, as well as from Marshall himself, we gather that, as a member of the Vatican Communication Commission, he had also written to Jacques Maritain about the role of the Roman Catholic Church in the modern world, particularly with regard to the *Papal Interval '70*. The cardinals with whom he had had earlier discussion on this subject, had shown little interest. Although Maritain responded to Marshall's letter, he didn't seem to have understood the issues. However, for the first six months after his election, Pope John Paul's pronouncements strongly suggested that he had both read and understood it; for he made reference to many things Marshall had outlined, even to the "Popemobile."

Marshall had also asked Gilson whether the question of personal salvation was doctrine, and Gilson was very upset, because no one else had ever raised the question. When we once asked him whether he was an optimist or a pessimist, Marshall promptly replied: "Neither! I'm an apocalyptic. I don't believe we can solve our problems without God's help." These are small examples of large theological questions that concerned him as a devout Roman Catholic.

Although, as a Christian, Marshall, it seemed to us, rejected the theology of neo-Platonists, we learned from him to imagine God in their terms as an eternal Being "with centres everywhere and boundaries nowhere." But, he always celebrated Jesus in historical terms as a Being, who "participated" both divine and human existence, eternally. His Faith made him whole.

CHAPTER Q

Plunging Ahead

At a Memorial Tribute to Professor Marshall McLuhan, held on January 27, 1981, at University of Toronto's Convocation Hall, we heard the President of St. Michael's College, John Kelly, the former President of the University of Toronto, Claude Bissell, and Carlton Williams, former President of the University of Western Ontario.[84]

Reverend John Kelly

One of the flippancies already in the McLuhan saga is the somewhat impertinent question: "What are you doin', Marshall McLuhan?" The world is well aware that he was doing something. There are different versions of just what that something was but there seems to be universal agreement that whatever it was, he was doing it differently. Marshall was not one to ignore the flippant; he was more likely to make it more flippant still. So, in the McLuhan spirit, I will add to the flippancy by adding two more questions, both flippant, and, with a touch of McLuhan irony, try to answer all three seriously. The additional questions are these: "How were you doin' what you were doin', Marshall McLuhan?" and "Why were you doin' what you were doin', Marshall McLuhan?"

I am well aware that Marshall would not answer any of the questions — not because he wasn't perfectly sure of the answers — but because he was convinced that serious questioners must first wrestle with the questions themselves. Involvement with the question is the necessary propaedeutic to the answer and even the route to the discovery of the obvious. Moreover, he was an iconoclast; an idol smasher living in an age when cracking barriers was the name of the game played on the frontiers. Breakthrough was the name of the game, and he played it to the hilt. Involvement and breakthrough, these were the McLuhan trademarks, and he was so wholly consumed by both that he had no time for answers to pedantic questions. Pedantry he would leave to the less agile; to fools like me who would rush into answers which angels might fear to give.

Marshall has been called a philosopher but the current connotation of that term is too left-hemisphere-oriented to really suit him. He was more truly an artist, impatient of the ratiocinative; more like an eagle, even a mystic, whose spirit thrilled to soar to the heights, swoop over the breadths and plumb the depths. He did not simply see and hear, he glowed and resonated with the sight and sound. He could not abide a partial deployment of perceptual powers: senses, mind, heart, faith and inspiration all fused together as he plunged into the inexhaustible and ineffable mystery of human existence. His life was filled with awe, the launching pad of enquiry. He was overwhelmed with the wonder and the marvel of the universe. The bored, in his mind, were asleep. To be awake was to be in dialogue with reality, taught by it, fulfilled by it, constantly challenged by it. You miss reality if you are simply a spectator. To be human is to be an involved participant in the drama of life — a sharer and a contributor. What was he doing? He was exploring on the turbulent sea of 20th century life, and he was doing it without the safeguard of a methodological rudder simply because he was in the process of trying to fashion an adequate one.

But no man is an island. McLuhan had roots deep in the main intellectual and artistic currents of the past. He insisted that human perception changed with the invention of print but he insisted more on the abrupt change in perception happening in the age of acoustic space. He was like a voice in the wilderness proclaiming the dawn of a new age and, just a few months before his voice was silenced, he observed about all of us that "we are the primitives of an unknown culture." Marshall did not exist on the periphery and he was attempting to apply the techniques of the artist to communicate his vision of the general condition of contemporary man.

But, if he had roots in the distant past, his immediate artistic forbears were men of this century. From Chesterton, he learned to be open to and even relish paradox. Leavis, Eliot, Pound and Joyce opened to him the doors of perception on the poetic process and its role in adjusting the reader to the contemporary world.

"My study of the media," he said, "began and remains rooted in these men." It was from them that he learned to search for perceptual links rather than discrete experiences, links which were psychological, rather than logical, associative rather than linear or grammatical. While his perception's and expression's bloodlines are traceable to these men, one cannot but feel that the lines have been freshened by the McLuhan spirit brooding over them.

In his public life, he developed a personal mask — a style which served the double purpose of protecting him in his venturesome and even reckless explorations, and, at the same time, turning on (or off) the mind of his audience. Instead of presenting a complete and realistic picture as the old proscenium stage did, he consciously disturbed the routine sequence of language, producing jagged thoughts and jagged sentences, engaging the imagination of his audience by a jolt not unlike an electric shock. He intentionally left gaps in his expressions, making his audience fill them in. "The action," he was wont to say, "is in the interval." He tried to present a dramatic mirror of the complex processes of the mind at work, drawing attention not to the words spoken but to the spaces between the words — stretches of silent subliminal suggestions — all to ensure audience engagement. That is my version of how he was doing what he was doing.

And why was he doing it? If McLuhan had a fear, it was the fear of fragmentation. The whole thrust of his educational effort was to make whole what tends to be discrete and disunified in most of us. Not only was he charting the "inner" landscape of the mind, but he was intent on restoring to unity the human person, rent asunder, first by forces bred in the Renaissance and second, by the contemporary technological and cultural magnets of our own time. That's why he was doing what he was doing — trying to overcome breakdown by breakthrough.

In closing, I beg your indulgence in mentioning the most memorable instant I know of the McLuhan art. It occurred about 10 years ago when he was on a panel with W.H. Auden, and the subject under discussion was the contemporary theatre. He said, to a startled Auden and an equally startled audience, "The Sacrifice of the Mass is the greatest form of theatre possible and the one in which the audience is necessarily participant—in which there is no audience." That statement is loaded with orthodox theology but spoken like an artist. It may well be the greatest statement McLuhan ever made and it is so perfect that I would dishonour his memory by offering comment. I only wish I could have said it. It was unrehearsed, spontaneous, brilliant: one sentence about which libraries could be and have been written. It was quintessential McLuhan, total involvement and ultimate breakthrough.

CLAUDE BISSELL

Marshall McLuhan, who questioned the primacy of the book in our electronic society, wrote many books, several of which are essential for understanding the nature of the world in which we live. But, like Harold Innis, his bias was towards the oral both in theoretical and practical terms; and in memory I see him always in a group of people, relaxed, dominant in an easy, unaggressive way, and I hear his voice, modulated, North American with some faint Cambridge echoes, with a gentle but firm persistence persuading us to enter the spacious room of his ideas. I first met Marshall in such surroundings, shortly after the war, when we were both recent members of the English department, and, in our domestic lives, were neighbours on the campus. He and Corinne, who brought with her to these northern climes the warmth and beauty and high courtesy of the old south, loved to entertain. Gatherings at the McLuhan home were relaxed symposia, introduced and led by Marshall: the subjects emerged naturally from the conversation, and ranged boldly across the whole sweep of the mental heavens, from the symbolism of the motor car (he was then working on that modern *Tale of A Tub, The Mechanical Bride)* to T.S. Eliot's theory of the auditory imagination. His mind moved with ease from subject to subject; he was confident and unruffled, with the assurance of a man who had thought deeply and widely on these matters and believed that he had reached sound conclusions.

The McLuhan of the 60s and 70s — the international figure, the most widely known Canadian in our time — was unchanged. The symposia had widened and had taken on a more formal structure but the essentials remained — spontaneity, dizzy leaps from subject to subject and from area to area, with Marshall probing, questioning, speculating, enunciating. Even telephone conversations with Marshall would turn into miniature symposia. He had a habit of calling me in the morning (I'm sure many others could tell the same story), often at a time when most of us are just beginning to grope our way into consciousness. There would be no ritual introduction, no opportunity to exchange pleasantries, no academic or domestic gossip. Marshall would begin with his most recent "probe." "By the way, did you know that the North American goes out to be alone and stays in to be social, and that, for the European, it's the exact reverse." Well, I didn't know, and I would wait for the explanation that was patiently and confidently given.

If you attend a formal conference with McLuhan, the high moments were likely to come during informal discussions. I recall vividly an international conference to which we were delegates. It was held in Elsinore, Denmark, an appropriate setting for Marshall, a Hamlet who knew his own mind, who had no fear of mounting the battlements in defence of his ideas. In the evening a number of us were relaxing in the hotel pub. The conversation turned to the problems of NATO, and an American delegate, who had recently stood at the very summit of the councils of his country, was critical of the Canadian attitude, which he thought was hesitant and unenthusiastic. Marshall rose to his country's defence. "Canada," he said, "is a land of multiple borderlines, psychic, social and geographic. Canadians live at the interface where opposites clash. We have, therefore, no recognizable identity, and are suspicious of those who think they have." A cloud passed over the face of the great pro-consul [Dean Rusk]. This was a kind of comment that he had not heard at the meetings of diplomats and that never darkened the familiar clichés of official memoranda. And yet it was the best explanation of the Canadian attitude that I had heard. Marshall's startling generalizations were, as he repeatedly said, "probes." They were neither true nor false; they were not designed to give ultimate answers; they were beams of light that never failed to illuminate some dark area.

I treasure a casual remark he made after returning from Mass in Elsinore: "In the global village, how stupid to celebrate Mass in the vernacular!"

Another "probe" came, during a brief conversation on the plane, between Marshall and a former senior official in the American state department. "The Vietnam war," observed Marshall, speaking with the characteristic jauntiness and assurance with which he tossed his verbal grenades, "is the American 20th century version of the wild-west frontier."

McLuhan was a humanist in action — a humanist in the great Renaissance tradition, who not only argued that the humanities were at the centre of knowledge, but demonstrated in his own words that this was so. And at the centre of these humanities was imaginative literature. He was, first of all, in time and interest, a literary critic. In his early work he wrote about poets — Poe, Hopkins, Eliot, Pound — who, he thought, best embodied the modern consciousness, who worked "backwards from the particular effect to the objective correlative or poetic means of evoking that precise effect"; and in his own social criticism, he followed the same method. He had the Renaissance humanist's belief in the power of literature to illuminate life and conduct. "The artist picks up the message of cultural and technical challenge decades before its transforming impact occurs. He, then, builds models or Noah's arks for facing the change that is ahead." But literature, he believed, cannot be studied fruitfully in its own context. The critic must be receptive to the physical sciences and the social sciences. He disliked narrow specialists and the narrow specialists responded to him in kind: he believed also that the engaged humanist had a broad social responsibility, to carry his perceptions to a wide audience, and to do so with care and humour (jokes, he said, revealed the besetting grievance of the day). In his last active year, for instance, he gave the Ezra Pound Lecture at the University of Idaho, a study of Pound's rhetoric that would delight the most austere textual critic, and he gave a general discourse on the problems of the electronic age to a conference of world bankers assembled in Monaco.

I return to the theme of McLuhan and the spoken word. I see him most characteristically stretched out in an easy chair in the living room of his Wychwood Park home, which, blot out a few distracting tall rises visible to the south, could have been an English country house on the southern downs or the Yorkshire moors. He sits close to the big fireplace, and he rises from time to time to make sure that the flames have not died down, as if he were at the same time rekindling the fire of his own spirit. Despite the sad deprivation of the last months, I believed that the inner fire always burned brightly, and that he continued to live in the glow of the ideas that had so powerfully illuminated his own age.

Carleton Williams

Marshall and Tom Easterbrook were already close friends when we were all undergraduates at the University of Manitoba in the early 30s. I came to know them both at that time and to value their friendship. But shortly thereafter we each went our separate ways until we were reunited at this university in the late 40s; Marshall in English at St. Mike's, Tom in economics and I in psychology.

Then in the mid-50s we came together more seriously along with Ted Carpenter in anthropology to plan an application to the Ford Foundation which had just announced a new grant program designed to encourage scholars to break out of their departmental cocoons and undertake a variety of interdisciplinary studies. We submitted a proposal whereby each of us would select four graduate students to work with us as part of aninterdepartmental seminar on "Culture and Communications." Our application was successful and each of our four departments was persuaded to accept student registration in our seminar as the equivalent of a regular graduate course. Then once we had won the agreement of Andy Gordon, the sceptical and peppery dean of graduate studies, we were on our way.

By common consent, Marshall was elected chairman of the seminar, a job he did in his own way to be sure: a way that proved to be extraordinarily effective.

It quickly became evident that the Ford Foundation was right, that interdepartmental barriers were real and very high, that we each spoke a different language, and that we had, consciously and unconsciously, adopted sets of assumptions about the world in general and our disciplines in particular that were widely and on occasion wildly at variance with each other. Marshall became very good at finding ways past flat contradictions, flaring tempers and latent suspicions. During those difficult days none of us doubted him whether we always wholly understood him or not.

But thanks to the serious efforts we all made and thanks to Marshall's intuitive capacity to seize on those concepts that facilitated rather than inhibited the cross-fertilization of ideas, we slowly developed a common language and common approaches to problems of mutual concern.

We even learned how to undertake joint research projects, and published them in a journal we founded, called *Explorations*. The seminar met every Wednesday evening, 52 weeks a year for the two-year life of the grant. If you wanted, or more likely needed, a holiday from its pressure-cooker atmosphere, you took it. Or if other responsibilities required your attendance elsewhere you went, but the seminar went on. Marshall missed few if any of its sessions.

I was present on the occasion when Marshall, leading a discussion on TV, standing beside the fireplace in the room the seminar used in St. Mike's, one arm on the mantlepiece and thoughtfully gesturing with the other, first said rather pensively, "well, of course, really, the medium is the message." No blinding lights flashed, no one shouted "Eureka!" but everyone's attention was caught by this unusual if casually-made remark.

As he often did with his sudden insights he returned to it during the week, phoning one or another of us to discuss new facets of the contemporary media which this touchstone had made manifest. The seminar then, was the launching pad from which Marshall began his famous "probes," and no spacecraft, no Voyager II ranged farther than he, nor discovered as much.

As many of you will know, Marshall was as famous among his friends for his sudden, penetrating insights into them and their affairs as he was to the general public to whom his name became a household word as The Media Man.

I remember one such occasion, when he and Corinne were staying with Peggy and me in London, he suddenly asked me if I liked the city. I replied that I had liked it from the start and added that while Peggy liked it too she had had rather more difficulty than I in adjusting to it. "Well, you know why that is, of course," he said, and I, puzzled and intrigued replied, "no, I do not know any such thing." "Why, Carl," said Marshall, "London is about the same size Winnipeg was when we grew up there as boys; of course it would be easy for you and harder for Peggy who was born and brought up in Toronto."

All of us have our favourite anecdotes; illustrating as they do various facets of Marshall's character. This next one, it seems to me, settles once and for all the controversy stirred up by Marshall's difficult prose style. I once tackled him on the subject directly, asking why the stuff had to be so obscure, so hard even for the interested and intelligent reader; so easy for the superficial and suspicious to dismiss as deliberate deception. "Well Carl," he said, "I will make to you the same offer I have made to all my publishers. I have tried to be as clear as I possibly can in my writing. If you can make it clearer, you're welcome to try."

Again, the public mind does not readily associate a scholarly mind like Marshall's — complete with its ferocious intelligence, daunting erudition, and soaring imagination — with a sturdy frame and robust physical stamina. While it is worth remembering that he rowed when at Cambridge, that stamina was even more evident in his mature years when, after a cruelly lengthy operation in New York to remove a benign tumor pressing on his brain, his surgeon entered the recovery room and asked, "How are you feeling?"; hoping at best for a mumbled word that would show a return to consciousness. Instead Marshall replied, "That depends on what you mean by feeling!"

One last tale, told at the risk of trespassing on John Kelly's territory. Marshall was always fascinated by dialogue but at one time he was almost obsessed with the idea, insisting it was at the root of all thought and imagination.

I contested this saying, "How can you of all people speak of dialogue, when so much of what you accomplish comes from your thinking-aloud monologues and from your quiet times, when no one is near you?"

"Ah, but Carl," he replied gently, "one is always in dialogue with God."

This was my friend, faithful and just to me.

I can never forget an incident a month earlier, just fifteen years after Marshall and I first met. We were enjoying a regular visit to "discuss" articles he had chosen for me to reread aloud from a large-print version of the *New York Times*; also one of his favourite books, *Caught in the Web of Words* (a detailed history of human problems encountered in creating the *Oxford English Dictionary*). We had read some of the *Web* before, when Marshall could still speak, and he had declared OED the greatest achievement of Western scholarship.

We normally followed reading with a "talk" and walk

around the park. On that day, however, Marshall led me downstairs to see a TV program: Peter Cook in *Bedazzled*. It was a Mephistophelian bargain in which Satan (a "city slicker") confesses to his victim that he had invented the Seven Deadly Sins on an idle Sunday afternoon. The eighth had taken much longer — Advertising! Never before, had I heard Marshall shout with laughter. Soon after, it was time for me to go home. He came out with me to the front patio, and we parted, waving *au revoir*.

Some months later, I wrote for my systems-science colleagues "Via Media With Marshall McLuhan."[85]

> Or say that the end precedes the beginning,
> And the end and the beginning were always there
> Before the beginning and after the end.
> And all is always now.
>
> (T.S. Eliot, *Four Quartets*, East Coker)

On the last night of 1980, Marshall McLuhan left history to enter eternity. In his end is a new beginning.

In sharing our playful Irish tradition, I once asked Marshall: "If, on some fine day, you wake up and find out you're dead, what would you do?" He promptly replied:

PLUNGE AHEAD, KEEP PLUNGING AHEAD!

ENVOI

We now learn how "effects precede causes," as in folk wisdom "actions speak louder than words."

As we replayed Baudelaire's *hypocrite lecteur* with Marshall, we already knew that there is no possible formula nor model for understanding the present. We knew this precisely because such understanding is of unique percepts, not repeatable concepts. We also knew that nobody can ever fully understand anybody, even ourselves. The reverberations of any human life, now and forever, are beyond measure.

Much perceived experience is almost, but not quite, impossible to replay in any conceivable language. Our comments are therefore intended only to suggest, not to define, what Marshall really thought or who he was.

Yet, the "laws" of natural languages do serve as "keys" — structural patterns — for exploring all human artifacts as communication media, including our very mode of exploration itself. This approach demands knowledge not only of the Grammars, but also of the Rhetorics and Dialectics of the dominant "extensions of man." Comprehensive awareness of their combined effects upon our psyche and society is mandatory to circumvent their powers over every one of us.

With fellow explorers, we grew beyond political ideologies and scientific theories, by employing approaches of both literate and non-literate, Eastern and Western, cultures. We learned to organize our ignorance deliberately to make fresh discoveries that sometimes led to "big breakthroughs" incidentally.

In our fields of interest, we explored not only logically, like Specialists and Generalists with "frozen categories," but also ecologically as Comprehensivists — concertmasters of the inter-penetrating harmonies of our boundless multiverse. In this GIANT PARADIGM SHIFT from visual categories to multi-sensory process patterns, we strove to harmonize man-made Nature with the maelstrom of nature itself by helping each other to discover the laws of media as figures in the ground of everything else imaginable.[87-91]

291

As more of us heeded Fuller's invitation to crew on Spaceship Earth, we began to appreciate Marshall's foresight that there would be no more space between audience and actors in the Global Electric Theatre. *The action is in the gaps, not the connections*, like the "play" between wheel and axle, or the interplay between people in dialogue. *Today, effects precede causes by design.*

Devoted like Marshall to the paradox, ambiguities and wonders of ignorance, we explore secure in the knowledge that we can't become McLuhanites. MARSHALL MCLUHAN *is the totality of effects he created beyond limit.*

With kindred spirits hoping to have "Fun again" like "Finn again" we playfully learned to explore "all space in a not shall ... where the hand of man has never set foot," with the Joycean "keys to. Given!" [91]

So ends *Finnegans Wake* and the nightmare of H.C.E. whose initials signal the arrival of everyone to the powerful dream of the electric age: Here Comes Everybody.

In our end is our beginning

APPENDIX A
(READING LIST 1966-67, WITH ADDITIONS)

Anshen, R.N.
Language:
Approached as an integral system for organizing space,
time and perception.

Bedini, Silvio A.
The Scent of Time:
Archaeolgical Treatise.

Bernard, Claude.
The Study of Experimental Medicine:
The classic prototype explaining the technique of
isolation of organs to observe the effect on other organs.

Brown, Norman O.
Life against Death:
Technology as neurotic sublimation and alienation of the body.

Canetti, Elias.
Crowds and Power.

Capek, Milic.
The Philosophical Impact of Modern Physics:
The cultural block of visual habit as impediment to
understanding physics in the Western world.

Chaytor, H. J.
From Script to Print.

Cherry, Colin.
On Human Communication:

Churchman, C.W.
The Meaning of Measurement, Definition and Theories:
Does for the bizarre world of measurement what
Ogden and Richards did for the meaning of meaning.

Clark and Sloan.
Classrooms in the Factory.

Danzig, Tobias.
Number, the Language of Science:
The extension of touch as manifested in the history of culture.

Deutsch, Karl.
The Nerves of Government:

293

A structural study of Models in present organization.

Dorner, Alexander.
Way beyond Art:
Approach to non-visual spaces in the history of culture.

Doxiadis, C.A.
Architecture in Transition:
A comprehensive Greek approach to world housing and city design.

Drucker, Peter.
The Age of Discontinuity.

Duncan, Hugh D.
Language and Literature in Society.

Dunlop, J.T.
Automation and Technological Change.

Ehrenzweig, Anton
Psychoanalysis of Artistic Vision and Hearing:
The Dissociation of Sensibility since the Renaissance.

Ellul, Jacques.
The Technological Society.
Propaganda.

Entralgo, Pedro.
Mind and Body: Psychosomatic Pathology.
The Therapy of the Word in Classical Antiquity.

Fincher, Jack.
Human Intelligence.

Foucault, Michel.
Madness and Civilization: History of Insanity in the Age of Reason.

Freud, Sigmund.
The Interpretation of Dreams.

Fromm, Eric.
The Forgotten Language.

Fuller, Buckminster.
Utopia or Oblivion.
Ideas and Integrities.
Operating Manual for Spaceship Earth.

Giedion, Sigfried
Mechanization Takes Command:
Space, Time and Architecture.
The Beginnings of Architecture.

Gombrich, E. H.
Art and Illusion:
A discovery of integral awareness amidst art
illsions based on isolated visual sense.

Hall, E.T.
The Silent Language.
The Hidden Dimension.

Havelock, E.A.
Preface to Plato.
Prologue to Greek Literacy.
Origins of Western Literacy.

Heisenberg, W.
The Physicist's Concept of Nature:
Contemporary physics finds much that is congenial
in archaic science.

Huizinga, Johan
Homo Ludens:
A study of the play element in culture.

Innis, H.A.
The Bias of Communication:
A pioneer work in exploring the psychic and social
consequences of the extensions of man.

Ivins, W. Jr.
Art and Geometry:
The Greeks did not succeed in separating visual
space from the tactile and kinetic spaces.

Jaynes, Julian.
The Origin of Consciousness in the Breakdown of the Bicameral
Mind

Kuhn, Thomas.
The Structure of Scientific Revolutions.

Leavis, Frank.
New Bearings in English Poetry.

Levis-Straus.
Structural Anthropology.

Lewis, Wyndham.
Time and Western Man.

Lusseyran, Jacques.
And There Was Light.

Mandler, G. & Kessen, W.
The Language of Psychology:
Model attempt to create a grammar of science.

Mazlish, B.
The Railways and the Space Age.

Mumford, Lewis.
Technics and Civilization:
The interplay of artefact and culture.

Pierce, J.R.
Symbols, Signals and Noise.

Polanyi, Karl. F.
The Great Transformation:
The struggle to disengage economic structures
from the Newtonian universe.

Pound, Ezra.
ABC of Reading.

Rubin, Edgar.
Visual Figures.

Schon, Donald.
The Displacement of Concepts.

Selye, Hans.
The Stress of life:
"The pharmacology of dirt" or an ecological approach to
human stress.

Simeons, A. T. W.
Man's Presumptuous Brain.

Straus, Urwin.
The Primary World of the Senses.

Usher, A.P.
The History of Mechanical Inventions:
A non-archeological approach revealing the background and
interrelation of seemingly isolated inventions.

Young, J.Z.
Doubt and Certainty in Science:
A view of the central nervous system as a new model for
understanding electric technology.

White, Lynn, Jr.
Medieval Technology and Social Change.

APPENDIX B
(FROM "MCLUHAN'S AND ORWELL'S 1984.")

What was happening in '34 was being noted in '43 by Orwell, and we noted again in '84 by

INSTANT REPLAY

BLAIR AS ORWELL	McLUHAN IS McLUHAN
• Ideologue as generalist	• Artist as comprehensivist
• Primacy of concepts and argument	• Primacy of percepts and dialogue
• Organizing knowledge for retrieval	• Organizing ignorance for discovery
• Start with "causes" like Doctor Watson	• Start with "effects" like Sherlock Holmes
• Unconscious visual sensory bias: ABCED-minded Western literate	• Conscious multi-sensory awareness: literate and non-literate
• Formal logic; "exact definition;" science; yes-OR-no thinking: Law of the Excluded Middle	• Ecologic; "exact word" for art, poetics, yin/yang, yes-AND-no thinking: Complementarity
• Deadly earnest	• Deliberately playful
• Old groundrules and new artificial intelligence	• New process patterns and old human wisdom
• Classify abstract figures without grounds	• Explore changing figures on changing grounds
• Visible plot minus invisible subplot in human situation	• Transformation of plot into subplot and vice versa in human drama
• Agnostic, confined to history forever	• Christian, touching eternity through history
• Criticizing conclusions	• Reconsidering premises
• Breakthroughs lead to breakdowns	• Breakdowns lead to breakthroughs

BLAIR AS ORWELL	McLUHAN IS McLUHAN
• Determined by technology	• Predetermining technolgy
• Descending to doom via rearview mirror	• Ascending from doom by understanding media
• All "Futures" past	• All "Futures" present
• Logical maturity that eliminates paradox	• Human maturity that savours paradox
• "Finn" slumbering and merely reacting to effects imposed by technologies	• "Finn,again" actively anticipating effects of his own technologies
• Humpty Dumpty in bits and bytes.	• Humpty Dumpty whole again
• Visual-space bias	• Embracing all spaces
• Thinking in terms of Western languages	• Thinking in both words and multi-sensory images
• Age of Reason and "wired city"	• Global Electric Theatre of "wireless world"
• Logical connections	• Resonant bonds
• Matching the Old	• Making the New
• Centralized authority in control	• Everybody a controller by understanding media
• City proletarians for "salvation" fearfully	• Country folk for "resurrection" playfully
• Passengers on the ship of fools.	• Crew on Spaceship Earth.

REFERENCES

1. Matie Molinaro, Corinne McLuhan, and William Toye (Eds), *Letters of Marshall McLuhan*. Toronto: Oxford University Press, 1987, p. 394.

2. Biographies published and planned include: Philip Marchand, *Marshall McLuhan: The Medium and the Messenger*. Toronto: Random House, 1989; and William Kuhns, in preparation.

3. Herbert Marshall McLuhan, *The Mechanical Bride: Folklore of Industrial Man*. New York: Vanguard Press, 1951.

4. Matie Molinaro on "Marshalling McLuhan," p. 93. in George Sanderson (Ed.), *Marshall McLuhan: The Man and His Message*. A Special Issue of *The Antigonish Review,* Summer 1988; (hardcover edition, Golden, Colorado: Fulcrum Commun-ications, 1989), p. 12.

5. *Letters,* see above Ref. 1, pp. 1-88.

6. Marshall McLuhan, *The Gutenberg Galaxy*. Toronto: University of Toronto Press, 1962; and *Understanding Media: The Extensions of Man*. New York: McGraw-Hill, 1964; "artist," p. 65.

7. Barrington Nevitt, "McLuhan's and Orwell's 1984," in (Ed.) Derrick de Kerkhove, *Understanding 1984. Occasional Paper 48*, Canadian Commission for UNESCO, Ottawa, Canada, 1983: 95-114.

8. Marshall McLuhan and Barrington Nevitt, *Take Today: The Executive as Dropout*. New York: Harcourt Brace Jovanovich, 1972, pp. 1-9.

9. Ibid, p. 293.

10. *The Art of Wychwood Park*. (Eds.) Curator Albert W.M. Fulton and Archivist Keith M.O. Miller, Wychwood Park Library, Toronto, p. 254 reprinted with kind permission of the Curator.

11. Ibid, p. 260.

12. *The Writings of Marshall McLuhan and what has been written about him: A Bibliography*, (Ed.) Robert Hittel. Wake-Brook House: 960 N.W. 53rd St., Fort Lauderdale, Florida, 1977.

13. Marshall McLuhan and Harley Parker, *Counterblast*. New York: Harcourt Brace, 1969 (with graphics mainly by George Thompson; but Alan Thomas refers to an "unpaged, side-stapled, nine-leaf, blue paper cover," and much shorter version, published

by University of Toronto Press, 1954).

14. Marshall McLuhan, initially with Edmund Carpenter (Eds.), *Explorations* (1953-1971) as an insert in *Varsity Graduate,* University of Toronto Press. Articles selected for *Explorations in Communication.* Boston: Beacon Press, 1966.

15. Jonathan Miller, *McLuhan.* London: Fontana/Collins, 1971.

16. Barrington Nevitt, "Problems of Communicating with People through Media," Gordon Thompson (Ed.), *THE* monograph 1. Ottawa: Northern Electric (now Bell-Northern) Laboratories, 1968. Compares the Shannon-Weaver mathematical theory of communication with McLuhan's approach to human communication, based on *Understanding Media.* Subsequently modified, see below Ref. 20. Indicates shift in Nevitt's pre-McLuhan approach outlined in "Predicting Scientific Prediction," in (Ed.) Marshall McLuhan, *Explorations,* Spring, 1967, pp. 49-64.

17. Barrington Nevitt, "Computer at Wits End Leads to Process Pattern Recognition," in Stanley Winkler (Ed.), *Computer Communication: Impacts and Implications (The First International Conference on Computer Communication,* Washington, D.C., ICCC '72). New York: IEEE publication: 56-57.

18. Marshall McLuhan and Barrington Nevitt, "Reply to Dr. Jonathan Miller's letter of July 15, 1971." *The Listener,* August 26, 1971.

19. Marshall McLuhan and Barrington Nevitt, "Reply to Dr. Jonathan Miller's letter of September 9, 1971." *The Listener,* October 28, 1971. (See above *Letters* for more.)

20. Marshall McLuhan and Barrington Nevitt, "Medium Meaning Message." *Communication 1,* (UK) 1974: 27-33; reprinted in Barrington Nevitt, *The Communication Ecology: Re-presentation versus Replica,* Toronto: Butterworths, 1982, pp. 140-144. Instead of considering old media as the "content" of new media, recognizing that people are the content of all media.

21. Marshall McLuhan, Kathryn Hutchon, and Eric McLuhan, *City as Classroom: Understanding Language and Media.* Agincourt, Ontario: Book Society of Canada, 1977; reprinted, *Media, Messages & Language: The World as Your Classroom* Skokie, Illinois: National Textbook, 1977.

22. Marshall McLuhan and Harley Parker, *Through the Vanishing*

Point: space in poetry and painting. New York: Harper & Row, 1968.

23. Marshall McLuhan and Barrington Nevitt, *Take Today*, see above Ref. 8, Chap. 8.

24. James Joyce, *Finnegans Wake.* New York: Viking Press, 1959. "allforabit," p. 19.

25. Jane Jacobs, "Making a Movie with McLuhan," in (Ed.) George Sanderson, *The Antigonish Review — Marshall McLuhan*, special issue 74-75, Summer-Autumn 1988: 127-129.

26. Marshall McLuhan and Barrington Nevitt, *Perception.* 1, November-December, 1977: 66-71. Reprinted in S.D. Berkowitz and Robert K. Logan (Eds), *Canada's Third Option.* MacMillan of Canada. Toronto, 1978, pp. 108-117; also Barrington Nevitt, "Canadian Cultures from Conflict to Complementary," Wallup, *Innis Herald*, February 20, 1978.

27. Harold A. Innis, *The Bias of Communication,* 1964; and *Empire and Communications,* 1972, reprinted by University of Toronto Press with Forewords by Marshall McLuhan.

28. Peter F. Drucker, *Adventures of a Bystander.* New York: Harper & Row, 1979, pp. 244-255.

29. Marshall McLuhan and Barrington Nevitt, "The Man Who Came to Listen," in (Eds.) Tony H. Bonaparte and John H. Flaherty, *Peter Drucker: Contributions to Business Enterprise.* New York University Press, 1970, pp. 35-55.

30. Marshall McLuhan and Barrington Nevitt, *Take Today,* see above Ref. 8, p. 234.

31. Barrington Nevitt, *Keeping Ahead of Economic Panic.* Montreal: Gamma Institute Press, 1985.

32. Marshall McLuhan, "Edgar Poe's Tradition," in (Ed.) Eugene McNamara, *The Interior Landscape: The Literary Criticism of Marshall McLuhan 1943-1962.* New York: McGraw-Hill, 1969, pp. 214-215.

33. Francis Bacon, *Advancement of Learning,* and *Novum Organon.* New York: The Colonial Press, 1899, pp. 21, 173-174; McLuhan normally cited the former from J.M. Dent, Everyman's Library, n/d, p. 142.

34. John Wain, "Incidental Thoughts of Marshall McLuhan," *Dear Shadows: Portraits from Memory.* London: John Murray, 1986,

pp. 77-110.

35. *Take Today*, see above Ref. 8, p. 8.

36. Robert Fulford, "The Age of McLuhan," in *The Best Seat in the House*. Toronto: W. Collins & Sons, 1988, pp.162-184.

37. W. Kuhns, *The Post Industrial Prophets: Interpretations of Technology*. New York: Harper & Row, 1973, pp. 169-70.

38. Eric McLuhan, "Postliteracy," *Indirections*, 14, 2, June 1989: 73-78.

39. T.S. Eliot, *The Use of Poetry and the Use of Criticism*. London: Faber Paperbacks, 1964, pp. 118-119.

40. Edmund Carpenter and Marshall McLuhan, "Acoustic Space," *Explorations in Communication: An Anthology*. (Eds.) Marshall McLuhan and Edmund Carpenter. Boston: Beacon Press, 1960, pp. 65-70; and Barrington Nevitt, "Problems of communicating with people through media," revised in *The Communication Ecology,* see above Ref. 20, pp. 150-153.

41. Edmund Carpenter, *Oh, What a Blow That Phantom Gave Me!* New York: Bantam Books, 1974.

42. Marshall McLuhan and Harley Parker, *Through the Vanishing Point: space in poetry and painting*. New York: Harper & Row, 1968.

43. Jacques Lusseyran, *And There Was Light*. Translated from the revised French original: *Et la lumière fût*, by Elizabeth R. Cameron. Boston: Little, Brown and Co., 1963, pp. 143-144.

44. Jacques Lusseyran, "Seeing Without Eyes", *The Idler*. No. 26, Nov./Dec. 1989, pp.43-46.
    See also Richard Wolkomir, "American Sign Language: 'It's not mouth stuff — it's brain stuff." *Smithsonian*, July 1992: 30-41)

45. Edward T. Hall, *The Silent Language*. Garden City: Anchor,1973.

46. Edward T. Hall, *The Hidden Dimension*. Garden City: Doubleday, 1966; "The Perception of Space," pp. 39-47; "Visual Space," pp. 61-69; "art and science," p. 70; "Art as a History of Perception," pp. 74-83; "The Language of Space," pp. 85-93; and he went further to examine "olfactory space" and territoriality in outlining a new science of "Proxemics."

47. Tony Schwartz, *The Responsive Chord*. Garden City: Anchor Press, 1973.

48. Elias Canetti, *Crowds and Power*. Markham: Penguin Books Canada, 1987, pp. 452-453.

49. E.H. Gombrich, *Art and Illusion*. New York: Pantheon, 1961, pp. 366-368.

50. Ward Cannel and June Macklin, *The Human Nature Industry*. Garden City, N.Y.: Anchor Press, 1973, p.p. 9-11 with modifications.

51. Fred and Barbro Thompson, "The Japanese Concept of MA," partially reprinted in *The Communication Ecology,* see above Ref. 20, pp. 61-68.

52. Marshall McLuhan and Wilfred Watson, *From Cliché to Archetype*. New York: Viking Press, 1970.

53. Ibid, pp. 139-141.

54. Thomas Eric Marshall McLuhan, *Menippean Thunder at "Finnegans Wake": The Critical Problems*. Ph.D. dissertation, University of Dallas, authorized facsimile, University Microfilms International, Ann Arbor, Mich., 1983, Abstract. To be published by University of Toronto Press in 1990s.

55. Marshall McLuhan, *Report on Project for Understanding Media,* commissioned by the American National Association of Educational Broadcasters, 1960; revised by Barrington Nevitt, *The Communication Ecology*, see above Ref. 20, pp. 155-161.

56. Winters, Yvor. *The Anatomy of Nonsense*, Norfolk, Conn., New Directions, 1943, pp. 212-213.
Wilson Bryan Key, *Subliminal Seduction*. Englewood Cliffs, N.J.: Prentice-Hall, 1973.

57. Siegfried Giedion, *Mechanization Takes Command: a contribution to anonymous history*. New York: Oxford University Press, 1948, p. vi.

58. Charles Baudelaire, *Les Fleurs du Mal*. New York: French and European Publishers, 1961; on the last line of *"envoi"* to the readers.

59. Herbert E. Krugman, "Electro-encephalographic aspects of low involvement: implications for the McLuhan hypothesis," *Meeting of the American Association of Public Opinion Research,* May 21-23, 1970.

60. Richard Aldington, cited by J. Isaacs in *The Background of*

Modern Poetry. New York: Dutton Paperback D17, 1952, p. 45.

61. Dennis Murphy, "Taking Media on their own Terms: The Integration of the Human and the Technological." Paper presented at the *Fourth International Conference of Systems Research, Information and Cybernetics,* Baden-Baden, Germany, August 1988.

62. *The Communication Ecology,* see above Ref. 20, p. 178.

63. *Take Today,* see above Ref. 8, p. 86.

64. George Leonard, *Walking on the Edge of the World.* Boston: Houghton Miflin, 1980; "Jamming with McLuhan," pp. 258-262.

65. Marshall McLuhan and Bruce Powers, *The Global Village.* New York: Oxford University Press, 1989, p. xii.

66. Margarita D'Amico, in (Ed.) Terry J. Leon, *McLuhan en Venezuela (April 1976).* Caracas, Venezuela: "El Mundo es un Poema en 'Multimedia', pp. 47-56; "Cada uno tiene el derecho de defender su propria ignorancia," pp. 201-209; "McLuhan y su ultimo libro," pp. 227-232. Selections abbreviated and translated from the Spanish.

67. Rosalie Colie, *Paradoxia Epidemica: The Renaissance Tradition of Paradox.* Princeton: Princeton University Press, 1966; Th. Stcherbatsky, *Buddhist Logic, Vol. 1,* New York, Dover Publications, n/d; Frederick L. Kumar, *The Philosophies of India.* Edwin Mellen Press: Lampeter, Dyfed, Wales, 1991; and Scott Eastham, "How Is Wisdom Communicated?" *Interculture,* Spring 1992, issue #115. Intercultural Institute of Montreal (4917 St. Urbain, Montreal, Quebec, H2T 2W1).

68. Barrington Nevitt, "Coping with Chaos," in (Eds) H. Burkhardt and W.E. Vanderberg, *Proceedings of the Interdisciplinary Conference: Preparing for a Sustainable Society. Toronto: Ryerson Polytechnical Institute, June 21-22, 1991:* 213-220.

69. W.A. Hurst, "Vision and Reading Achievement," *Canadian Journal of Optometry* , April 1964: 3-19; and "A Basis for Diagnosing and Treating Learning Disabilities within the School System," ibid., 29 (September 1967):46-59; also "Vision, Brain Hemispheres, Learning Disabilities," *CDNTACTO* (January, 1981): 30-40; introduced McLuhan to his colleague Abraham Kirshner whose methods of "Vestibular Stimulation" are now curing other "incurable" mental diseases. Dr. Kirshner cites the following references in his article for our book.

1. Marshall McLuhan, *The Gutenberg Galaxy*. Toronto: University of Toronto Press, 1962; and *Understanding Media: The Extensions of Man*. New York, N.Y.: McGraw-Hill Book Company, 1964.

2. Sir W. Stewart Duke-Edler, *Textbook of Ophthalmology*, Vol. 1, 8th edition. Philadelphia, Pa.: W.B. Saunders Company, 1960.

3. A. Gesell, *Vision: Its Development in Infant and Child*. New York, N.Y.: Paul B. Hoeber, Inc., 1949.

4. K.J. Ciufredda, A.T. Bahill, R.V. Kenyon, et al. "Eye movements during reading: case reports." American Journal of Optics and Optometry, 1976; 53:389-95.

5. L.A. Lefton. "Eye movements in reading by disabled children." In: J.W. Senders, D.F. Fisher, R.A. Monty, (Eds.) Proceedings of conference on eye movements and higher psychological functions. Hillsdale N.J: Lawrence Erlbaum Assoc, 1978:225-37.

6. Pavlidis G.T. "Eye movements in dyslexia: their diagnostic significance." Journal of Learning Disability. 1985: 18:42-50.

7· "Treatment of Hard Core Offenders," Stan Herrin, O.D., (ed.) *Review of Optometry*, Nov. 1982, Vol. 119, No.11

70. Ross Hume Hall, *Food for Nought: The Decline of Nutrition*. New York: Harper & Row, 1974.

71. Carolyn F.A. Dean and Robert F. Dean, "Body Percept in Electric Times," presented at the *Conference on Simulation and Modelling,* University of Pittsburg, May 5, 1988.

72. Barrington Nevitt, *A B C of Prophecy: understanding the environment,* Montreal: Gamma Institute Press, 1985: how dominant metaphors both help and hinder current thinking in art and philosophy and science; converting breakdowns into breakthroughs to bypass hitherto "inevitable fate." See also Max Jammer, *Concepts of Space* and *Concepts of Force.* Cambridge, Mass.: Harvard University Press, 1957, and Barrington Nevitt, "Space in Physics and Cosmology," *Explorations*, Summer 1967, pp. 74-78 concerning *apeiron*, and above Ref. 68 on chaos.

73. Karl R. Popper, *The Logic of Scientific Discovery*. New York: Basic Books, 1959, pp. 43, 59, 314-315.

74. Niels Bohr, cited by Werner Heisenberg, *Physics and Beyond: Encounters and Conversations*. New York: Harper Torchbook, 1972, p. 102.

75. Johan Huizinga, *Homo Ludens: A Study of the Play-Element in Culture.* Boston: Beacon Paperback, 1955, p. 1.

76. *Kybernetes* articles by Barrington Nevitt:

    1973 "Cybernetics and Management." *Kybernetes* 2, Editorial, with Marshall McLuhan.

    1976 "Anticipating Fate: Beyond Feedback to Feedforward by Process Pattern Recognition." *Kybernetes* 5: 221-228.

    1979 "Ecological Rationality beyond Cybernetics." Summary in *Proceedings of the Fourth International Congress on Cybernetics and Systems,* Amsterdam, 1978. Springer, Berlin: 337-340. Complete paper in *Kybernetes* 9: 275-281.

    1981 "Via Media with Marshall McLuhan." *Kybernetes* 10: 235-240.

    1985 "Thinking and Feeling in the Atomic Age," discussion paper for the conference of *Health Professionals for Nuclear Responsibility on Hope in the Nuclear Age,* McGill University, Montreal, November 8-10, (published in 1987 by *Kybernetes*, 16: 99-105).

    1987 "Futures for Cybernetics," *Cybernetics and Systems: The Way Ahead: Proceedings of the Seventh International Congress of Cybernetics and Systems,* (Ed.) John Rose, Lytham St. Annes, Lancs., England: Thales Publications: 725-729.

77. Frederick Engels, *Dialectics of Nature.* Translated and edited by Clemens Dutt with a Preface and Notes by J.B.S. Haldane. New York: International Publishers, 1940.

78. Marshall and Eric McLuhan, *Laws of Media: the new science,* Toronto: University of Toronto Press, 1988; Marshall McLuhan, "Laws of the Media." *et cetera*, June 1977, pp. 173-179; "McLuhan's Laws of the Media," Communication to the Editor, *Technology and Culture,* January 1975: 74-78: invites readers to "disprove" his "postulates" and to "get a dialogue going from which all might benefit;" Marshall McLuhan and Barrington Nevitt, "The Future of 'New' Media," commissioned by Helstar, Geneva and Paris, for publication in a proposed Encyclopedia of the Future, submitted in December 1973; formulates thirty-six "grammars" or "laws" of the media by asking "four basic questions" (subsequently called a "tetrad") that expose the dynamic effects or "message" of any human artifact ("hardware" or "software," past or present or future), considered as a communication

medium.

79. Kamala Bhatia and Baldev Bhatia, *The Philosophical and Social Foundations of Education*. Delhi, India: Seema Offset Press, 1974.

80. Marshall McLuhan and Barrington Nevitt, "Causality in the Electric World." *Technology and Culture,* 18, January 1973:1-18.

81. Alexander P.D. Mourelatos (Ed.), *The Pre-Socratics*. New York: Anchor Press/Doubleday, 1974; a rich source of references for further study.

82. Barrington Nevitt, "Percept, Participation, and Pattern." Series of seminars and the *Hill Family Lecture,* United Theological Seminary of the Twin Cities, New Brighton, Minn., 1974.

83. Pierre Babin and Marshall McLuhan, *Autre Homme Autre Chrétien à l'Age Electronique*. Lyon: Editions du Chalet, 1977. Translated from French to English.

84. John Kelly, Claude Bissell, and Carleton Williams, "Herbert Marshall McLuhan: The University's tribute," *University of Toronto Bulletin,* Monday, February 9, 1981.

85. Eric Koch, *Inside Seven Days*. Scarborough: Prentice Hall/-Newcastle, 1986. pp. 219-21.

86. Barrington Nevitt, "Via Media with Marshall McLuhan." In (Eds.) George Sanderson and Frank Macdonald, A Special Issue of the *Antigonish Review: Marshall McLuhan*, Summer-Autumn, 1988: 153-161 (Republished from *Kybernetes*, 1981, 10: 235-240).

87. _____, *Neues Sein und altes Denken und vice versa* (New Being and Old Thinking and Vice Versa)," (Ed.) Peter Noever, *UMRISS* 1, 1987, Vienna, Austria: 25-26.

88. _____, "Global Design and Experimental Aesthetics," discussion paper for *SEMINAR 88 — THE OTHER DIMEN-SION,* School of Industrial Design, Carleton University, January 6-8, 1988.

89. _____, "Retuning the Global Theatre," seminars in Spanish and English organized by the Canadian Commission for UNESCO and the Canadian Embassy in Argentina for University of Buenos Aires, April 12-15, 1988; published in *Kybernetes* 19, #16, 1990: 42-53.

90. _____, "Laws of Implementation: Glasnost and Perestroika," workshop for *Teleconference on Glasnost and the Global Village,* York University, Toronto, February, 1991, published in (Ed.) Eric McLuhan, *McLuhan Studies, Vol.1,* 1991 (c/o Dept of Italian Studies, University of Toronto, Toronto, Ontario, Canada, M5S 1A1), pp. 203-212; "Thinking Machines: possible and impossible," (discussed by Dennis Murphy at an international symposium on *Communications, Cybernetics and Consciousness,* Baden-Baden, Germany, August, 1993); "What is Good Designing?" (presented at a symposium on *The Good, the Bad, and the Ugly*, School of Industrial Design, Carleton University, Ottawa, February, 1994); "Introduction" to *Harold Innis and India's Ancient Culture and Civilization* by Kamala Bhatia (Delhi, India: Doaba House, 1994), pp. 1-11.

91. *Finnegans Wake*, see above Ref. 24, p. 628: "Finn, again" by "resurrection" with the "keys to. Given!"

Index

CONTRIBUTORS

We gratefully thank colleagues, friends, and students who have generously donated their time in presenting this mosaic of Marshall McLuhan as they knew him. Our book and its chapter references here give barely an inkling of their vast qualifications and talents. We also acknowledge our indebtedness to others who wish to remain anonymous, as well as to those who contributed much without writing. (The letters indicate the chapter in which contributions appear, followed by the page number.)

Raymond Affleck, Architect, Montreal, Quebec: H-161

Earle Beattie, Professor, founder of *The Canadian Journal of Communications*, Toronto: D-89

Bede (Sullivan), Benedictine Sister, Victoria B.C.: I-169, P-277

Kamala Bhatia, Professor, Hamilton, Ontario: D-90, P-275

Claude Bissell, Professor and former University President, Toronto: B-28, J-188, Q-283

Harry Boyle, Radio Broadcaster and Journalist, Toronto: J-196

John Cage, Musician and Poet, New York: O-268

Adrienne Clarkson, TV Broadcaster and Publisher, Toronto: J-191

John Robert Colombo, Encyclopedist, Toronto: G-126

Wayne Constantineau, Nonverbal and Media Research, Toronto: H-156

Sandra Conti, Author and Educator, Society of Emissaries of Divine Light: P-278

Tom Cooper, Professor, Lawrence, Massachusetts: D-74

Margarita D'Amico, Professor and Journalist, Caracas, Venezuela: M-230

Derrick de Kerckhove, Professor, Toronto; D-86

Carolyn Dean, Medical Doctor; and Robert Dean, Radio Journalist; Toronto: N-257

Denis Diniacopoulos, Professor, Montreal: L-221

Peter F. Drucker, Author and Management Consultant, Claremont, California: G-122

Gerald Mason Feigen, Proctologist, San Francisco, California: J-198, P-272

Robert Fleming, Encyclopedist and Editor, Toronto: L-215

Donald Forgie, Professor, Toronto: B-40

Northrop Frye, Professor, Toronto: G-126

Jacques Giard, Director of Industrial Design, Ottawa: L-219

Sister St. Michael Guinan, Consultant in Gerontology, London, Ontario: D-69, P-276

Edward T. Hall, Cultural Anthropologist, Santa Fe, New Mexico: H-148

Ross Hall, Environmentalist, Danby, Vermont: N-253

Robert Hittel, Construction Contractor, Fort Lauderdale, Fla: B-36

Arthur Hurst, Doctor of Optometry, Gravenhurst, Ontario: N-253

Kathryn Hutchon, Teacher, Toronto: D-76, P-272

Jane Jacobs, Author and City Planner, Toronto: E-101

Yousuf Karsh, Master Photographer, Ottawa: D-85

Rev. John Kelly, former University President, Toronto: Q-279

Joseph Keogh, Professor and Media Consultant, St. Catharines, Ontario: D-70

Wilson Bryan Key, Author and Media Consultant, Steamboat (Reno), Nevada: K-208

A.J. Kirshner, Doctor of Optometry, Montreal: N-248

Eric Koch, Producer and Director of Public Affairs, Toronto: G-134

Murray Koffler, Entrepreneur and Philanthropist, Toronto: D-79

William Kuhns, Journalist, Alcove, Quebec: G-141

Thomas Langan, Professor, Toronto: D-84

George Leonard, Author and Editor, Mill Valley, California: M-227

Robert K. Logan, Physics Professor, Toronto: B-38

David Mackay, Motion Picture Producer, Guelph, Ontario: E-99

Philip Marchand, Author and Editor, Toronto: D-71

Teri McLuhan, Author and Film Maker, New York: E-104

Eric McLuhan, Author and Media Consultant, Toronto: G-139, M-240

M.B. McNamee, S.J., Professor, St. Louis, Missouri: G-119

Jean Mercier, Professor, Quebec, Quebec: J-194

W.G. Mitchell, Computer Educator, Toronto: D-95

Matie Molinaro, McLuhan's Publicist, Literary Agent, Toronto: E-103

Dennis Murphy, Professor, Montreal: L-223

Samuel D. Neill, Professor, London, Ontario: G-140

Peter Newman, Author and Journalist, Toronto: F-108

David Ogilvie, Adman "extraordinaire," Bennes, France: K-210

Walter Pittman, former University President, Toronto: F-112

Arthur Porter, Operations Research Pioneer, Toronto: B-26

B.W. Powe, Author, Toronto: G-137

Bruce Powers, Professor, Lewiston, N.Y.: M-230

Fred Rainsberry, TV Producer, Toronto: K-205

John Rose, Cyberneticist, St. Annes-on-Sea, Lancashire, England:
  J-194

E.A. Safarian, Professor, Toronto: L-219

Carl Scharfe, Editor, Toronto: C-42

R.J. Schoeck, Visiting Professor, Universität Trier, Germany: J-188

Tony Schwartz, Media Consultant, New York: H-151

Mary Jane Shoultz, former Women's Liberation leader, Ann
  Arbor, Michigan: D-82

Michael B. Smart, Toponomist, Toronto: H-154

Margaret Stewart, former Secretary to Marshall McLuhan,
  Washago, Ontario: B-23

Nelson Thall, Media executive, Toronto: D-76

Alan Thomas, Adult Educator, Toronto: B-25

Fred Thompson, Japanese Scholar, Waterloo, Ontario: I-177

George Thompson, former Research Assistant to Marshall
McLuhan, Toronto: B-34

Gordon Thompson, Fellow Emeritus, Ottawa, Ontario: N-247

John Wain, Author and Poet, Stratford-upon-Avon, England: G-130

Wayne & Shuster, TV Producers of Satire, Toronto: J-199

Eric Wesselow, Stained-Glass Window Creator, Montreal: L-221

Carleton Williams, former University President, London, Ontario:
H-143, Q-284

Lela Wilson (Mrs. York Wilson), Artist, Toronto: B-36

Elwy Yost, Motion Picture Historian, Toronto: D-86

Frank Zingrone, Professor of Communications, Toronto: F-114

SAMPLER

Marshall McLuhan took a first glance at page 69 of any book that attracted his attention. Any "good" book written "in Method," he explained, is full of repetitions and redundancies; skipping every second page is more than enough to find anything worth a second look. But if it is a book of poetry, or of prose written "in Aphorism," every word may deserve savouring.

User's Index

SOFTWARE AVAILABLE

Who Was Marshall McLuhan?
For Your Computer

The companion software product, available from Thought Company, includes carefully selected files of short quotes, passages, a comprehensive index, reading list and more. The software is a combination of an abridged version of the book and an entertaining screen-saver. All files can be searched and are cross-referenced, making this software truly interactive and an invaluable complement to the book.

This easy-to-use software runs on IBM-compatible PCs and requires Windows 3.1™ or higher.

To order, please send your check or money order (US funds) for $14.95 plus $5.00 S&H to:

Thought Company - Order Desk
4104 24th Street, Suite 149
San Francisco, CA USA
94114

Email: thought@io.org
Web: http://www.io.org/~thought
Phone: (416) 964-8770

OF RELATED INTEREST . . .

THE ESSENTIAL McLUHAN
Edited by Eric McLuhan and Frank Zingrone

Interest in the work and ideas of Marshall McLuhan is on the rise, yet most of his major works are no longer available. *The Essential McLuhan* fills this vacuum, gathering together in one concise volume McLuhan's key ideas, drawn from his books, articles, correspondence, and published speeches. McLuhan's insights are even more applicable today than they were twenty to forty years ago; by their prescient accuracy, they have become fundamental to the way we perceive the world today.

Eric McLuhan teaches writing, communications, and literature. He is the co-author of *Laws of Media* and *The City as Classroom* (both with Marshall McLuhan). **Frank Zingrone** is a professor of communication and senior scholar at York University in Toronto.

The Essential McLuhan
(published by House of Anansi Press;
ISBN 0-88784-5657)
is available through bookstores, or directly from
House of Anansi Press
34 Lesmill Road
Toronto, Canada M3B 2T6
(416) 445-3333
Fax (416) 445-5967